You will always
lovely to Jesus!

[illegible signature]

Songs of the Heart

An Intimate Journey of Love from the Song of Solomon

Florli Zweifel Nemeth

WestBow Press
A Division of Thomas Nelson

All Scriptures are from the King James Version unless specified otherwise

WestBow Press books may be ordered through booksellers or by contacting:

WestBow Press
A Division of Thomas Nelson
1663 Liberty Drive
Bloomington, IN 47403
www.westbowpress.com
1-(866) 928-1240

ISBN: 978-1-4497-4631-5 (sc)
ISBN: 978-1-4497-4632-2 (hc)
ISBN: 978-1-4497-4630-8 (e)

Library of Congress Control Number: 2012909052

Printed in the United States of America

WestBow Press rev. date: 06/26/2012

Table of Contents

Endorsements

Florli Nemeth is a woman of God whom I deeply respect. I have known her since I was a brand new Christian and have always admired her as a passionate lover of Christ who has faithfully sought the heart of God in pure devotion.

Songs of the Heart is a valuable tool for your intimate sacred times with the Lord's. Florli's insights and meditations into the Song of Solomon will indeed enhance and deepen your understanding of Christ's eternal love for you.

I highly recommend adding Songs of the Heart to your devotional library.

Patricia King, Author of a number of books, including "*The Bride Makes Herself Ready*" and "*Dream Big*"
XPmedia.com

Florli's heart and passion for God is reflected in her meditations on the Song of Solomon. Rather than a strictly theological exposition of this challenging portion of Scripture the writer presents it as a conversation of love between believers and their Lord. This has been a work of worship.

Rev. Linda Wegner
Owner, Words of Worth: writing for and about business
Powell River, BC
www.wordsofworth.ca

Florli has brought many refreshing and insightful perspectives to the Song of Songs. I have known Florli for many years and I know that these perspectives come from the depths of her own spirituality.

She writes with transparency and candor as we are allowed to peer into the author's personal journey of faith and intimacy with God. This is a great book, Florli, thank you for sharing it with us!

Rev. Kenneth Parker, National Director, ACOP of Canada and Apostle to the Nations
www.acop.ca

Foreword

Our Lord's instruction to love Him "with all of our heart, soul and strength" and then to "love our neighbour as ourselves", sets an undisputable priority and order for what should take place in every life on planet Earth. While this is a command, it is mingled with the notion that loving God and having a relationship with Him, through Jesus Christ, is both the highest privilege and greatest life changing experience we can come into in this life.

The most empty life is one void of the presence and embrace of the Creator. Being alienated from the life of God is not what was planned at creation. David said it well when he cried out, "Cast me not away from your presence". So many people live their lives with a feeling of emptiness. A 20th century author, H.S Vigeveno, in his book "*The Revolutionary Jesus*" said it well, "There is a God-shaped vacuum in the life of every man that only God can fill".

Christ coming to fill our hearts is just the beginning of a life-long journey with the One who desires to be our best friend, closest associate and confidant. God's perfect plan is that there be a growing relationship which develops seamlessly right into eternity. As relationship develops here and now with Christ, we engage in just a little bit or maybe better said, a lot of heaven on earth because we are in His presence in a relationship that is friend to friend. "We love Him because He first loved us."

The Song of Solomon brings so many clear illustrations as to how this happens when we relate openly to Jesus. Salvation's plan is to reconcile us to God so we can have unhindered communion with God because of the work of Christ on the cross. That work opens the door to an ongoing, growing relationship.

Depth of relationship does not happen overnight, it takes time and there is a process and path for this to happen. Our Lord is patient. He grows us in His grace, drawing us to run after Him. He affirms us amid our sin scars, failures and insecurities; unfolding His plan for us as we move forward with and in Him. As we behold Him we are changed into the same image and are able to relate in a growing, mature way with the Lover of our soul.

"SONGS OF THE HEART – An Intimate Journey of Love" is well titled by the author of this devotional. I have come to know and admire Florli as a member of Gateway, an employee, a labourer in the Gospel and as a friend. Her service to the Lord is undoubtedly born out of true intimacy with her Lord.

Florli writes from the vantage point of a life journey that is very human, yet exemplary of responding to her Lord who has passionately pursued her. She has responded in a personal, loving, Biblical way, sharing the truth and lessons of her journey and experience with the Lord.

Contained in these pages are timeless truths that will inspire you on a daily basis to become like the beloved apostle John, who was able to draw near enough in confidence to place his head on the breast of our Lord with intimate - pure desire. This devotional, drawn out of truth and experience, will assist you in becoming intimate with the Lover of your soul, thus achieving life's greatest joy.

Rev. Timothy A. Osiowy, Founding Pastor
Gateway Christian Ministries in Prince George, British Columbia, Canada

Dedication

To Mrs. Sylvia Sirag, a dear mentor and friend who introduced me to the study of the Song of Solomon when I was 16 years old and a junior in high school at Prairie Bible Institute.

She was born in 1909 and served with her husband as a missionary to Indonesia. Suffering imprisonment during World War II along with her three boys and separated from her husband, she learned to draw into that intimate place with God where He strengthened and sustained her.

At the end of the war, finding that her husband had died in prison, she returned to North America with her three sons and for a time resided near Prairie Bible Institute in Three Hills, Alberta.

I first met her when she offered to teach a Bible study for girls who wanted more of God. She introduced us to the study of the Song of Solomon. We read Jesse Penn Lewis's book on this Song, and we studied the Song verse by verse. The seeds planted in my heart at this young age took root and gave me a strong desire to know the Lord more intimately.

When introduced to Mike Bickle's Song of Songs material there resounded a "yes" in my spirit, and the seeds planted so long ago began to germinate and bear fruit, the result of which you will see in this book.

My precious friend, Mother Sirag as I loved to call her, went home to be with her Lord on May 7th, 2005. To her I dedicate this book. She was a friend to me in my youth, a mentor and counselor, a loving servant of Jesus Christ, and a passionate lover of God. Today she stands before her Lord, her Friend and Lover, and enjoys intimate, face to face communion with God.

Thank you, Mother Sirag, for your faithfulness as a teacher of the Word, as an intercessor, and as an intimate lover of God. To you I dedicate this book.

Acknowledgements

I wish to thank my pastor, Rev. Timothy A. Osiowy, for his profound encouragement as a mentor and friend, and his assistant, Mrs. Shelley Poulin. They were the first to proof-read my work and express appreciation for it.

Thanks to others who read some of this material, gave me great ideas and offered timely advice. Among them were Rev. Elsie Welch, involved in ministry to the nations, Rev. Kenn Parker, another mentor and friend, Rev. Abe Friesen and his wife Olga, missionaries and teachers, Mrs. Dixie Hoffman, Prayer Pastor at my local church, her husband Ernest Hoffman and my life-long friend Theresa Burge and her sister and brother-in-law, Rosie and Bill Stoppenbrink who used the material as a devotional on a holiday we shared together at the ocean in Northern California.

Thanks to my friend, Rev. Marja Kostamo, who introduced me to Mike Bickle's work on the Song of Songs, and whose passionate pursuit to become a lover of God constantly challenges me to keep moving in that direction!

Thanks to Pastor Mike Bickle whose teaching on the Song of Songs has gone around the world and has opened up a door to intimacy with God that many of us have desired to enter into for many years. The study of his material challenged me to go deeper into this book for myself. I am indebted to him for much of my understanding of this book and for the outline I have used which is totally his.

Thanks to my sisters – Ruth, Sue, Betty, and Esther – and my brothers – Paul and David - who have always encouraged me in my writings and poetry.

A very special thank you to my editor, Rev. Linda Wegner who worked with me, prayed with me, and did for me what only she could do in helping to produce the finished product you see today.

Thanks to Ruth Barbin, a friend and former co-worker who volunteered to do the final line edit for me. You came to my rescue, and your expertise was greatly appreciated.

Thanks to my dear friend, Patricia King, her life a living example of a lover of God whose ministry flows out of intimate relationship with God. In all the years we've known each other, she continues to inspire me to higher heights and deeper depths in my relationship with God!

Thanks most of all to my late husband, Dr. Rev. Stephen Nemeth, who supported me in the initial beginnings of this endeavor and whose love for God continues to challenge me to become a more passionate lover of God.

Introduction

As a teenager studying the book of the Song of Solomon I never in my wildest imaginations dreamt that one day I would write anything at all on this book of the Bible!

You will be reading my personal spiritual journal as I have studied, prayed and wept my way through the Song of Solomon, verse by verse.

You possibly have never read a book quite like this! But this book is not only for me! It is for YOU!

The "*KISSES OF LOVE*" are the kisses of God's Word as it touches our lives. May you experience many such "kisses" as you open your heart to this book.

This is my prayer for you -

1. That you will read it as a daily devotional, one verse at a time, letting your heart soak in the truth of God's Word to YOU personally.
2. That you will take my prayers and make them yours!
3. That you will take His words to me, and receive them for yourself because they ARE for you too!

The greatest benefit of this book to you will be when you take off from what you read here, and you begin to form your own prayers, and you begin to record in your own journal what God is saying to ***YOU***.

When this happens, I will be delighted to know that what I have shared of my personal spiritual journey has encouraged you to go on your own spiritual journey in this book, the Song of Songs!

I know you are excited to begin your journey to become a more intimate lover of God. Go for it! I bless you in Jesus' name!

Love,
Florli Nemeth

Chapter One

Introduction

Verse 1

The Song of Songs [the most excellent of them all] which is Solomon's.

My prayer:
Lord, Solomon wrote so many songs, reportedly over a thousand, yet this *one* alone was preserved for us in the canon of Scripture, the *one* song meant for the whole body of Christ.

Lord, I ask You to give me songs for the bride. You have given me many songs that I have sung to You alone; thank You for giving me a song for the whole body of Christ. I open my heart to You to receive Yours—whatever You choose to give me. Open my heart to sing this new song, a sound coming forth from my heart, O Lord.

Father, give me a greater understanding of this book, this song. Let it become the song of *my* heart, not just Solomon's; let it be a song sung from *my* heart! I want to grow in my love relationship with You. I want to know You intimately, personally, firsthand. Make me passionate in my love for You.

My heart is often prone to become "hum-ho," complacent in my relationship with You. But God, stir my heart once again with this song of all songs. Take me deeper. Lift me higher. Let me see and know and love You, Jesus. Give me eyes for only you!

He said:
I prayed that you would see My glory and that the Father would reveal His love to you. He loves you just like He loves Me! Revealing that truth is My commitment to your life. My promise to you and to all My people is that I will continue to reveal the Father's love to your heart.

In your desire to continue your study of this song, I urge you to keep on pursuing the Father's love and the understanding and experience of My love for you. It is an everlasting love with no end, a love that will continue to grow forever, into eternity. Even after the official marriage of the Lamb in the ages (or Age) to come, your continued pursuit of me will cause you to grow in the understanding of My love for you.

Yes, I will give you a new song. I will give you songs in the night, songs that will bless My body, songs that will bless Me! My heart is so passionately in love with you, and your songs are so dear to My heart. Sing your songs of love, dear one, and I will come to you and anoint you to sing as never before.

Your destiny is to call My people to love and to worship. Your alp horn will sound near and far—across the mountain, from peak to peak and valley to valley. Till now, your songs have been primarily for Me with a few for your local body of believers. But I'm redefining your life and ministry; in My timing, you will find yourself catapulted into a more public ministry.

Wait on Me for the songs of love that I desire to release to My body. Sing to Me. Spend time with Me. Spend your life on Me. O, how much I love you!

The Divine Kiss and the Awakening of Love

Verse 2

Let Him kiss me with the kisses of His mouth: for Thy love is better than wine. Kiss me again and again, for Your love is sweeter than wine. (Living Bible)

My prayer:
Lord Jesus, I long to feel Your love again and again. Every morning when I wake, I look for You and long for the sense of Your presence. The more You kiss me with Your love, the more I want to feel Your embrace. The more You kiss me with Your Word, the more I want to be kissed!

And Lord, the word *love* denotes "loves"—plural in the Hebrew. The many expressions of Your love are sweeter than anything the world may offer. The wine of Your Word is refreshing and exhilarating! It causes my heart to rejoice, relax, and be at rest. I love to drink Your Word and then lie down to rest, trusting my heart to Your Word.

Your Word refreshes me, brings rest to my heart, and reassures me of Your faithfulness, Your mercy, and Your loving affirmations over me. Your Word opens my eyes to see You in all Your glory; I long to see Your bride as You are preparing her for Yourself. I long to see those who still sit in darkness and in the shadow of death, waiting for someone to show them the way to life and love—to Jesus!

O Jesus, kiss me with Your presence and Your Word. There is no one like You. My heart cries out for You, for Your love, for Your Word. Kiss me again today! Your love is so much better than the best this world can offer.

He said:
I, too, look forward to your times with Me. I delight in you and in your love. As you come and sit daily at My feet, waiting in My courts, My heart is overwhelmed with your devotion. I will kiss you as you come to Me again and again and morning by morning. I love you, My child. I delight to fill your heart with My love today.

Verse 3

Because of the savour of Thy good ointments Thy name is as ointment poured forth, therefore do the virgins love Thee.

My prayer:
Why do I long to know You better, my God? Because Your love is better than anything this world has to offer and because the odor of Your ointments is fragrant. You are fairer than the children of men, and graciousness is poured upon Your lips.[1]

You are a good God, faithful to Your Word and showing mercy to thousands, forgiving sin, and filling hearts with joy. Your ointments—Your graces—adorn You and refresh those who draw near to You.[2]

Jesus, You were anointed to preach a gospel of good news to the poor and afflicted. You were sent to bind up and heal the brokenhearted, to proclaim liberty to the captives, and to open the prison of those who are bound.[3]

You came to proclaim the year of God's favor, *not* God's anger! You came to comfort and to give joy to those who mourn. You came to give beauty instead of ashes, oil of joy instead of mourning, and the garment of praise instead of heaviness and depression.[4]

O God, Your heart is like that of the father who waited and longed for his younger son to return home. He desired to favor his son and pour out blessings upon him. He desired to provide for him and cover him with his love and forgiveness. Most of all, he desired his friendship and companionship. He was a good father with a heart of love for his son.

You, too, are good, and Your message is one of love outpoured. It is Your very goodness that draws me to You. You, in turn, long for my response so that You can bless me. Nor is Your desire for me alone, this is Your heart for all mankind! O Jesus! The fragrance of Your goodness is so intoxicating. It draws me to desire You above all others.[5]

---

1 Psalm 45:2
2 Jeremiah 32:18
3 Isaiah 61:1
4 Isaiah 61:2,3
5 John 3:16

He said:
I stand with arms outstretched toward every human being. None has strayed too far or sinned too deeply for Me to save and heal and deliver. I am good and I am love. I gave My life to bear the sins of all and to die their death so that they might live. And I come today with a message of hope and healing for *all*. This is good news! And as you proclaim it, many will be drawn to the fragrance of My ointments.

You have longed to be refreshed in heart. Come and sit a while with Me and bask in the fragrance of My presence. As you go from this place, others will be drawn to you because of the fragrance of My ointments flowing from you.

I am kind and loving, gentle and caring, patient and forgiving. These graces are within you, too—a sweet attractiveness that draws people to you and eventually to Me! So live in My presence, and the fragrance of My ointments over you will grace your life and fill you with My joy.

Verse 4A

Draw me, we will run after thee . . .

My prayer:
Draw me, my Father. I desire to be near You, very near You. I have no desire to walk at a distance. I want to love you more, like John who was closest to You. Because no casual relationship would satisfy, John laid his head on Your breast in a longing to know Your heart and feel Your love.

Father, I recognize I do not have the strength to follow You closely. I need You to draw me, to make me willing, to give me the deep desire to be close to You. I do not depend on my own self-sufficiency.

> I in myself am nothing—
> I cannot even cling
> To Him who bought me with His blood
> And makes my heart to sing!
>
> *Poetry written by Florli Nemeth*

It is Your clinging to me that matters, Lord Jesus. It is Your visits and the allurement of Your love that draws me to new levels of prayer and purpose, worship and praise, love and adoration. You are always running and skipping on the high places. Take me with you! I want to run!

I want to run in prayer, in ministry, in love for You and for Your people. I want to run the race You have set before me, but I need Your enabling to do it! So draw me again and again; empower me again and again.

He said
I was looking for you this morning - listening for your voice. There is only one like you! I say, Come! And yes, I will draw you, enable you, empower you to run today. And as you run toward Me, others will be encouraged to follow and to run toward Me, too.

Every day that you run you advance in your own personal journey with Me, and I rejoice in your spiritual progress! As I lure you by My love, you are enabled to go higher in prayer, in love, and in all the graces that need to be added to your faith. My work in your life is never ending as I continually add to your life - always enriching - always leading higher - always causing you to make progress even on your high places of difficulty. Nothing is too difficult for Me! How I love you, My dearest beloved![6]

I hear your cry and your desire. I'm holding your hand so run with Me! Come with Me! Walk with Me! Climb with Me! Explore with Me! Pouring My indescribable love upon you, I long for you to enjoy My presence even as I waft My perfume over you. Leaving your high place, remember that you leave *with Me* as well as with My fragrance upon you!

Verse 4B

. . . . the king hath brought me into his chambers . . .

My prayer
Lord Jesus, You are crowned with glory and honor - crowned a King by the God of all the earth!

For the Lord declares, This is the King of my choice, and I have enthroned him in Jerusalem, my holy city. His chosen one replies, I will reveal the everlasting

---

[6] Habakkuk 3:19

purposes of God, for the Lord has said to me, You are my Son. This is your Coronation Day. Today I am giving you your glory.[7]

You were chosen by God to be King, and I, too, choose You as my King! I choose to love You and submit my life to You. I choose to live under Your reign! You are the King of my heart. You are enthroned in the praises of Your people, You are the chosen Son of God, You are King of all the nations! God has blessed You forever.[8]

You brought me - picked me up and carried me into Your palace, a place I could not reach on my own. Many barriers proved to be a hindrance to intimacy, yet You overcame every difficulty. Your life and shed blood brought me near to God. Father God, You chose Jesus to be King just as You chose David, taking him from feeding sheep and from following the ewes with the lambs.[9]

You gave David as a shepherd for Your people - a shepherd whose true heart and skillful hands provided and cared for them. Likewise You anointed Jesus King. As a Shepherd He cares for His people as could none other. Thank You Father, for giving me such a wonderful King. Thank You for giving me to Him! He cares for me. He brings me into His chambers daily. He loves me - He cares for my needs - He answers the cry of my heart for nearness to God!

He said

> Yes, I truly am your God and your King.
> Yes, I am committed to make your heart sing.
> Yes, I have paid the price to ransom your soul.
> Yes, I forgave you and made your heart whole.
> Now I can bring you, gather in My arms
> Right into My palace, safe from all harm.

Poetry written by Florli Nemeth

My child, you are the child of the King! I have overcome every obstacle the enemy put before Me in My journey to the cross. There I died for

7 Psalm 2:6,7 Living Bible
8 Psalm 45:1,2
9 Psalm 78:70, 72

your sin and purchased your salvation. Would I leave you now? No, for I have overcome every obstacle in your life that would keep you from enjoying intimacy with Me.

Each day I pick you up and carry you over every mountain and hill to the closeness of My chambers! When you come each morning in your weariness, I meet you at My gates with arms spread wide and I call out, Come! I long to bring you close to Me and my desire is toward you. One day, when your time on earth is completed, I'll be at the gate of heaven to carry you into My eternal presence. I long for that day - to show you off as My purchased possession, My Bride!

Dear one, I see your weariness and I am here today to strengthen and encourage you. You are not alone, and you are greatly loved. Child of My heart, lean hard today. Lean hard on Me! Lean on Me for strength, for wisdom. I know the questions you need answers for today. I am your Wisdom - your Help - your Counselor and Confidant - Your Husband!

Verse 4C

. . . .we will be glad and rejoice in thee . . .

My prayer

Lord, I'm so grateful to You for hearing My prayer and drawing me into Your presence. I find the closer I come to You, the more my heart is at peace. I rest, happy and content just to be near You. But as I come closer, I realize there are many others who are drawing close to You and are rejoicing in You, as well. This confirms Your promise that "in His presence is fullness of joy and pleasures forevermore."[10]

Increasingly I experience the pleasures of drawing near to You! And Lord, I see there are degrees of joy and steps in coming into communion with You that bring new and increasing joy and rest previously unknown. Your joy is deep and touches every area of my life, bringing rest even in the midst of stress and busyness.

[10] Psalm 16:11

But joy of all joys, I know there's more! That's what keeps me going - from one degree of joy to another! I confess to You, however, there are times when my joy is diminished, not nearly as full as at other times.

Sometimes You lead me to a level I haven't experienced yet, and You say, "Here, taste this!" Then You lead me back down to the place I've already known. It is then I grasp a new revelation of something more in God that can be mine. I have experienced this before, My Lord, when at conferences and prayer gatherings Your presence and joy descended upon Your corporate body. It is as if You have displayed possibilities in prayer that we have not known before and then You say, "Now go and make this higher level yours."

Lord, the object of my joy - the reason for any joy I have - is *You*! You so delight my heart. This joy I have - this joy You give - does not depend on any earthly circumstance. Your joy embraces my heart and strengthens me in the way. O Lord, Your joy is my strength today. I will rejoice and be glad in You. I *choose* the attitude of my heart - and I choose joy today![11]

He said
Now you are truly coming to understand how My love works! As I bring joy to your heart, you partake of My strength and peace and stability. A joyful, loving person is a stable person in their emotions. My love stabilizes you emotionally, and My love in you - released in you and through you - adds to your life and to the lives of those you touch. I want to take you to higher levels, to greater experiences in My presence. I am committed to you to do that for you.

Dear one, I am so pleased with the way your heart reaches out to Me. Continue in My love. Continue to open your heart to Me, to come into My presence, to be around people who have experienced more of Me than you have. Stay close to the shepherds' tents. And My dearest Child, I touch you today with My joy! It is your strength - the source of your power. Be strong! Be blessed! Be a blessing today. O how much I love you! You are so beautiful!

---

[11] Nehemiah 8:10

Verse 4D

. . . . we will remember thy love more than wine . . . .

My prayer
Lord, when I remember something, I don't forget. I acknowledge Your love and mercy over me. I am so grateful to You for all Your blessings and answers to prayer. I will never forget or lay aside Your precepts, Lord, for You have used them to restore my joy and my health.[12]

Your faithfulness extends to every generation, just like the earth You created. Your Word stands forever in heaven. These are things I want to remember forever and I am so grateful to You. Your love and provision for mankind is amazing! I don't ever want to forget Your love because You are so good! There is no one like You.[13]

But it is when times are tough and when you may choose to hide Your face that I never want to forget Your love and goodness. When my emotions defy my trust it is then that I need to remind myself of Your love, Your faithfulness, Your goodness and kindness, Your provision. But joy of all joys, I know there's more! That's what keeps me going - from one degree of joy to another! But, I confess to You, there are times when my joy is diminished, not nearly as full as at other times.

It is in those moments or days when I need to recall that Your left hand is under my head protecting me and Your right hand embraces me, holding me fast.

Lord, help me to forget what I should forget - what You Yourself have forgotten and forgiven– my sins, and my faults and failures. Help me remember Your daily mercies - the little graces, little expressions of Your love that accompany Your great goodness and faithfulness and mercy! Jesus, I love You so much!

He said
You are awesome as an army with banners. When I look at you, I'm overwhelmed with your heart of love toward Me. My banner over

---

[12] Psalm 119:93 Living Bible

[13] Psalm 119:89-91 Living Bible

you is love. I see you as a victorious army coming home with all its banners.

And I say to you, dear one, that you walk in victory today because you remembered to sit with Me, to talk with Me, to worship Me, to receive My Word into your heart. It is My Word that works to transform your life. Because You have remembered to look daily into the mirror of My Word, My words are released to work changes in you and to conform you into My image.

So dear one, don't forget -

> I carry you - I love you, I hold you close to My heart.
> I need you - I value you, I've given you a part.
> I chasten you - I discipline, I draw you back when you stray.
> I teach you - I guide you, I shepherd you day after day.
> I use you - I fill you, I strengthen you to do My will.
> I call you - I challenge you, to climb the mountains still.
> I love you, I love you, I love you, dearest child of My heart!
>
> *Poetry written by Florli Nemeth*

Verse 4E

. . . . the upright love Thee.

My prayer
O dear Shepherd, dear Jesus, it is You I love above all others! You are loved dearly by those You love. Look upon us, Your struggling people, and see with joy our desire to love You in purity and sincerity.

I am sustained, dear Jesus, by the knowledge that You see me and all Your people as pure and sincere, even when we fail. I am strengthened knowing that You are not looking for perfection but simply for those whose heart is pure, overflowing with earnest love for You. If that's how You see Your people, then help me to see Your people in that way, as well. Sometimes I see people in a negative way, but I want to see them as You see them. Open my eyes Jesus, to see as You see!

He said
I view the ones I love as chaste virgins, pure and sincere in their love for Me. Dearest Child, My heart aches when you allow the enemy to demean you and strike you down. Remember that the wound

you suffered last night is not an unknown thing on this journey. Not everyone will be drawn to you or even like you; for reasons they themselves may not understand there are those who will find their spirit at war against yours.

In all of this remember above all to keep your heart pure before Me. It is better to be wounded without just cause than to be wounded for one that was just! Give this injustice to Me and let Me be the judge of all that has transpired. Dear one, I see the uprightness of your heart, and I know you love Me. I love your commitment to honor Me in your work and, indeed, in all you do.

Will you allow Me to purify you? Sometimes the instrument I use is the pain of criticism deserved or even undeserved. You see, dear one, I'm a partner with you in this, and by allowing criticism to touch your soul, My refining work will make of you an even better person!

I see you as a pure virgin, and an upright person. I know your love for Me and I am blessed. Sometimes I have to look away from you because I am so overcome with love for you. Come, run to Me, I long to envelop you in My love.[14]

---

[14] Song of Songs 6:5 and Ephesians 3:18,19

The Bride's First Crisis Experience

Verse 5

I am black, but comely, O ye daughters of Jerusalem, as the tents of Kedar, as the curtains of Solomon.

Psalm 45:13
The King's daughter is all glorious within . . . .

My prayer
Lord, when I see shades of darkness in my life, help me not to despair. And when I see Your beautifying graces within me, keep me free from becoming proud and from the temptation to claim what is nothing of **my** doing.

Father, where there is darkness in me that offends others, deal with my heart, draw it out of me. Wash my feet daily, Jesus. I need the probing of Your Spirit because my tendency is not to see my faults at all, or to see them so clearly that I am consumed with them and driven to despair.

Help me never deny what You see - that I am beautiful, even when I am blinded by my shadows. Yet help me never forget my humanness, my darkness, when I see Your graces in my life. Help me live before others in humility, knowing that they may see my faults before they see Your beauty in me. Let me display the truths that honor You: I *am* dark, I *do* fail, I am not perfect *but, because of Your grace upon me, I am beautiful!*

Help us, Your people, understand both aspects of who we are. You know our temptation to despair or to become sinfully proud. Jesus, You want me to see both darkness and beauty in myself and in others. I cry to You for help with this.

He said
It is good you see yourself as dark. So often My people do not struggle with seeing themselves as dark - they struggle with believing themselves to be beautiful and lovely in Me! You struggle with the same thing. So why do you go to pieces when someone points out a darkness in your life? If others can see your weaknesses, should you not be grateful when someone points out a weakness you may not even be aware of?

Could your despair at seeing your weakness be the result of your forgetting My grace? Forgetting My redemption? Forgetting My work on the cross for you? You will always be dark *but* lovely. And it is your correct view of your darkness that will enable you to see your beauty without becoming proud and haughty. O My dear, sweet, lovely child! You are so beautiful within, so awesome! When you see your darkness, or when others point it out (kindly, or otherwise) just run to the Cross.

The cross is your place of refuge - the place where My blood atones for your sin, the place of forgiveness, the place where I commission you to get up and go again. The cross is the place where you obtain My covering, My beauty, My beautiful robe of righteousness. Yes, there will always be shadows of darkness, but you are so very beautiful! I want My people to see their beauty as well as their darkness. Tell them for Me, won't you?

Verse 6A

Look not upon me, because I am black, because the sun hath looked upon me . . . .

My prayer
Sometimes our weaknesses obscure the beauty of Your grace in our lives, Lord. And sometimes, we all spend more time looking at people's weaknesses and infirmities rather than looking for Your graces. Lord, help me to spend more time looking for Your beauty and Your grace in others' lives. Cover my darkness. May others never be made to stumble by any weakness or infirmity in my life.

And Father, I pray for the body of Christ in general that we would not be stumbled by the sins and failures, weaknesses and infirmities of those in places of leadership. Lord, You know there is enough weakness in any of us to cause others to stumble. But particularly where those you have called to be leaders - pastors, apostles, prophets, evangelists, teachers - have fallen into sin because of weaknesses in their lives, help Your Body to **cover** them - to release them to Your dealings - and to continue to follow after You!

Father, help the young ones especially to get their eyes off the darkness they see in others and focus their eyes on Your grace, Your love, Your forgiveness, Your power to restore and Your power to heal. Deliver us Lord from bad-mouthing Your prophets because of their infirmities and failures.

He said
This is an awesome thing - a critical issue in My Body. I have leaders who, like Samson, have great power and strength and anointing yet struggle with great flaws and weaknesses in their character and in their lives. Because they are so visible in their ministry, people see their flaws and weaknesses and some become disillusioned, frustrated and bitter because they suppose My servants should be perfect!

The truth of the matter is that *none* of My servants are perfect. That is why I work in your life, My child. If you allow Me to prune your life and to catch the little foxes, you will never need to feel the shame of your weaknesses and infirmities. If you allow these things to be exposed to Me, I will deal with them so they are not exposed to others!

Keep humble before Me. Come often to the Cross. Lay down your life before Me. Spend much time in My presence for yourself - *not* for your ministry!

As you spend time with Me, I will pour My life into you and you will be strong in My power and anointing. And My glory will cover you. I always cover those who spend much time with Me. When you sense a lack of covering and you see your weaknesses, run again into My arms - into My presence. Let the passion of your life be to *be with Me!* O how I love you, My dear child! I bless and strengthen you today.

Verse 6B

My mother's children were angry with me; they made me the keeper of the vineyards, but mine own vineyard have I not kept.

My prayer
Father, there are times when I feel I have been given more to do than I can accomplish. Sometimes I fail to meet others' expectations and they become frustrated with me.

They may not even be angry with me at all but when I feel I fail to meet others' expectations, I can easily believe they are - even without knowing!

Sometimes, though, our feelings are justified and our brothers and sisters can become our greatest enemies because we fail to be or to do what they expected we would be or do. I have experienced this a few times in my life, Father, and it is so painful to feel one's self accused wrongly. And yet, no matter what others expect of me, my most important commitment is to keep my own vineyard - to spend time in fellowship with You.

Sometimes, Lord, it's not even others' expectations, but my own busyness and my own expectations that keep me from You. At this season in my life I need primarily and most importantly to be in Your presence, worshipping and loving You. My heart needs You more than it needs anything else. Come to me, my dear Shepherd. Help me tend my own vineyard so I can adequately care for other vineyards.

He said
Come to Me and sit at My feet like Mary, the sister of Martha did. Ponder over the things I have spoken to you like My mother, Mary did. You may feel like you haven't kept your vineyard, but I see much fruit in your life My Child. There are things you cannot always see yourself. So you need to rejoice in the fruit that **is** there!

You know dear one, if you will keep a thankful heart, that alone will keep out many weeds of self-pity, discontent, fear of the unknown, and frustration with yourself and with others. My Word says the joy of the Lord is your strength. You keep your vineyard when you speak My Word regardless of your feelings or circumstances. Just embrace those around you, receive My enabling and continue in My joy!

So especially now, dear one, guard your thoughts, your words, your attitudes. Don't let anything negative take root in your heart. Keep the vineyard clear of all that stuff . . . and you know what? I will help you! *You are an awesome, beautiful, stunningly beautiful bride!*

Don't worry about how you're going to look after your vineyard. Just let Me help you moment by moment, morning by morning, hour by hour, and day by day. You can't look after others if you're not well cared for yourself. Don't expect others to do this. *You must do it with Me!*

I'm here for you - to help, to strengthen and to sustain you. Today go out and leap over mountains with Me! Don't try to do it on your own; you might fall and break your bones. I love you! Have fun!!! Enjoy your life today.

Verse 7A

Tell me, O thou whom my soul loveth, where thou feedest, where thou makest thy flock to rest at noon . . .

My prayer
O Thou whom my soul loves, where *do* You feed Your flock? Where *do* You rest at noon? I want to be fed by You - I need to find Your rest in the heat of the day. I need to know where to lie down and rest when everything in my life is in disarray and I feel I cannot cope another day. I need to know where to go when the pressures I feel hinder me from every kind of rest.

Dear Shepherd, I need Your nourishment and Your rest. You alone can meet my deepest and every need. I need to be upheld by You. I need to be kept safe and secure within Your hand.

A song I memorized many years ago came back into my consciousness today, and I was so blessed by it! It's an old hymn written by Joseph Swain in 1791.

> "O Thou in Whose presence my soul takes delight
> On Whom in affliction I call
> My Comfort by day and my Song in the night,
> My Hope, my Salvation, my All!
>
> Where dost Thou, dear Shepherd, resort with Thy sheep
> To feed them in pastures of love?
> Say, why in the valley of death should I weep
> Or alone in this wilderness rove?
>
> O why should I wander, an alien from Thee
> Or cry in the desert for bread?
> Thy foes will rejoice when my sorrows they see
> And smile at the tears I have shed.
>
> Dear Shepherd, I hear and will follow Thy call;
> I know the sweet sound of Thy voice.
> Restore and defend me, for Thou art my All
> And in Thee I will ever rejoice."

Lord, Your Word affirms those words for You have said *"My presence shall go with thee, and I will give thee rest".*[15]

When Your people needed respite from the journey, *The ark went before them during the three days journey to seek out a resting place for them."*[16]

It is You, oh Lord, alone who leads me to a place of rest.

He said
I seek out resting places for you. This season is one of quiet restoration, a time to shut the door and be with Me. Your circumstances are no surprise to Me. In fact, I prepared you for this and led you even without your knowing of it. So do not chafe at the seeming delay but rather, rest during this time and season in your lives. Enjoy your husband's presence, do things together, and be drawn into My presence together. I spoke these words so long ago to the Psalmist and they hold true for you: *". . . . my body too shall rest and confidently dwell in safety."*[17]

My prayer

Wherever You are - that's where I want to be!
Wherever You rest, that's where I too can see
Streams and clear water
Life-giving drink
Grass and green pastures
Nourishing food.
So feed me, my Shepherd, and cause me to rest
Lying my head down, upon Your breast.
Let me drink deeply, deeply of love
Let me feast daily, daily on love.
Let me rest gently, gently on Your shoulders
Let me live wholly, wholly for You!

Poetry written by Florli Nemeth

Jesus, I just don't have the words to tell You how much I love You, how much I need You. I cannot face a single day without Your love, Your

[15] Exodus 33:14
[16] Numbers 10:33
[17] Psalm 16:9

strength, Your provision, Your protection, Your rest. Lead me to Your resting place and let me stay forever there. I must join You wherever You are. I must be with You. I must feel Your strong arms supporting me and drawing me close to Your heart. Gentle Shepherd, truest Friend, Your love is my resting place forever.

He said
Yes, dear one, I see your heart. I know the sweet thoughts of your heart toward Me. My heart is overwhelmed at the way you reach out for Me and look for Me.

I am here, My child - here for you! I will never leave you nor forsake you. I draw you to My heart today. I lead you to quiet streams and beautiful resting places in the valley. Today there are no mountains for you to climb, just grassy pastures and clear streams of water.

Yes, dear one, you shall live quietly and at peace in your own home. You do not need to fear a thing. I have promised to prosper you and give you peace. I put the cloud of My presence over your house. That cloud is My presence, My peace, My protection over you. Know the prosperity of my presence with you.

What the enemy has stolen shall be returned to you because I am a prosperous God and I desire My people to walk in My prosperity. Do not worry, dear one. Don't think about tomorrow or the next day. I'm your Shepherd. I'm here for you today and every day of your life. You need not fear. My grace does not run out. My strength is not in short supply! My peace is ever increasing. It gets better and better!

Your strength will ever increase as you *rest* in Me! My heart is your home and you will live in peace and in prosperity in your beautiful home. I love you so much, My dear child!

Verse 7B

. . . for why should I be as one that turneth aside by the flocks of thy companions?

My prayer
Lord, I don't ever want to turn aside or wander alone by the flocks; I don't want to miss the mark. Help me, Lord, in the heat of the day

and in the midst of the pressures of life, to maintain a leaning, trusting heart - resting in Your love, drawing from Your strength, finding my help and consolation in You.

Father, under the scorching sun of trials and tribulation it is so easy to lose my way - so easy to give in to a negative mind set, to succumb to the weakness of my flesh, and so easy to give way to stress, weariness and the pain of isolation.

Lord, help me to know and to remember that in times like these You carry Your people. You comfort, You refresh, You strengthen, You encourage, You make me equal to every situation I face no matter how scorching the sun may be! Bring to my mind those truths that are hidden deeply in my heart.

It is Your job to lead me into safe pastures, to give me cool, refreshing places in the heat of the day, to tenderly care for me, especially in times of suffering. O, dear Shepherd, forgive my lack of faith and trust. How could I ever mistrust You? I quiet myself in Your presence today that I might find Your peace and help and direction.

Lord, there are so many of Your flock who follow after their own way. They may know You, but are not following You closely, nor are they in loving communion with You. Jesus, keep me from wandering from You! I cannot bear the thought of wandering like a vagabond in the wilderness! I want only to be with You - wherever You are.

Joseph Swain wrote this beautiful hymn, and my heart beats as his:

"O why should I wander an alien from Thee
Or cry in the desert for bread?
Thy foes will rejoice when my sorrows they see
And smile at the tears I have shed.

Dear Shepherd, I hear and will follow Thy call
I know the sweet sound of Thy voice
Restore and defend me for Thou art my all
And in Thee I will ever rejoice."

Verse 8

If thou know not, O thou fairest among women, go thy way forth by the footsteps of the flock and feed thy kids beside the shepherds' tents.

He said
I will lead you by the hand and comfort you. I will refresh and strengthen you. I have so many things to share with you. You may not always feel My presence as you do now, but remember this one thing - I will always love you, no matter what weakness or imperfection you may see in yourself! You are My Bride, and I love you - I carry you - I hold you close to My heart today.

The Bridegroom's Affirmations

Verse 9

I have compared thee, O my love, to a company of horses in Pharaoh's chariots.

He said
I see you as stately, strong and courageous. You are bold as a lion with a fearless spirit. I see you as unconquerable by the enemy. You are one who will *not* be overcome by anything the enemy throws at you.

The reason for your strength is simple: I have made you so! As you allowed Me to conquer your heart, I put within you a strength and boldness that no one or no other thing can defeat. You are a mighty conqueror My daughter, My son, and as Paul said, you are **more** than a conqueror![18] No matter what the enemy may throw at you, you are never without a place of safety and a sanctuary of peace.

As Pharaoh cared for his horses, so I will care for you, ensuring that you have everything you need. The devil lies to you, proclaiming you weak, helpless and insignificant. But I say to you today, in spite of the weakness you feel, you are as strong as the most beautiful horse in the world because you have allowed Me to conquer your heart. How I love you, My child! And dear one, you are not like just one horse - *you are like a company of horses!* You are powerful and strong today in the power and strength I pour into you.

My prayer
Thank You, Lord, my unfailing strength and faithful warrior. I ride into this day in Your power and strength. I hide myself in Your place of safety. I can face whatever comes my way because I am a conqueror - I am *more than a conqueror because of* what Your Word tells me I am.

> I will not fall, I cannot fail
> With Christ my Lord and King
> *I will not conquered be!*
> I will not doubt, I cannot miss

[18] Romans 8:37

The song He gives to sing
I will not conquered be!
I will not cry, I cannot stop
Declaring He's my Strength
I will not conquered be!
I'll not despair, I can't give up
He's with me for the length
I will not conquered be!
I will rejoice, I will look up, the Risen Christ in me
The Conquering Lamb, the Son of God in power and majesty -
Goes forth to fight my battles sore, to conquer every foe
He rides in strength and victory His might and power to show!
You are awesome, You are strong - You are faithful, You are sure
You are gracious, You are kind - You are *LOVE* forever true!
Poetry written by Florli Nemeth

Thank You for giving me the strength to ride in victory and triumph this day. I rejoice in Your awesome strength and Your powerful love!

Verse 10

Thy cheeks are comely with rows of jewels, thy neck with chains of gold.

He said
O My Child, you are beautiful! It is My grace that has made you so. You may think yourself black and full of weaknesses, but I see only that which I have placed within you and upon you. My beauty, My gifts of gold, silver and precious stones adorn you.

Remember how you adorned your granddaughter with a beautiful necklace on the day of her wedding? Expensive? Yes! But your heart would have paid almost any price to give it to her. She was truly a beautiful bride!

You are My Bride, and you, too, are adorned with the gifts and the fruit of My Spirit. I have given you many other gifts as well as My beauty upon you. My beauty has been imparted and placed upon each of My believers. This beauty comes from Me, and as a Master Designer, I work it into your life.

My grace is beautiful, resting upon you for always. It is incumbent upon you, however, to put these ornaments on! As you sit in My presence and draw from My heart my beauty and grace is bestowed upon you. Every act of submission and obedience is another precious jewel in your necklace; your neck is graced with many priceless gems. O how I love you, My beautiful bride!

My prayer
O my Beloved, even in this time of difficult circumstances in my life, You are pouring Your grace over me. Thank You for the beauty You place within me and for the jewels You have given to me.

I want to be beautifully adorned when I stand before You, neither naked nor ashamed at the lack of Your embellishment. I long to stand before You dressed in Your righteousness and gilded with ornaments of Your grace. I want to be proud to be Your Bride, Your love! I want to be confident in the beauty You place in me, the beauty You see in me. Help me to see myself as You see me, and help me to see others as You see them.

Verse 11

We will make thee borders of gold with studs of silver.

My prayer
Father, You are saying "I am making gold and silver jewelry for you that will mark and accent your beauty".[19] You promise to add to my beauty and gloriously complete it. And as James Durham, another of Your servants, said in his book, "this thing promised is the *increase, continuance and perfecting* of my comeliness and beauty". [20]

You are promising to continue to beautify and perfect me! O my precious Jesus, I am so happy with Your work in me. It is a *good work*, and Your promise is to keep on helping me to grow in grace until Your task within me is fully finished.[21] It is a *daily work* You are doing in me, adding to my beauty each new day.

---

[19] Song of Songs 1:11, The Message
[20] "The Song of Solomon" by James Durham, page 110
[21] Philippians 1:6

Each day, I receive a gift from You as You add to my beauty by the work of the Father, Son and Holy Spirit within me. Even as You were involved together in the creation of the first man, so is this a work You are all involved in, a joint design and purpose and work.

Yes, Lord, my growth in grace will never be of my own doing. It is Your work that You have undertaken to do - a work You have committed Yourself to do. Thank You for the gifts You give me every day of my life!

Father, I have never thought of Your work in my life in this way before. What a beautiful gift You have given me today! As You perfect Your work and design within, You beautify me daily with Your love and grace, constantly creating Your design within me. Thank You, my God! How dearly I love You, how greatly I honor You today. My heart cries out to worship You!

He said
I bless you today, My child. I bless you with the strength you need to be a blessing because I know that is the desire of your heart. Your desire to give is so much greater than your ability to give, yet you tend to over-extend yourself again and again in wanting to give gifts and love and hospitality and warmth and companionship to others. So dear one, I plan (in human terms) to over-extend Myself in giving to you today!

You will have the physical, mental and emotional strength you need to make this a great day for the people you've invited into your heart and into your home. Again, you've over-extended yourself in ministry because of your desire to serve. You give and give until you have nothing more to give! But I give and give and give because My resources are totally and completely limitless!!!

I never run out of strength or grace or love - I am limitless, boundless, a never-to-be-exhausted Source of whatever you may need!

My prayer
O Jesus, You are awesome! I can hardly comprehend Your vast resources and Your heart so expansive. I need You so desperately today. It is true - I have over-extended myself. But I did not know in advance all the circumstances of my life that would stretch me to the limit. I did not

know that when I opened my heart and home to a guest, but You knew! You knew I would need You!!!

Help me today, Jesus. Make me a blessing to all who enter our home, especially to the husband and family you have given me. I need Your strength.

He said
I bless you today, My child, with joy, with love and with strength! I bless you with My anointing and My presence. My heart is enamored of you; You are precious to Me. Be strengthened in your body and mind and be encouraged, knowing that I am doing a good work in you, and I will perfect it. I am committed to your good, your happiness, your growth and your perfection.

The Bride's Desire for Intimacy Expressed

Verse 12A

While the King sitteth at His table . . . .

My prayer

My prayer is to my King, the Shepherd who prepares the table for me, even in the presence of my enemies. [22] In the middle of the things that would distract me, He prepares a table for me!

In aeons past the prophet Isaiah proclaimed Your message: "*In Mount Zion He will prepare a feast in the wake of a background of gloom, judgment and terror*". [23]

In the midst of whatever chaos is happening around me, even as in the days Isaiah spoke about, You are always preparing a place where Your people may be encouraged and refreshed. Lord Jesus, You are not at a distance nor do you remove me from Your feast. We feast together, You and me. Nor do you ask *me* to prepare the feast! This banquet comes from You - from its initiation to the execution of our communion together. It is You who prepare it all for me!

We talk together at these meals of grace and our hearts are joined as You whisper the privileged words of lovers. You speak to me of loving preparation and intimate times with You. Your gifts of heavenly food and wine refresh me. You know what nourishment I need; You know my need to converse with You. You are a wonderful listener! As I open my heart to You unreservedly, I can look into Your eyes and read Your heart. I love these wonderful feasts You prepare for me and I rejoice in knowing that every day is a feast with You. Even the ordinary table set for a meal is a feast when You join me and fellowship with me.

And it's not even *my* table - I have nothing to do with it! It is *Your* table - *Your* food - *Your* nourishment and refreshing - *Your* friendship and fellowship!

---

[22] Psalm 23:5

[23] Isaiah 25:6 Amplified

He said
I welcome you as My special guest for you have understood the truth of My coming to you and being *your* special guest. [24] You have welcomed Me into your heart and into your home. Now I welcome you to My table, My feast, My celebration of love!

Just as you welcome My presence, your visits never fail to delight me. I love to hear your heart as you pour it out before Me; I love to nourish you and sustain you out of the abundance I possess. There is no time when You would fail to be welcomed by Me.

I am reminded of an old hymn - one I learned as a teenager -

> "I hunger and I thirst
> Jesu, my manna be
> Ye living waters burst
> Out of the rock for me.
>
> Thou bruised and broken bread
> My life-long wants supply
> As living souls are fed
> O feed me, or I die.
>
> Thou true life-giving vine
> Let me Thy sweetness prove
> Renew my life with Thine
> Refresh my soul with love."[25]

Verse 12B

. . . my spikenard sendeth forth the smell thereof.

My prayer
Lord, it is when I sit with You that the graces You have given begin to flow out of my life. It is Your presence that draws the fragrance out, Your presence that causes the fragrance You have imparted to flow out to others. Where You are, everything flourishes and blossoms!

---

[24] Psalm 23:5 Living Bible
[25] Written by J.S.B. Monsell

The perfume, Lord, is first for You and then for others. You give it to me, and You are also enchanted by it as I sit in Your presence. I have learned to understand the fragrance is connected to my sitting at Your table and feasting in Your presence.

Lord, I want forever to sit at the table of the King, receiving Your nourishment and graces over my life. Let Your fragrance flow forth to bless You and enchant Your heart today. I sing with another of Your servants: "*Thanks be to God…who through us spreads and makes evident the fragrance of the knowledge of God everywhere. For* ***we*** *are the sweet fragrance of Christ which exhales unto God [discernable alike] among those who are being saved and among those who are perishing."*[26] Let Your sweet fragrance minister life to everyone that touches my life today, oh God.

He said
O My beloved child, My friend, how I love for you to come and sit at My table. I love those who linger long - who allow the sweet fragrance of My love to do its beautiful work in their lives. For it is from the lingering, the remaining in My presence, that fragrance flows. Stay with Me at length for it is the overflow of My fragrance that will bless others around you. *But do not forget, the fragrance is first for Me!* Receive My fragrance and My beauty; then share it with Me as you sit at My table. You bring Me such joy, My dear friend!

My thoughts
In light of His beautiful words to me, My thoughts were drawn to several hymns I have treasured -

> "Here, O my Lord! I see Thee face to face
> Here faith can touch and handle things unseen
> Here would I grasp with firmer hand Thy grace
> And all my weariness upon Thee lean.
>
> Here would I feed upon the bread of God
> Here drink with Thee the royal wine of heaven
> Here would I lay aside each earthly load
> Here taste afresh the calm of sin forgiven.

[26] 2 Corinthians 2:14, 15 Amplified

This is the hour of banquet and of song
This is the heavenly table spread for me
Here let me feast, and feasting still prolong
The brief, bright hour of fellowship with Thee.

Too soon we rise; the symbols disappear
The feast, though not the love, is past and gone
The bread and wine remove, but Thou art here
Nearer than ever, still our Shield and Sun.

Feast after feast thus comes and passes by
Yet passing, points to that great feast above
Giving sweet foretaste of the festal joy
The Lamb's great bridal-feast of bliss and love!" [27]

Another hymn -
"Come ye yourselves apart and rest awhile
Weary, I know it, of the press and throng
Wipe from your brow the sweat and dust of toil
And in My quiet strength again be strong.

Come ye and rest: the journey is too great
And ye will faint beside the way and sink
The Bread of Life is here for you to eat
And here for you the Wine of Love to drink. [28]

And then another hymn perhaps better known -
"The King of love my Shepherd is
Whose goodness faileth never
I nothing lack if I am His
And He is mine forever.

Where streams of living water flow
My ransomed soul He leadeth
And, where the verdant pastures grow
With food celestial feedeth.

---

[27] Written by Horatius Bonar. - a song written to celebrate the ordinance of communion - the table of the Lord

[28] Written by Bishop Bickersteth

Thou spreadest a table in my sight
Thy unction grace bestowed
And oh, what transport of delight
From Thy pure chalice floweth.

And so through all the length of days
Thy goodness faileth never
Good Shepherd, may I sing Thy praise
Within Thy house forever." [29]

My prayer
O Father, these songs so express the emotions of my heart today. You are such a good and wonderful Shepherd. Your love never fails me. Forever I will sing Your praise; I will play skillfully my song of praise to You...and yet it will take an eternity to rightfully extol the glories of Your name and the limits of Your fame!

O Jesus, in Your quiet strength I am strong today. Great Bearer of Burdens, on you I cast my weariness for you alone are ALL I need and ALL I could ever want!

Verse 13 & 14

A bundle of myrrh is my well beloved unto me; he shall lie all night betwixt my breasts.
My beloved is unto me as a cluster of camphire in the vineyards of Engedi.

My prayer
O my Lord, my Beloved One, You are so special to me! Myrrh as the primary ingredient in the holy anointing oil was very precious. The bundle of myrrh speaks of Your excellency, Your worth, and Your preciousness to me! There is none other in all of earth or heaven who can compare to You!

I embrace You this morning. Holding You close to my heart, I will not let You go. My heart is Your home; be at rest, Oh God, within my heart. I hold fast to Your promise that You will never leave me nor forsake me. I truly could never part with You!

---

[29] Written by Sir H.W. Baker

I embrace Your sufferings in whatever way You allow them to come into my life. I know You will only do me good all the days of my life. All fear has been replaced with trust in You and in Your work in me. You hold me safe within the palm of Your hand. You will never let me go and there is no one who can ever pluck me from Your hand. Likewise, I hold You to my heart and I will not let You go. I've discovered not only is *Your heart* my home, but *my heart* is Your home!

He said
Beloved one, My heart responds to your embrace. I am a tree of life to you[30] and to all who will hold Me and not let Me go. In holding Me you remain connected to Me, growing daily as you get your strength and nourishment from Me. [31]

Yes, I live in you, dear one, My temple and My home. Just as you love and care for your earthly home, so I care about My home, your heart. Your efforts in cleaning, beautifying and repairing your home are more than matched by the work of My word and My spirit in cleaning and healing the broken parts of your heart. I keep you clean through My Word; I minister My healing power; I care for you! Thank you for holding Me to your bosom. You are so very dear to Me! And I will never let you go either. So rest your heart in My love and in My care.

---

[30] Proverbs 3:18

[31] Colossians 2:19 Living Bible

The Bridegroom's Declaration of the Bride's Beauty

Verse 15

Behold, thou art fair, my love; behold, thou art fair; thou hast doves' eyes.

He said
You are My love, Mine, and Mine alone. And, as true lovers know, your heart is Mine, and Mine alone with eyes for only Me. I pronounce My beauty over you and I declare before the whole of heaven and earth - You are ALL fair - you are beautiful!!!

There are many who look to see your blemishes, blackness, weaknesses and imperfections. But I see you as beautiful. Because in your human frailty you also need to feel the affirmation of My love and to hear the expression of My love, you will hear my voice again and again - declaring your beauty and My love. Listen closely to My voice when the enemy tells his lies, causing you to focus on your darkness.

Yes, some dark spots remain in your life, but it is My purpose and intention to refine your beauty, leaving you without spot or wrinkle. I esteem My Bride very highly and it is My estimation of you that holds eternal value. Guard your heart and your inclination to estimate your own worth - that evaluation will always come up short.

Be careful to remember that it is in My strength that your weakness is covered, in your sinfulness that My grace is revealed and it is when your lack of loveliness is most evident to you that I am most overwhelmed with your beauty. Look often to My grace and know how highly I esteem you; all human valuations fade beside Mine!

I Prayed
O my Lord, my dear Shepherd, my King, I nestle in Your arms of love; my heart sings at the sound of Your voice, my heart soars heavenward at the sound of Your commendations. Your affirmations of love and acceptance bring healing to my heart. To know Your love and acceptance has been the quest of my life yet how many times I stumbled in the darkness for lack of comprehension of the depths of Your love.

He said
Yes, and you are single minded in your love for Me. In My eyes, yours are as doves' eyes, single in your vision, centered on Me in your heart and mind. You are not easily distracted, but your heart is focused totally on Me. I love that about you!

There is no blurring of vision with you, no distortion or misdirection. It is My Word that gives you this kind of vision. Because you are a lover of My Word your eyes can see aright, because you are an avid devourer of My Word, My ways are clear. O dearest one, you are all fair with eyes that are soft as doves!

Verse 16A

Behold, thou art fair, my beloved, yea, pleasant . . . .

My prayer
Dear Lord Jesus, there is none so lovely as You. If there is any beauty in me, it is because You have put it there. You are the lovely One, the beautiful One. You are the sun around which my life revolves, depends upon, draws life and beauty and gains its light. As the moon reflects the light of the sun and has no light of its own, so I am content to reflect Your light, Your beauty, Your life, Your strength and majesty.

O Jesus, You are so delightful! If only everyone in the world could see how beautiful You are. Shine on me today, Jesus. I need Your grace and Your love to beautify my life. Jesus, You are awesome! You are pure love, and I hold You to my heart today.

Verses 16B & 17

...our bed is green.
The beams of our house are cedar, and our rafters of fir.

My prayer
Jesus, our bed is the place where we fellowship, the place where I am nearest to You. You love to comfort me and encourage me in this place of rest, and I love just to be near You. I flourish in Your presence; I wane and languish without our times of intimate fellowship.[32]

---

[32] See Psalm 92:12, 13 and Jeremiah 17:8

I find my true goodness in being near to You. In nearness to You I'm made fruitful in everything I do. It is our secret place, a lovers' tryst shared only by us two, and it is there in Your secret place that I am safe, under the shadow of the Almighty God.[33]

Yes, I want to live within the shadow of the Almighty, sheltered by the God who is above ***ALL*** gods! And Jesus, the beams of our house are cedar. ***WE*** are Your house - the Body of Christ - we are one family. You have known us in our humanity, and have gained the right to be our great High Priest. Because You carry Your people on Your heart, Your house is a beautiful house. A day in Your courts is better than a thousand elsewhere![34]

You have placed each of us in a family and You are the One who is building us together. Thank You for Your love and care for Your whole Body, the entirety of Your household. Your house is my dwelling place and how I love Your house, the place where Your glory dwells.[35]. My heart has one desire - to dwell in Your house forever [36] for it is there I know Your protection and provision. [37] It is there that I know the pleasure of Yourself.[38]

Jesus, we are Your house according to Your Word. I honor You as Master of Your house and in honoring You I submit to Your authority, offering You my love.

Together we, You and the members of Your body, fill Your house with strength and beauty. We're made of fir for You have made us strong. How good and how pleasant it is for us to dwell together in unity! [39]

The ***BED*** - to rest with You
The ***HOUSE*** - to live with You
The ***GALLERIES*** - to walk with You

---

[33] Psalm 91:1

[34] Psalm 84:10

[35] Psalm 23:6/Psalm 26:8

[36] Psalm 27:4

[37] Psalm 36:7,8

[38] Hebrews 3:6

[39] Psalm 133:1

In every part of my life I am with You and You are with me. O Jesus, Jesus, Jesus! How I love You!

I take Your hand
You help me stand
You'll walk with me tomorrow.

I see Your face
Receive Your grace
Your love removes all sorrow.

I hear Your voice
Make You my choice
I'll follow You forever.

My heart is Yours
Removed all fears
For naught from You can sever.

I'll live with You
I'll walk with You
Enjoy Your love forever!

Poetry written by Florli Nemeth

Chapter Two

The Bride Begins to Understand Her Beauty in God

Verse 1

I am the rose of Sharon, and the lily of the valleys.

My prayer

Lord, I'm a common rose that grows by the roadside, a lily rooted in the valleys. I'm not a rare or exquisite flower, just an ordinary human being, a common flower, and yet you say that I am beautiful. Though not of rare beauty or design, I am crafted by Your hand, content to blossom in Your garden for it is there that I am readily available to all, crafted by Your design to bring beauty and joy to Your heart!

Verse 2

As the lily among thorns, so is my love among the daughters.

He said

Dearest Child, your beauty and purity are beautiful to Me but even My choicest lilies lie among thorns. Though in this world you will suffer pain and anguish, sorrow and grief and even persecution, there is nothing that can tear your heart away from Me. Thorns will hurt you, injuries and injustices will come, but I take special note of your sufferings and of how you patiently endure.

My prayer
Father, my heart is so full on this last night of the year. It is a night to put the past behind me and to venture out into the new. Thank You for a wonderful year. We've had so many good things happen to us. Even in the challenges we've faced, we have seen Your goodness and Your love and protection.

You are an awesome Father. Your care of me is so great. Thank You for Your love. My heart is overwhelmed with Your love tonight! Thank you for opening Your heart, Your Word to me. Thank You for the friends You've given me. Though I feel lonely tonight, I know there are many who love me - and above all, You!

Verse 3

As the apple tree among the trees of the wood, so is my beloved among the sons. I sat down under his shadow with great delight, and his fruit was sweet to my taste.

My prayer
My dearest Lord, You are the only One in all of creation and in eternity to give both shade and fruit! I have known the scorching of the sun, been wounded by difficulties and thorns but in them all Your shadow provided shade and shelter for my heart. It is under Your protection that I find a place to sit and rest. And best of all, it is there that I partake of Your delicious fruit - sweet to my taste, filled with all I need for refreshment and strength.

I am scorched sometimes by outward heat and sometimes even by inner heat - with fiery darts launched by Satan against my mind and heart. But Lord, You are an awesome Refuge from the heat, protecting me and providing for me even in the greatest of trouble or afflictions. No matter what happens in my life, I am sheltered under the "apple tree" of Your grace where I may quiet my heart, finding refuge and renewal, protection and provision, comfort and love!

He said
Dearest Child of My heart, My tree is here for you each day of your life and it is there that I wait for you. Because I AM the apple tree, it is to Me you come for shade and nourishment. When you eat the fruit, you partake of Me! Beware of coming to me without partaking as some do - and yet I know that you are one who loves to take My fruit and savor it.

Yes, dear one, as you contemplate the days that lie before you, you do not know what Refuge you may need. But you do know that whatever happens in your life or in the world around you, there is a place in My heart for you - a shadow from the heat and a provision for your every need.

My Reply
Thank You, Lord. I love to sit under Your shade each morning. It is the place where You meet me and feed me. I love these precious moments in my day where it's just You and me! I love Your Word. It is strength and nourishment to my soul. I cannot live without Your Word, without Your love!

Hide me in the shadow of Your wings (of Your branches) as You hover over me for it is there that I take refuge and there I put my trust. In the shadow of your wings I take refuge until calamities and destructive storms are past; it is there my soul finds shelter and confidence in You. How I rejoice through the night, hidden beneath the protecting shadow of Your wings.

Lord, Your Word says You hide me in the shadow of Your hand! That's how close You are to me. That's how much You care about me! You are truly my "apple tree" and Your Word is so sweet to my taste. [40]

Verse 4

He brought me to the banqueting house, and his banner over me was love.

He said
Yes, I brought you - and I bring you daily to My banqueting house. My banquet hall is the place of abundant provision, provision that I have purchased, provided and prepared for you! Where your resources are limited or even non-existent, Mine are unlimited; when your strength fails, My omnipotence prevails. I bless you today with grace and strength and joy as well as with every material provision.

My banner over you is love. It is love that brought you in and love that continues to be written over your life. My love adorns you, makes a way

[40] Psalm 17:8/Psalm 36:7/Psalm 57:1/Psalm 63:7/Isaiah 49:2 - suggested meditation

for you and covers you completely. The demons of hell cringe and slink away when you stand under My banner of love. My love will conquer anything and everything that is *not* love!

I put My banner of love over you because I want everyone to know how much I love you. I take full responsibility for you, My Child. You are Mine to love and cherish forever!

Verse 5

Stay me with flagons, comfort me with apples; for I am sick of love.
Sustain me with raisins, refresh me with apples, for I am sick with love. (Amplified)
Oh feed me with Your love - Your raisins and Your apples - for I am utterly lovesick. (Living Bible)

My prayer
O Lord, there are times when I am overwhelmed by Your love and intoxicated with its delights - so much so that in my frailty I must partake of a little at a time. Think what it will be like when I see You in glory and feel the full extent of Your love! I cry to You to strengthen me and to support me so I can repose beneath Your apple tree, surrounded by the harvest of Your love for me. Dizzy under the weight of Your wine of love. I stagger in pure delight!

Jesus, You are incomparably wonderful. Your love has overpowered me, leaving me defenseless against the power of Your presence. What am I to do? I can never live without a sense of Your love. Life is meaningless without You!

Lord Jesus, my vessel is weak and able to handle only limited portions of Your wine. Keep filling me to overflowing with Your love; keep feeding me with the succulent fruit of Your love. Utterly weak and famished for Your love, I find nothing else to satisfy. I truly want Your love more than anything else in life!

He said
Stay - stay under the tree of My love. Rest - rest in My shade.
Be strengthened with the fruit of My love and be encouraged by My Word.
I spread My blanket of love over you today.

Let each part of your being be strengthened by My love today. I cover you as Boaz covered Ruth, signifying his intention to take her as his wife. [41]

You are My Bride, My chosen one. I spread My blanket of love and care and protection over you. You are My desire, My bride, My spouse. I will truly do for you all that you require - all that you need. Your smallest need is My concern and My joy to fulfill.

I see the need in your heart to be cherished, to be wooed with kind words. I see the way you wither in relationships at the slightest affront or impatient word. I see your desire to please your earthly spouse. I see the frustration you feel at times and it is in those times that I cover you.

My dear one, My beautiful rose, I counsel you to run into My arms when you feel pain. Let Me cover you with My love. Place your life in My hands, dear one. Entrust Me with your dreams, your desires, your expectations, your hopes and your ambitions, knowing they are safe from the enemy of your soul. In My hands You are safe, protected from anything that would harm you.

I have dreams and desires for you, too, My love, and I am committed to fulfilling every purpose in My heart for you. Your way is ***not*** hidden from Me. I see, I know, I ***love***!

Verse 6

His left hand is under my head, and his right hand doth embrace me.

My prayer
O Lord, when I am weakest, You come alongside me, put Your strong arms around me to sustain and strengthen me. You support my heart in the moments of greatest weakness; it is when I cannot see You that I am most aware of Your strengthening presence.

He said
Yes, dear Child, there have been many times when My left hand, the hand you could not see - was holding you, guiding you, protecting you in ways you could not imagine.

---

[41] Ruth 3:8,9

My left hand often has prevented and protected you from harm and danger, accident and tragedy. Although sometimes you've felt My protection and at other times you've had no knowledge of it, I have been there for you throughout your entire life! Rest in the assurance that My left hand - my strength and protection - remains firmly placed underneath your head.

It is My right hand that embraces you and holds you close to My heart. As we have walked together you have learned that it is there to be seen and known. I have said to you that I am your refuge and your dwelling place, and that underneath are My everlasting arms, promised you that I will be with you all the days (perpetually, uniformly, and on every occasion, to the close of the age).

You can stake your entire life on My promise to be with you, to *never* leave you nor forsake you, and although you have proven this over and over again, be assured that today I carry you in My strong arms and My right hand holds you close. And as if that wasn't enough, My embrace is accompanied by whispered words of love and encouragement to your heart! This I do for those I love.[42]

My Reply
I am overwhelmed with Your love but there are others who have not yet begun this journey of love. Help me, My Beloved, to rightly share the drawing power of Your love. You know how to do Your work; give me wisdom and grace to do that which You have given me to do.

He said
As you follow Me and run after Me, others will follow. As you worship and praise Me in the sanctuary, others will see and know how dearly you are loved.

As the fragrance of My love is over you, it will envelop those around you. They cannot get away from the fragrance. As you draw closer to Me, others cannot but be touched by your life as it overflows with My love and it is My overflowing love through you that will entice them to know Me, too.

---

[42] Deuteronomy 33:27/Matthew 28:20 (Scriptures for meditation)

Be much with Me and I will draw many to My heart through you. It is My love that makes you kind and gentle, gracious and caring, thoughtful and understanding. Allow Me to continue to embrace you with My love and as you do I will see you through every day of your life, upholding, strengthening and encouraging you, whatever the circumstances may be. Remember what I did for My servant, Joseph:

> *"But his bow remained strong and steady and rested in the Strength that does not fail him, for the arms of his hands were made strong and active by the hands of the Mighty God of Jacob, by the name of the Shepherd, the Rock of Israel."*[43]

My Reply
I am resting in the Strength that does not fail me!

Verse 7

I charge you, O ye daughters of Jerusalem, by the roes, and by the hinds of the field, that ye stir not up, nor awake my love, till he please.
[He said} I charge you, O you daughters of Jerusalem, by the gazelles or by the hinds of the field [which are free to follow their own instincts] that you not try to stir up or awaken [my] love until it pleases. (Amplified)[44]

My prayer
Lord, I feel that sometimes You stand up in my defense and say, "*Enough is enough! It is time for rest. I want My loved one to be uninterrupted in times of intimate fellowship with Me. I want you, My loved one to bask in My love for a season."*

Lord, I feel I am in that season now. I'm in no hurry for it to end. As a deer or roe is distracted by the smallest movement in the bush, so easily do I turn away at the slightest interruption! Yet even in my human limitations You take note of my desire to entertain Your presence. As a spouse would protect their sleeping lover from noisy children, or from anything that would waken them, I seek to hush the world around me, quiet myself and present myself with You!

---

[43] Genesis 49:24Amplified

[44] Differences of opinion exist as to whether the Bride or the Bridegroom is the speaker in this passage. The writer believes that a central truth remains, regardless of who is correct - times of intimate fellowship with Christ must be guarded against distractions.

Still these anxious thoughts within me,
Quiet my heart
Rest me in the arms of Greatness,
Never to depart.
Speak Your peace and quiet o'er me,
Calm the raging seas
Stir not up, do not awaken, O my love,
Until you please!

Poetry written by Florli Nemeth

He said

Come apart, this is the time
Come and rest awhile
How I long to see your face
View your lovely smile.

Just for Me, for Me alone
Wait in silence here
I would stay, and stay awhile
Wipe your every tear.

Lie you down, be still My Child
All My loved ones rest
Find your weakened strength renewed
Resting on My breast.

Truth be known, the eagle flies
Mounting up with wings
There she waits upon her God
Resting while she sings.

Lavish all your love on Me
Seek My face alone
Rest within My secret place
Quietly at home.

Here you'll see Me, touched by love
Held within My arms
Here protected, quiet, still
Kept from all alarm.

Thus in confidence draw near, My Child
Wait serenely here
Bask in love - in love divine
Banished every fear!
Poetry written by Florli Nemeth

The Bride's Comfort Zone is Challenged

Verse 8

The voice of my beloved! Behold, he cometh leaping upon the mountains, skipping upon the hills.

My prayer
Lord, I often feel a sense of distance between us - not that You have actually left me, but my ***sense*** of Your presence is not always strong. If I could ***feel*** Your presence all the time, I'd be so happy! But I know and have experienced that feelings cannot be trusted when it comes to knowing Your presence is with me.

The amazing thing is that You are always bridging the gap, shortening the distance between us, by coming to me. But one day - and how I look forward to that day, dear Jesus - You will come to remove the distance forever. On that day You will claim Your Bride and take her to live with You forever. Until then, let me hear Your voice, O my dearest Beloved Lord![45]

He said
O My dearest Child, how I love you! My heart skips for joy when I see how you trust Me. Even when your feelings cannot sense My love or presence, you trust Me implicitly - never speaking ill of Me behind My back, but always loving Me and speaking well of Me. How I love you, dear friend!

Do you know how many of My children question Me and draw away from Me when troubles come? But you, My Child, are one who simply draws closer when difficulties or tragedy hits your life.

---

[45] John 14:3

Do you know how that makes Me feel? When others would blame Me or become bitter or disinterested in Me, you always come running to Me, you've always called out to Me in your desperation. I commend you for trusting Me even when you can't see or feel Me, even when the enemy does his work and then accuses Me to you. If only you could see how much I delight in you, My Child! You are awesome in your love for Me!

And guess what! I leap over mountains of huge, insurmountable difficulties. They are nothing to Me! And I skip and jump over the hills - the smaller difficulties and problems.

There is *nothing* the enemy can put before you that can hinder or deter Me! One day you too will be leaping over mountains and skipping over hills. But you're in training for that now. I have you just where I want you to be!

My Reply
Lord, I'm reminded of a song I love and one we sing occasionally -

> "O Most High, You who are my Refuge
> When troubles come, You're my Hiding Place
> O Most High, those who know You, trust You
> You will not forsake the ones who seek Your face."[46]

I'm also reminded of a few lines of poetry I wrote as a teenager, not even fully understanding the full extent of what I wrote!

> In the darkness I will praise Thee
> When Thy face is hidden from view
> Stepping out in faith I'll trust Thee
> For Thy life in me renewed.
>
> *Poetry written by Florli Nemeth*

Verse 9

My beloved is like a roe or a young hart: behold, he standeth behind our wall, he looketh forth at the windows, showing himself through the lattice.

---

[46] Written by Mark Altrogge

My prayer
Lord, You are loving and kind as a roe or a young hart, so gentle is Your desire toward me and Your dealings with me. When my heart withers and shrinks at impatience, unkindness, and harsh misunderstanding, You never misinterpret my motives because You know my heart. In those times when I fail or need to be disciplined, You gently draw me back, when chastising me becomes necessary, I have learned to trust You for You never wound my heart. I long to be kind and gentle and understanding with others as You are with me!

Lord, You are *standing behind our wall - ready for action*. You are always ready to defend me, to fight my battles, to protect me. And right now You are standing, ready to leap into action.

I see You *standing for the help and comfort of Your people* who are suffering, and for the help of all who cry to You.

He said
Don't let the walls we built together for protection become a prison to you! I am outside, on the other side of the wall, calling to you, knowing you will see and hear and follow Me! The walls of your home are meant to protect and shelter you, and your home is meant to be a place of peace and rest and security. But the walls of your beautiful home could become a prison if you never set foot out into the world! Together we built this home and these walls for its protection. But now it is morning - it is a new season in your life, and I am beginning to draw you outside of your comfort zone. I am wanting to show you the beautiful expanse of My wonderful world, and I need you to labor with Me in My world!

My Response in Prayer
I think I'm understanding now in a way I never have before. You want to draw me out of my home, my comfort zone, to show me new and beautiful things so that You can use me to minister to others. I cannot minister "out there" if I refuse to go beyond the walls of my home.

And yet You are not asking me to "give up" my comfortable home. You're just asking me to join You in whatever You have for me "out there". You'll always bring me back to "our walls" of safety and protection.

You'll always bring me back to our strong base of love and communion where I can bask in Your presence. It is true that in everyday life a person with a good, solid home and family is more productive, more contented, more secure. I see it, Father!

As long as my relationship with You is solid and secure, I can go out in whatever You call me to do and be secure in who I am and in what You've called me to do. You will always bring me back home to rest in Your love, to feed on Your Word, and to bask in Your presence!

He said
You are beginning to understand, My beloved Child! You will always have a home in My heart, and You'll always find Me there. But I see a world of weak, wounded, broken people who need the touch of My love. I need you to touch them for Me, to love them with My love.

When you venture out of your comfortable walls to see and respond to their needs, I will lead you and take you to them. It is I who will lead you and none else. Rest assured that when the task is done I will always lead you back to be home alone with Me!

Verse 10A

My Beloved spake, and said unto me . . . .

My prayer
Lord, my heart is so encouraged when You speak. As the hymn writer so aptly wrote,

> "Speak Lord, in the stillness
> While I wait on Thee
> Hushed my heart to listen
> In expectancy." [47]

I hear You calling me to rise up, and when you speak You affirm me, assure me, of Your love. When You speak, my fears are stilled, my heart is filled with joy! Your words refresh, comfort and console me. Cause me to hear Your voice again today as I quiet my heart before You.

[47] Written by E.M. Grimes

He said

I will speak, and speak again, My words of affirmation
Until your heart hears and believes My loving commendations.
I will speak as each day dawns My comfort, consolations
Until your heart is filled with peace and joyful exclamations!
I will speak throughout the day discernment and direction
Until your heart is one with Mine, the Word in your possession.
Then **you** will speak the words I say - make it your heart's confession
All fear be gone, your faith be strong, and no more apprehension.

Poetry written by Florli Nemeth

So come to Me and let Me make you strong. I'm speaking to your heart right now and will continue to speak. "My voice shalt thou hear in the morning!" [48] I will speak what you need to hear. Ask Me for what you need. And you will hear Me clearly. My Word will sound as a trumpet in the land - blasting out My Word and My voice. You cannot miss it. Listen for it today - Child of My heart - I love you!

My prayerful Response
Lord, I need Your rest and Your strength as I face another challenging day. I also need your direction. Let me hear Your voice, Father, directing me clearly. Pour Your strength into me as I lean on You.

Verse 10B

...Rise up My love, My fair one, and come away.

He said
You may feel distant, dear one, perhaps disconsolate or even discouraged or depressed. You are not alone for these emotional states are common to mankind. My answer for you is this - get up and come away with Me! Let Me take you to a place where you will be refreshed in your spirit and strengthened in your body and mind. As a bridegroom plans to take his bride to a very special place, perhaps secretly planning to surprise her, so I have plans to woo you and wow you and totally astonish you!

My heart's desire is to bless you today. So come - wake up - rise up and run into My arms. I'm taking you away to My secret place today. I have

[48] Psalm 5:3

many such secret places in My presence, and I delight to take you there and refresh your heart.

My response
It sounds so wonderful, Lord! My heart is tired and in need of being refreshed in Your presence. You have chosen me to come near and to dwell in Your courts. Thank You, Lord, for causing me to come near.[49] As I come into Your sanctuary, I come under Your guardianship[50] and I welcome Your love and protection, Your care and provision. I just want to run away with You - just want to be where You are!

He said

Come away My loved one,
    Come away, My dove
I've prepared a place for you
    Where I'll reveal My love.

In that blessed secret place
    You will be renewed
Find that I have plans for you
    Precious things in view.

You are not alone, My child
    I am very near
Calling you to come away
    Removing every fear.

How My heart, it yearns for you
    Longs to hold you close
Comfort and delight your soul
    With things you treasure most.

Come away, beloved friend
    Rise and take My hand
I will take you far away
    To a promised land.

---

[49] Psalm 65:4

[50] Psalm 118:26 Amplified

There I'll give you peace and rest
Promised joys secure
There you'll find My faithfulness
True from year to year.

Until that day I come for you
In bridal full array
Taking you to that fair land
Where night gives way to day!

Poetry written by Florli Nemeth

Verses 11 - 13

11 - For lo, the winter is past, the rain is over and gone.
12 - The flowers appear on the earth; the time of the singing of birds is come, and the voice of the turtle is heard in our land;
13 - The fig tree putteth forth her green figs, and the vines with the tender grape give a good smell. Arise, my love, my fair one, and come away.

Dear Lord
You are calling me to rise because You want deeper intimacy and communion with me. And the things that once hindered intimacy with You have fled! The signs of Spring are here. The winter cold that brought the wind and bitter storms are gone. I am immersed in pure joy and anticipation as You call me forth to deeper intimacy. You really do want me close to You! It is a time for love, a time for basking in Your presence!

He said
Rise up, My love! I call to you again and again because I long to see your face and hear your voice. The birds sing their praises, but none sing as beautifully as you do! The flowers and trees and plants are budding and showing promise of a good harvest, but none are arrayed as ornately as you! I call you forth to life and health and love. I call you forth to a place of deeper intimacy with Me.

This is a day of favor and grace. I am calling forth My body, My people, to deeper intimacy with Me. Many have slept through the storms of winter and the dark nights of that season, but Spring is here! Everything is coming alive, warming to the sun and in like manner, I am calling forth My people to waken - to rise up - to come away with Me.

Abandon yourselves to intimacy with Me. Allow Me to take you to a deeper place. The call is going out throughout the land and around the world. I am calling you, My Child, to partner with Me in taking this message to the world.

This book embraces and encompasses ALL of My Word.

So do not think it wasted time to lavish love on Me. And do not think you may be putting too much focus on these meditations on My Word. Take these truths, pursue them, consume them, and embrace them to your heart night and day until I release you to do otherwise! I will continue to reveal things to you and give you fresh revelation daily. I will continue to lead you into a deeper, more intimate relationship with Me. Your heart has longed for this for many years. Now is the time! Arise! Come away with Me!

My Response
I'm coming, Lord! I'm just a bit slow getting moving, but wait for me—I'm coming!

Verse 14

O my dove, that art in the clefts of the rock, in the secret places of the stairs, let me see thy countenance, let me hear thy voice; for sweet is thy voice, and thy countenance is comely.

He said
Call to Me, My Child. Sing to Me, My Friend. You are so very special to Me. I listen for your voice in prayer. I've recorded every prayer you've ever prayed. I've kept every song you've sung to Me. I wait for you to come and show your face, and I long once again to hear your voice.

Your songs may not have been on anyone's "Hit List" or on the "Top Ten", but each song you have ever sung to Me is on *My* list, in My vault, where one day it will be sung in heaven!

O My Child, don't look at your frailties. Yes, you are small and fragile as a dove, but you are beautiful, guileless and pure before Me. My blood has made a way for you to draw near without fear - in boldness and in confidence. Your prayers ascend as sweet incense to Me[51]. The angel mixes the incense with your prayers, so no matter how weak or insignificant you may feel, your prayers are sweet to Me!

Your voice rings in the courts of heaven when you pray or when you worship and sing praise to Me. I see you as a dove whose wings are covered with gold! You are so very precious to Me. I would never, never turn you away or ignore you. My precious child, you are so precious and lovely to Me! So come, dear one, pour out your heart in prayer and in song to Me. Let Me hear your voice today - let Me see your lovely face!

My response

O sweet Lord, I come, I bow
Before Your Throne today
Look on me with favor now
And do not turn away.

All that's in my heart I tell
All that's on my mind
The praises of my lips to swell
The worship redefine.

O my Love, I come to You
My arms are opened wide
You give to me a song that's new
I run to You and hide.

So here I am, bowed low again
My heart at one with Yours
To worship You, my truest gain
To love You much, my joy!

Poetry written by Florli Nemeth

Here I am Lord! I love you, I need You, I want you. You are **ALL** I'll ever need.

---

[51] Revelation 8:3

Verse 15

Take us the foxes, the little foxes, that spoil the vines, for our vines have tender grapes.

Father,
I don't want the vines in the garden of my heart spoiled by anything. I'm asking You to deal with every sin or weakness that could destroy the tender vines because You have pledged Your care and protection over Your church, Your Bride - both individually and corporately.

Are there any little destructive things in my life that need to be dealt with? Any subtle errors or misjudgments that only You would know about?

Jesus, You are the Shepherd and the Keeper of our garden. You have the right and the authority to deal with whatever would injure or destroy Your vineyard. So catch them, take them, get rid of them! I don't want any even seemingly harmless little foxes roaming at will in our garden! Be ruthless in Your detection and destruction of such harmful things, no matter how small they may be.

He said
I will do as you ask, My Child. As you keep your heart humble before Me, I will uncover any hidden, subtle thing that would bring injury to you. I also will help you to deal with whatever intruding thing would bring destruction to your heart. I am concerned even more than you about the garden of your heart. I will guard it and keep it night and day!

Verse 16

My Beloved is mine, and I am His. He feedeth among the lilies.

My prayer
Lord, I am not and never will be for another. YOU are my Love, my true Husband. YOU are my desire, my life, my strength, my all! You have wrapped Your cloak around me to legally declare Your marriage vow to me. [52]

---

[52] Ruth 3:9/Ezekiel 16:8

You signed a covenant with me - my name is written on Your hands! Lord, You care for Your church. You nourish and cherish it.[53] I am Yours - I belong to You - I am a member of Your body, of Your flesh, of Your bones. Though this great mystery almost defies human understanding My heart says, YES for You loved me and gave Yourself for Your church - and that includes me!

You love me - You love me - You love me!

Jesus, how I need the assurance of Your love over and over again. And yet I know that You are covenanted to the Church, Your Bride, and to me! My heart is overwhelmed at such love! You, the true Lily and purest of them all, feed among the lilies. And You make us pure as You are pure. You make Your home among us. You love to be with Your people, feed on our love, our praises, our worship; You walk among the churches, holding each leader in Your hands. [54]

I may not always feel You, I may not always see you, but You are there, identifying with us - sharing the joys and sorrows, aches and pains of Your people. You know what we are going through right now at this stage in our lives, and You are with us, loving us, feeding us, protecting us, caring for us with a mother's love and care.

O Jesus, Your love and beauty have bound me to You forever. How can I tell You of my love?

He said
When I saw you, I loved you, put My protective robe of righteousness over you and claimed you for Myself. I knew your heart would never be happy with another.

You are flesh of My flesh, bone of My bones, truly one with Me. Your comprehension of all I have done is not limited to time, I have prepared eternity for you to enjoy and live out your union with Me.

I am here for you today, though you cannot see Me with your eyes - you may see Me with the eyes of your heart. Listen to your heart, for

[53] Ephesians 5:27-30
[54] Revelation 2:1,2

I will speak My Word deep into your heart and I will hold You in My hands, close to My heart. I will never let you go!

I will never fail you nor cause you a needless tear. I am pure love, patient in speech, gentle and meek. I woo you gently, and I understand you perfectly. My counsel remains direct and right, My love constant throughout your days and nights. You are beautiful!

Verse 17

Before the dawn comes, and the shadows flee away, Come to me, my Beloved, and be like a gazelle or a young stag upon the mountain of spices. (Living Bible) "...mountains of Bether - meaning division" in KJV.

My prayer
Lord, there is a dawn to come, a day to come, where shadows will flee away and night will be no more. I long for that day of the Lord - that great day when I shall see You face to face. Lord, when mountains separate us from time to time, I cry to You: "Come to me like a roe or a young hart upon the mountains."

Mountains of difficulty, of frailty, of imperfection can never separate You from me; even those mountains of my own making cannot keep You from me! You come leaping to me - bounding over every mountain of separation or division.

I know there is a day coming when I will be in Your presence forever. But until then, I hunger for our daily trysts (or love visits) in the secret place.

As You come morning by morning I am encouraged and comforted; as we meet together Your love strengthens, reminding me that it is Your love for me that causes You to spend time with me. How I treasure the times we share; my heart unceasingly calls for You to meet with me each day. And on those days when strength to cry for help is gone, I ask You still to come, Lord Jesus, come.

He said
There is no mountain - man-made or demonic - that can keep Me from you! No matter what difficulty you may encounter, I will come to you in that place, jumping and skipping over that difficulty. I came to My

disciples on the waters of the sea, and in that very place taught Peter how to walk on water. I come to you to comfort and strengthen you, to encourage and empower you to skip and jump on your mountains of difficulties. I come to take you with Me - over the mountains!

I will always come at the sound of your voice, and I will come every morning to meet with you. These times are so delightful for you! I see your face light up when I come, and My heart skips a beat for you. Your beauty is so intoxicating, and even one look of your eyes totally overwhelms Me.

I am so delighted to be with you. And throughout the day as you go about your business, I am only a call away - a breath away! When you call, I come running to you, My love. I bless you today, and I empower you to be a blessing. May every life you touch be touched with love.

Chapter Three

The Bride Experiences Chastisement

Verse 1

By night on my bed I sought Him whom my soul loveth; I sought Him, but I found Him not.

My prayer
Lord, I do not enjoy the dark night of the soul. There are days when listlessness sweeps over me, taunting my inability to rise up to follow You in obedience. My heart yearns for You, yet my feelings fear that You have hidden Your face as You did from the maiden here.

You called her to rise up, to come with You over the mountains, but she hesitated. I do the same at times. Even in my darkest night I love You more than any other, yet I too struggle to rise up out of my comfort zone to seek you with all my heart. What are You saying to me, my Beloved Lord?

He said
I come to you in the night, in the storm, in the midst of chaos, pain and affliction. In these times My chosen ones cannot always see Me. The fog hides My face. But even in those times be assured (or, you can know) that I have not left you nor forsaken you. I am just calling you to rise up and follow Me even when sense and sight cannot see Me.

It is not crying in the darkness that will unveil Me to you. *It is rising up from that p*lace of pain and suffering, chastisement and disappointment - rising up to follow Me, rising up to find Me, rising up to worship Me!

I see the disappointment you feel in your own weaknesses and failures. That disappointment with yourself will keep you from finding Me. Do not look at yourself or others. If you look at others not as spiritual as you, you will become proud. And if you look at others who are ahead of you spiritually, you will despair.

Don't look to others or for others. Look to Me - look for Me! And you will find Me because I will reveal Myself to you in a tangible way. I see what you have been going through. You have relied on Me, and My heart is so touched by your love and devotion. Not even your weakest prayer gets by Me. I hear every prayer - see every tear - feel every concern of your heart.

You will truly find Me when you rise up from your bed of affliction and truly seek for Me with all your heart. Worship Me in the very place of your pain, and I will reveal Myself to you there.

Verse 2

I will rise now . . . .I will seek Him whom my soul loveth . . . . I sought Him, but I found Him not...

My thoughts
There is a sense of urgency here, an immediacy that cries: I *must* see Him! I'll pray more fervently, I'll fast, I'll do whatever I must do to find His sweet presence. But even that is not enough at times, for it is not our fleshly effort that brings Him near.

I believe I must just continue to seek Him with all my heart by continuing to pray and meditate on His Word. No matter how dark the night, the morning will come! He will reveal Himself to me.

My prayer
My heart so longs to feel Your touch, hear Your voice, see Your face. Reveal Yourself to me today, dear Lord, You whom I love with all of my heart!

He said

Watch and pray
I come today
To touch your life afresh.

Look and see
And come to Me
Run into arms outstretched.

Dry your tears
Your Love is near
My heart is yours alone.

Lift your eyes
I'm not disguised
I'm here for you alone.

Poetry written by Florli Nemeth

Verse 3

The watchmen that go about the city found me, to whom I said, Saw ye Him whom my soul loveth?

My prayer
In this instance, Lord, I see the watchmen were tender and caring toward her and tried to help and encourage her. She is encouraged to go a little further - not to give up! You have given me watchmen, pastors, elders etc., committed to my care. They have varying degrees of responsibility, but they are all to watch over believers committed to their trust.

It is important that watchmen themselves experience intimate relationship with their Beloved and are acquainted with the different seasons of the soul. For how can we help another if we know nothing of heart love relationship with Jesus! And sometimes in trying to help someone, we need to be able to diagnose the problem and give the answer to it.

Father, I so desire to be a tender-hearted watchman. When people come to me for counsel or advice, may they fall into tender hands that will not break a bruised reed, not rough and uncaring hands that will further harm their hearts.

Help me, Lord, to be that kind of a watchman - one with a caring, sensitive heart that will speak the truth in love. Make me as those watchmen who saw her, struggling, lost and desperate, and gathered round her. Make me an encourager and a guide to point the way to You

He said
Be much with Me! That's how you get a caring, tender heart. That's how you can speak truth in love. That's how you can discern where people are at and what they need.

Spend time with Me yourself - develop your love relationship with Me. Be open and honest and bask in My presence for yourself alone. Spend time praying for those in your care, in your sphere of influence. Watch over the souls of those committed to your care.

Let Me encourage you, dear one. You are a tender-hearted watchman. You have endured much, traveled far, experienced many things. Commit the things you have learned to faithful men and women, even as Paul instructed Timothy to do. I have called you to do this. It is not something you have assumed to do on your own.

This season in your life, however, is a season to bask in My presence and revel in My love, a time to search out and study My Word more deeply. Time spent reading My word and journaling those thoughts we share will speak deeply into your heart in all your days (or, days to come).

Would you be a good watchman? Then be a good listener and learner as you sit at My feet. And I will bring watchmen to you who will speak into your life and encourage you to go further in your seeking for Me.

Verse 4A

It was but a little that I passed from them, but I found Him whom my soul loveth . . . .

My prayer
Lord, I see the importance of venturing further in my search for You. Thank You for the watchmen you have put in my life, but I realize they cannot take me to You. I must find You for myself! Spiritual authorities in the church can counsel and give advice or direction, but they cannot reveal You to me.

This is good for You desire that I look to You and You alone for answers, for love, for fulfillment. I've found in times of grief and pain, disappointment and questioning, that You alone can ease the pain, comfort the heart, restore the hope and give direction and answers.

You ordained watchmen to point people in Your direction, not to be what only You can be - the Source of all our questions and the place of refuge for our souls. Leaning hard on You for answers and safety, I ask You to be my comfort and help in the things I face.

There are times in Your wisdom that You allow us to be disappointed in people, no matter how godly they are, because You are training us to run to You alone. In those times when I turn to others for help, continue to beckon me to come closer, to go further, to seek You with just a little more abandonment.

He said
You will always find Me when you seek for Me with all your heart. I have placed My servants in My Body to edify, exhort, encourage My people but they cannot reveal Me to you! They can only point you in the right direction.

You learned this many years ago, but there are many of My people going from this watchman to that watchman, thinking to find Me thus. Encourage My people to seek Me - to search for Me with all their hearts. The maiden knew this truth for she could have stayed with the watchmen! Yet in her hunger for Me she pursued Me with increased vigor and her faith and perseverance paid off as she found Me searching for her. So be encouraged, dear one. Learn from My servants and from those who watch over your soul, but put your faith and your trust in Me alone!

Verse 4B

. . . .I found Him, I held Him, and would not let Him go . . . .

My prayer

> Yes, Lord, I have found You,
> To be faithful, to be true
> I have found You, I have seen You – Face to face!

Lord, I've found You - I will not let You go! There is absolutely no one like You. I've longed for Your presence, I've so desired to know You more intimately.

Jesus, I put my arms around You and will never let You go! You promised You would never leave me, no matter what! I cling to You on the basis of Your love and Your Word that will never change. Things around me have always changed, but You are truly the same - You *never* change!

And so, having found You, I will *not* let You go until You bless me. I hold You close to my heart. Please - do *not* leave me, ***ever***! I must have You in my life. Nothing else really matters.

Love of my life, I hold You to my heart
Jesus, my Shepherd, Never depart.
Now that I've found You, I won't let You go
You are my life, my all - You're all I know.
Jesus, my whole life long I've sought for this
Simply to feel Your love, Experience Your kiss.
I've found You - I've found You, My Lover divine
I hold You - I keep You, Forever You're mine!

Poetry written by Florli Nemeth

Verse 4C

. . . .until I had brought Him into my mother's house, and into the chamber of her that conceived me.

My thoughts
The maiden here had a deep revelation of the presence and love of Jesus, and she wanted to bring this to the church - to share Him with the body of Christ - the particular local expression of the body of Christ to which she belonged. It is important that we reverence and respect the "mother" that has given us life. God is our Father, but the church is our mother!

How many believers speak ill of the "mother" and dishonor her by having nothing to do with her. The maiden here brought Jesus into her mother's house - even into the very chamber where she was conceived (the very local group of believers where she was born-again).

My prayer
Lord, there are many of Your children who do not yet know Your intimate love. I want them to realize how wonderful You are. I want them to be touched and changed forever by Your love. Take me deeper in Your love, Lord, so that I can bring others with me. Help me to take You into the house of my mother.

I thank You for the church! What a wonderful "mother" You've given us! I desire to be rightly related with Your church and may I bring only blessing to Your church. May I never be guilty of disrespect or dishonor toward Your church. May I bring Your presence, Your love, Your grace, Your blessing to Your church at all times.

I've always felt Your church was important in my life. Now I realize it is absolutely essential for my well-being! How can I curse my "mother" and be blessed by You? So Lord, enable me. Deepen this revelation in me. Make me a great blessing to Your church.

He said
As you bring Me into the chamber of her who conceived you and brought you forth to life, I will continually reveal Myself to you more deeply. Since conception is realized in intimacy, it is from our shared communion that you will conceive and bring forth children for My glory. Would you be used by Me to birth others into My kingdom? Spend much time with Me; the time you give to Me is never wasted for out of our intimacy I will fill you and send you to pour My love into the lives of others.

But you must always be filled up first; there is no ministry possible on "empty". Allow your sense of emptiness to drive you to seek Me and My fullness. Let your very feelings of emptiness draw you *to* Me and not away from Me. It pains Me when you allow these feelings to draw you away because of the lack you feel emotionally or spiritually. Your emptiness and poverty are known to Me, but it is those who recognize that they are poor in spirit who are truly blessed and prosperous.[55]

My Response
How can this be? How can I be poor and prosperous at the same time?

---

[55] Matthew 5:3

He said
When your spirit is poor - empty, lonely, feeling insignificant and lifeless - come to Me and I will fill you up! It is just that simple! You are blessed because you know you are poor in yourself, and you know where to go to be satisfied! I see your loneliness and frustration these days, but I also see you have chosen to come to Me! You have chosen Me; I choose to bless you with My presence, My love, My strength and My joy.

Yes, you are blessed when you are rightly related to Me and rightly related to My Body. There will again be times where you can bring Me "into the chamber of her who conceived you". There will again be times of ministry. But as you spend this time with Me - alone with Me - I will deepen your ministry and give you an even greater impact.

So dear one, just bask in My presence and let Me fill you up today. You are so very precious to Me! You have honored and cherished My church, My Body. I will honor and cherish you!

I will bless you today with a joyful heart –

- Not depressed - but joyful
- Not impoverished - but made rich
- Not empty - but full
- Not alone - My presence with you

My prayer
Your Word says that by Your becoming poor, You have made me rich.[56]

I have been abundantly supplied with every favor and every blessing I could possibly receive! Thank You, my Father, my God! I am inwardly and outwardly rich. I am very well-provided for! I don't have to provide for myself. You are my great Source of Supply, Protector and Director. I love You, Jesus!

Verse 5

I charge you, O ye daughters of Jerusalem, by the roes, and by the hinds of the field, that ye stir not up, nor awake my love, till he please.

---

[56] 2 Corinthians 8:9

He said
I'm here to protect you, My Child. My heart is gentle and kind toward you. Your heart aches for understanding and gentleness but don't make the mistake of looking to others to meet this need for tenderness in your life.

Give Me again your expectations and your needs. I am a gentle God, a gentle, caring Husband. I wrap My arms around you and hold you close to My heart. I whisper My love into your heart. None other can minister to you as I do. My word to you is *rest, dear one*! Lie down in My green pastures and let Me restore your soul.

My prayer
Yes, Lord, You give me rest in green pastures. You nurture me in a place of comfort and abundant nourishment. You have not called me to lie down in a desert, but in the solace of lush green meadows! You feed me and nourish my soul as I rest in You. O Lord, I lie down - I rest my heart on You. You are the only One who can feed me, refresh me and restore me. [57]

Lead me, Jesus, in the right way; call me to the paths that You have prepared for me. I so long to be directed by You!

He said
Not only will I lead you in the right way, I will protect you and comfort you. You do not need to fear, for I am with you, even on the dark days, even in the difficult mountain trails. I will never *leave* you nor forsake you![58]

So be encouraged! Lift up your eyes. Lift up your face so I can see you, and hear your lovely voice. I do not grow weary of your failings nor do I tire of your struggles. I am proud of you! You have come a long way, and now you need to rest, My dearest Child.

---

[57] Psalm 23

[58] Hebrews 13:5

He said

I will give you rest
For the journey has been long
I will come to you
I will make your spirit strong.

Resting in My arms
A shelter strong and sure
Resting in My love
You can - and will - endure!

Storms and shadows, wind and rain
Floods and rivers, sickness, pain
Suffering, sorrow, judgments wrong
In the midst of all - a song!
For even now I hear that strain
Coming from the midst of pain.

Poetry written by Florli Nemeth

She said

O how sweet to rest again in the arms of love divine
Every loss is naught but gain
Yes, the sun again will shine!
Rock divine and Refuge dear, lay me down in love so near
Here forever let me stay
Held in love's divine sweet sway!

Poetry written by Florli Nemeth

He said

'Til you please, My lovely Bride
Safe within My arms abide
Here forever you may stay
Resting 'til the break of day!

Poetry written by Florli Nemeth

Scriptures to meditate on
Isaiah 32:18 - Matthew 11:28,29 - Jeremiah 6:16

The Bride Receives a Fresh Revelation of Jesus

Verse 6

Who is this sweeping in from the deserts like a cloud of smoke along the ground, smelling of myrrh and frankincense and every other spice that can be bought?

My thoughts
The Bride here is gliding in from the desert with her Lover with the cloud of His presence over her, covered totally with His presence and fragrance.

Emerging from the wilderness experience, she is a different person bearing a different presence and exuding a different fragrance and influence.

My prayer
O God, thank You for Your presence over me and for the fragrance of Your love in me. Your presence is so awesome in my life! Thank you for the transforming power of Your love in the desert places of my life. I always come out of the desert with more of You in my life!

Mount Sinai was wrapped in smoke when You descended upon it, and the smoke ascended like that of a furnace.[59] Lord God, wrap me in the smoke of Your presence today. Let others see it and be changed by Your loving presence.

He said
I will do as you ask. You will know that I the Lord your God have touched your life. I will never leave you alone. I will always be with you - a fire and cloud about you, a fragrance upon you! Go in the joy and fragrance of My love today.

Verses 7 & 8

Behold his bed, which is Solomon's; threescore valiant men are about it, of the valiant of Israel.
They all hold swords, being expert in war: every man hath his sword upon his thigh because of fear in the night.

---

[59] Exodus 19:18

My prayer
Lord, You bring Your loved ones to Your bed, that wondrous place of rest and refreshing, of comfort and of fellowship (communion). It is a place of nearness to You that we cannot conjure up ourselves. The psalmist said that You make me lie down in green pastures.

You watch me as a mother who puts her child to bed because she knows he needs to rest! And then she watches over him while he rests. She is so near she hears any movement or noise - even his breathing!

It is Your peace and love that I enjoy as I rest in Your bed. You have prepared it for me, but You don't claim it as Yours, but rather as "our bed", since everything You have, You have given to me! I am made a partaker - a joint heir.[60]

This intimate communion is not for me alone but for all Your loved ones . . . and yet You make me feel as if it were for me alone. How can we all be loved so much, and yet loved so individually?

Yes, the Greater than Solomon invites me to His own bed and gives me His own peace and protection! Jesus, You guard me not only from real danger and from the evil one, but You shield me also from my fears in the night. You have twenty thousand chariots and thousands of angels. Yes, the angel of the Lord pitches His tent over me![61]

So Lord, I am totally secure in Your presence. Nothing can harm me - not even my own fears!

He said
Yes, you understand it well. In the darkest night of your soul you will find rest and peace and security with Me. Your times with Me in the mornings are "the bed" - "our bed" where you can share your heart with Me and where I can share My heart with you! I love these times with you, and I want you to know you are totally protected and loved.

---

[60] Canticles 1:16, "our bed"/1 Corinthians 10:17/Romans 8:17/Ephesians 3:6
[61] Psalm 68:17/Psalm 34:7

I have provided for your rest, your fears and your refreshing. I personally will meet every one of your needs. And you may go from this place of rest to face your day, knowing you have a "bed" to come back to - a place where you may again be refreshed and strengthened.

So many of My children - My loved ones - have not yet learned to meet Me thus. But you, My dear one, have learned to come daily to Me, and I love you so dearly!

My peace is an armed guard, a garrison around your mind.[62]

My peace is yours! You need never fear condemnation or accusation from Me. I am *not* your Accuser *but* your Redeemer and Saviour. I am your beloved King and Lover of your soul. This day I place My peace around you.

No matter what this day may bring, go knowing that My peace and love are over you, around you, above and beneath you. You are My Bride, and I love you!

Verses 9 & 10

King Solomon made himself a chariot of the wood of Lebanon. He made the pillars thereof of silver, the bottom thereof of gold, the covering of it of purple, the midst thereof being paved with love, for the daughters of Jerusalem.

My thoughts and prayers
The one who made the chariot was King Solomon - that is, Jesus! Why did He make it?

1. For His own glory[63]
2. For the daughters of Jerusalem - for those who are weak and fall short of perfection. He wanted to further them on their way.

The chariot itself is described as made from wood of Lebanon, with pillars of silver, a bottom of gold, the covering is purple, and it is completely paved with love.

---

62 Philippians 4:7
63 Isaiah 43:7 & 21

Lord, You have a chariot to safely and conveniently carry me through my journey until I come to my complete rest. Your work of redemption is signified by this chariot. It is what You have done to communicate Your love and to carry us through - it is a work paved with love for poor sinners.

I am borne up and sustained by You, and You cause me to ride in triumph! Your redemption is made of wood - excellent, durable, and based on an everlasting covenant that will never fail. The pillars of silver signify stability and strength.[64]

Your promises and Your Word support me. They will never give way. Your word is eternal, final, and sealed. Lord, You constantly look after my safety and success.[65]

The bottom of the chariot is made of gold, the metal known for its stability and preciousness. This covenant You have made with us boasts a sure foundation. I'll not fall through the cracks. And the covering is of purple, typifying the blood of Jesus - Your blood that covers me. My sins are forgotten so I will never be called to a reckoning of them. I will never be reminded or accused of them by You!

And Jesus, all this is paved with love! Your goodness and kindness toward me breathes out love. I walk in Your love, I sit on love, I rest in love, I breathe in love! Your love has made Your riches available to me.

If I fall, I fall on love. If I fail, I fail in the arms of love.

I sit, stand, and lie down on love. No matter where I go or what I do, I'm in the hands of love - love that does not condemn or reject me when I fall short. There may be something better than gold, but there is nothing better than love! All this provision is for the daughters of Jerusalem.

Lord, since You have made me Your friend all this provision is for me. You carry me in my times of weakness and in my infirmities - You

---

[64] 2 Chronicles 3:17 - Jachin means *stability* and Boaz means *strength*.

[65] 2 Samuel 23:5 Living Bible

carry me when my sense of sin and failure would sting and disquiet me. You carry me in every challenge and perplexity of life. Your love will always have the last word!

Lord, thank You for Your wonderful provision - a bed by night for rest and refreshment, a chariot by day for rest and contentment.

You are such an awesome God! Your chariot is for the daughters of Zion - plural! I'm not alone! I'm on this journey with my sisters and brothers - we, Your family, are in this together!

He said to me

You are the object of My love
You are My sole desire
You bring Me joy and great delight
My heart, it burns with fire.

For you I died, for you I live
For you I've given My all
For you I left My Father's home
And answered His great call.

This fiery love I cannot hide
It rides to all the earth
This chariot paved with love divine
For daughters (sons) of new birth.

The passion of My heart is still
And evermore will be
To bring My ransomed Body home,
My Bride to live with Me.

So yes, I hold you in My love
I carry you today
No matter the perplexity
Love has the final say!

So rest in Me and trust Me, Child
I'll not relax My hold
You're safe, secure, serenely loved
Your preciousness, pure gold!

Poetry written by Florli Nemeth

My response
Thank You, Lord! I breathe deeply of Your love. I sit back and relax in this chariot of redeeming love. Take me where You will. Fulfill Your purposes in my life. I'm Yours, and forever Yours alone!

Verse 11

Go forth, O ye daughters of Zion, and behold king Solomon with the crown wherewith his mother crowned him in the day of his espousals, and in the day of the gladness of his heart.

My prayer written on a Sunday
Lord, Zion is the city You love more than any other. And today we gather together to crown You King - to behold You! One look at You, and all my problems disappear. Jesus, I want to see You - truly see You. Open my eyes, the eyes of my heart, to see You in all Your glory. It is Your city - Your people who crown You. May we truly crown You with the worship we bring today.[66]

Lord Jesus, You are formed and brought forth in Your people, as it were conceived in each of us.[67]

And we crown You when we bring forth children to You, as You are begotten in them. In this sense, we, Your church, are Your mother.

We crown You Lord when -

1. We bring forth children to You
2. We accept You as our King, consenting to God's crowning of You as King, submitting to Your scepter and government - we make You King as Judah and the Ten Tribes made David King[68].
3. We yield ourselves to You[69]

So we, Your church, are Your crown, even as a virtuous wife is a crown to her husband[70]

---

[66] Scripture to meditate on: Psalm 87:2
[67] Galatians 4:19
[68] 2 Samuel 5:1-5/1 Chronicles 11:1-3
[69] Isaiah 62:2,3
[70] Proverbs 12:4

I am a crown and a joy unto You, dear Lord. And You hold me aloft in Your hands for all to see. I'm a crown of glory in Your hand, and a royal diadem in the hand of my God!

[It is interesting to note that when we go forth to behold the King, we find that we ourselves are His joy and crown - so highly does He value our love, worship, obedience and submission.]

He said
I loved My church! I gave up My life for My church. You are My church - My bride! You are My joy and My crown! Just even one little act of obedience brings Me such joy. I see you as a glorious Bride without spot or wrinkle, My Bride! And I hold you aloft in My hand for all the world to see. You are My pride and joy. You are a splendid crown for Me, your King. I open your eyes today to see yourself and My church through My eyes.[71]

You are My Bride, My delight, the one I have claimed for My own! My heart rejoices in you, the one I have chosen to be mine forever.

My prayer
My Lord, it is incumbent upon the daughters of Your choosing to *go* forth and behold. Until then, I cannot rightly gaze upon Your beauty or discern Your glory until there is a going forth - a getting up to look upon Him. Your Word exhorts me: "*Forget thine own people and thy father's house, so shall the King greatly desire thy beauty.*"[72]

More of my thoughts
When my belief in Him draws me to Him, it is then that I truly honor and reverence Him as Lord and crown Him King in my life...and it is then I bring gladness to His heart. His word to me: "Draw near to God, and He will draw near to you."[73]

It was in that first, tentative, going forth, that I first beheld Him; my heart was overwhelmed by His love espousing me to Him. It was then He claimed me for His very own.

---

[71] Isaiah 62:4,5

[72] Psalm 45:10,11 "Your royal husband delights in your beauty" Living Bible

[73] James 4:8

But there is more to our love than that first embrace. The joy and peace of our daily trysts come not from compulsion but from adoration-filled communion. He invites me; I respond. I open my heart; He reveals Himself in all His glory

My prayer
Jesus, I rise up to meet You this morning. You are my royal husband! You delight to come to me morning by morning as I draw near to You. You've shown me today that I reverence You by coming to You, by going forth, by beholding You.

I reverence and honor You not by degrading myself or by lying in the dust, but by coming to You in full recognition of You as my royal husband and my King. I am here to fellowship with You and it is in that fact alone that we share our mutual delight. I'm here to behold You today and to lavish my love on You, my Lord.

He said
I see your heart, My child and understand the craving of your heart for more of Me. But be assured that our coming together is for Me as well! I greatly desire your beauty and yet I cannot force you to come to meet with Me.

Your coming to me is made more precious because it is of your own volition. You come because you love Me, come even on those mornings when you would rather sleep or read another book. But you choose to read My Word, to study My Word, to sit in My presence and wait for Me to speak to you. Do you know how few of My people do this - regularly watching at My gates?

You have honored Me today by coming to Me, by going forth to behold Me. And I will honor you with My love, My presence, My companionship, My wisdom, My strength. I honor you also with peace and joy and laughter. Why should you not be joyful in the presence of your King? I strengthen you to face each task of this day with joy.

Chapter Four

Prophetic Affirmations of the Bridegroom over the Bride

Verse 1A

Behold, thou art fair, my love; behold, thou art fair . . . .

My prayer
Lord, You said these exact words in Song of Songs 1:15 in the earlier part of the maiden's walk with You. In the next chapter the maiden cried for You to come to her, and here You are - speaking gracious, loving words into her life.

Jesus, You have come to me like that so many times in my life, speaking words of love and commendation. You delight to reaffirm what You see in me. I have known You to be kind in Your dealings with me; even when I've needed correction, You always preface it with love. You have never belittled or demeaned me, even though I may have deserved it! Instead, Your eyes have looked upon my beauty now and what, by Your grace, I shall be one day. It's as if You take Your finger and put it on the ugliness of my life, smooth Your finger across the ugliness, and through Your words of love create beauty where once there was only the ugliness of ashes.

Jesus, I believe You want Your church to hear these words. You are trying to entice us to hear the words, "Behold....behold". Then Lord, why do You repeat these words? Is it because the enemy has so lied to us we see nothing but our ugliness, our weaknesses and our imperfections? Is it because You are calling Your church to see her beauty in You so she may rise up and take her place as Your Bride in this dark, sinful world?

He said
Would that all My people could hear My voice so clearly. To me, My church is spotless; there are no wrinkles. My Bride is beauty-filled, completely fair, yes, all fair. Until My church sees what I see, it will continue to live far below what I have said it would be in this world. My church is glorious and victorious, a mighty force on this earth.

When My church lifts its eyes to focus on Me, then no longer will it be consumed by its failings or absorbed in its sins. Until My church lifts its eyes to see Me rather than focusing on its sins – those you classify as petty differences and those that are gross imperfections, it will never fulfill its destiny on this earth.

You are My called out ones – chosen, called and appointed to bring forth fruit. You are My Bride - beautiful beyond description, powerful in your position, awesome in your possession of the gifts and graces that only I can give. You stand in favor with Me because My blood has set you free. I have clothed you with the beauty of My righteousness.

Would that all My people would see My church, My Bride this way; if only they could see the need to view My church as I do. You need also to see My individual maidens the same way; each one is precious to Me. You tend to look at people's appearance, success or lack of success, position and station in life but I just look at hearts. I want to teach you to look for My beauty in My people.

My prayerful response
Yes, Lord, I understand what You are saying to me. I haven't always seen Your beauty in Your people. It's true; I have regarded their station in life, their success or failure in life, and their imperfections. It's a struggle for me to look beyond these things and see You in Your people. And I am not alone in failing to behold Your beauty in others and in displaying Your love to those around us. Many of us in Your church need to heed your voice calling: "*Behold* . . . . *Behold* . . . . !"

He said
Yes, dear one, and for you it is a struggle to see beyond your own weaknesses and imperfections, is it not? And if you cannot see your own worth to Me, how can you see the worth of others? You see, it's not "*self-worth*" you need – it is a deep sense of your "God-worth". Just as this maiden in the Song of Songs needed to see herself as I viewed her, so do you. That's why I declared it again over her and over you!

"Behold, you are fair, My love, behold, you are fair."
For now it is enough for you to know you are beautiful! You are fair! You are lovely! You are awesome! You stun My heart! You make Me sing! And I sing over you today My dear one.

You are beautiful, My love
You are fair and charming too
You are covered with My love
You are beautiful, My love.
Poetry written by Florli Nemeth

Verse 1B

. . . . thou hast dove's eyes within thy locks; thy hair is as a flock of goats that appear from Mt. Gilead.

My thoughts
So important is it to Him that we grasp these truths, He repeats and expands His Word to us[74]; so vital is it to Him that our eyes are open to discern and understand, Paul prayed for our hearts to be flooded with light so that in gazing into His face we could know and understand: [75]

- The hope to which He has called us
- The richness of His glorious inheritance in us
- The greatness of His power in and for us

Jesus also spoke of a single, or an evil eye, showing that the affection of the heart is set forth in the eye.[76]

---

[74] Song of Solomon 1:15
[75] Ephesians 1:18-20
[76] Matthew 6:22,23

Paul said a spiritual man has insight, and that baffles the man of the world who can't understand him at all.[77]

The King observed that His bride had insight and understanding. She was single-minded in her love and devotion to Him, and her heart was filled with wisdom.

My prayer
Lord, I want to be single-minded in my love and desire toward You. I want to know and understand Your hope, Your purpose, Your inheritance in me, and the surpassing greatness of Your power at work within me and for me. You are awesome in Your love and power.

I desire to be like the dove - gentle and with a single focus for You and for Your purposes alone. May I not be double-minded and tossed about, but single-minded in my love and desire toward You.

My thoughts
He commends also her hair - not an essential part of the body, but very conspicuous as a decoration of the body. Hair adorns the body in the same way a well-ordered life commends and adorns the beauty within. Paul spoke of the need for women to adorn themselves with good works[78].

Peter also spoke of the inward adorning of the heart with a gentle, peaceful spirit which is very precious in the sight of God.[79]

A heart adorned with a gentle, peaceful spirit is not anxious or overwrought. Being beautiful on the inside is so important to God. He sees this inner beauty as beautiful; the world around sees that which is outward.

The goats appeared from mount Gilead - from a fruitful place where they had fed and become strong and beautiful. He sees this, too, in us.

---

[77] 1 Corinthians 2:14 & 15
[78] 1 Timothy 2:9, 10
[79] 1 Peter 3:3-5

He said
I want you to shine as a guiding star and as a beacon light in a dark, dark world to be a bearer of light to those who still sit in darkness.[80]

I want you to look beautiful to those who need Me. This begins in your home where your attitudes and demeanor should reflect My life and graces within you.

Your hair (your outward adornment) is very important because it symbolizes those outward graces seen by others. By feeding on My Word in My presence (on Mt. Gilead), you will become and then be known as one who is cheerful, kind, gracious and winsome.

People will only see what is in your heart by what they see in your actions and attitudes. So dear one, you need to feed at My table in Mt. Gilead daily so you will be strong; you need to let Me arrange your hair! I'll make you beautiful on the outside as well as on the inside, so that when you "appear from Mt. Gilead" you will appear with My glory and presence, My sweetness and love upon you. Those around you will be attracted to you because of the graces they see on the outside, but you will have something more to offer because of the gifts and graces and beauty that dwell within.

There are those who display the outward attributes of love and graciousness yet because they have not spent time with Me on Mt. Gilead, they are not strong inside and have nothing to share with those who hunger for reality. Then there are those who spend time with Me daily and are strong and beautiful on the inside, but because they are unkind, grumpy and short with people on the outside, people are not drawn to them and see no beauty in them.

I want you, My bride, to be beautiful both on the inside and on the outside for it is not enough to be just one or the other; to be complete there must be both. I see you with dove's eyes - single-mindedness in your love for Me and in your desire to please Me; when I look into your eyes I see love, hope and passion.

Do not fear to look deeply into My eyes, for as you do, you will penetrate the depth of My love for you and your heart will understand

[80] Philippians 2:15

anew the power and love that is available to you. Never forget that it is in looking and gazing into My eyes that you will become like Me for that is when the transference of life takes place. The mystery by which You apprehend the depth of My love and understand anew the power and tenderness of Who I am costs nothing more nor less than time spent with Me. Gaze long into My eyes so that I may gaze into your eyes and fill you up to overflowing.

Stay in My presence (on Mt. Gilead) long enough to feed and drink deeply; allow Me to adorn you outwardly. Come into My beauty parlor daily and ask Me to adorn your inner and outer life with My gifts and graces. Then leave Mt. Gilead to go down into the valley and pour out My love and graces and gifts on those who need Me so desperately.

You understand this, beloved one and I know that even now your heart is responding joyfully to My words of love and encouragement. I love you so dearly. Go in My strength today, give away My love to everyone you meet - but not just today. Let every single day be filled with excitement, joy and anticipation.

My lament or complaint
Father, I need to talk with You. I feel such heaviness in my spirit and I do not understand why. I can't even explain it to You. Speak to me about where I am my dear Father.

He said
Come to Me, My dearest Child! Let Me take the load you have been carrying. It is too heavy for you. I never meant for you to carry another's load. Don't compare yourself to your spouse, or to anyone else. I am doing a deep work in your friend's life, but it is not what I am doing in your life at this time. I am drawing you into a deeper place of intimacy with Me. I have hidden you so you can be with Me alone.

Furthermore, there are some to whom you are not called to minister, for there are others in My Body as well whom I have chosen to use. That does not diminish what you mean to these ones, or what you have given to them. You are a unique person with unique gifts. Because you have a special ability to get close to individuals and pour your life into them, this does not mean you will be close to everyone! Some will not connect with you at all; others will connect for only a season. There will be others, however, who will be drawn to you more permanently for mentoring.

Right now you are feeling at a loss because you feel that one has closed her heart to you. But dearest friend, you poured your life into this one - you did what you could. Her actions have nothing to do with you!

There will always be some who come to you for a season and then go to another for a season. Don't be dismayed or disappointed or disillusioned. Know that this will happen again and again. Just be sensitive to My leading and to the voice of the Holy Spirit. Minister only to those I bring to you. In that way your heart will rest and you will not be stressed out wondering if you've missed My purpose in it all.

This is a season of rest for you, a time to hide under the shadow of My wings. Right now it is you who needs refreshing, recreation and blessed quietness for your soul. You will always find respite when you come to Me - rest in your mind and soul and body.

My yoke in your life is not harsh, sharp or pressing, Likewise those things you minister to others should be in kind - comfortable, gracious and pleasant, not harsh, hard or pressing. Always minister in a spirit of graciousness and you will thus touch others as I touch you and as I touch them. I will lead you to those you should touch each day. Depend on Me to do this for you.

Verse 2

Your teeth are like a flock of sheep that are even shorn, which came up from the washing, whereof everyone bear twins, and none is barren among them.

My thoughts
I see three things here -

1. Teeth signify a person's disposition as good or evil[81]
2. Teeth evidence what a person feeds on
3. Teeth evidence a healthy or unhealthy complexion, depending upon what we eat

[81] Psalm 57:4 & Daniel 7:5

God has given us teeth, a zealousness, endowing our words with a "bite" to those who hear. Our conversation is not always soft and yet we have teeth like sheep, not like lions or tigers or bears. We are to be moderate, free from the sin of biting and devouring each other.[82] As we come from meditating on God's Word, we have been washed clean.[83]

The Bridegroom speaks of the maiden's spiritual health and fruitfulness. Like a flock of sheep bearing twins enriches their owner, so the Bride here is seen as fruitful and productive, a profitable servant who is not barren. She comes with fruit for her Lord, her Lover, her Friend.[84]

My prayer
Lord, I want healthy teeth that I may chew on Your Word for it cleanses my life as I meditate and consume it. Moreover, I was meant to eat Your Word as was the prophet Jeremiah. [85] Your Word is sweet to my taste, making me fruitful for You and fulfilling my longing to be beautiful for You.

He said
Dearest One I see you as a sheep, harmless, always in need of the Shepherd's protection and care. You are one who has learned to obey My Word and My Word washes you daily. It is a lesson too few have learned.

I desire that your words have a "bite" to them, but never to be voiced in spite against My people, never to bite and devour My sons and daughters. Like a mighty sword, use them only to bite and devour any enemy that would dare to come against My people and against My Word. You are able in prayer to speak words that will demolish the work of the enemy. Be soft and gentle toward your brothers and sisters who love Me, but as you come to the place of prayer, always be zealous to stand up for My truth and righteousness.

Yes, you are beautiful with a smile that ravishes My heart. Your desire to eat the meat of My Word beings Me joy and satisfaction because I

---

[82] Galatians 5:15
[83] John 15:3 "Now you are clean through the Word I have spoken unto you."
[84] John 15:8
[85] Jeremiah 15:16

know the power of My Word to keep you clean and make you fruitful. As you eat, you will never be barren or alone.

There will always be someone in your life who is receiving your care; be careful not to assume responsibility for those whom I have not committed to your ministry. Even then, hold those I have given you loosely; don't hold them to yourself. My calling on your life is to simply nurture and care for them as long as they need you; then release them back to Me. I may give them to another, or they may be ready to bear lambs (twins) themselves.

But whatever happens, do not languish when some leave you for another. It is not because you've failed, but because you've done a good job with what I have given you, and now it's time for another to pour into their life. This attitude will allow you to rejoice in their growth and advance in the kingdom.

Don't worry - you are not beyond the age of bearing fruit in My kingdom! You will bear fruit even into old age. [86] So keep in My Word, and maintain your gentle spirit. You are beautiful, and I love you.

Verse 3A

Thy lips are like a thread of scarlet, and thy speech is comely . . . .

My prayer
Cleanse my lips, Lord, that my words may bring joy to Your heart and comfort and kindness to the hearts of others. May my speech be profitable and kind. May my voice be sweet and beautiful to You and to all who touch my life. When I cry to You may it be with unfeigned and guileless lips.[87]

I've sought to speak truth, Lord[88] for I have purposed that my lips shall praise You with joyful lips.[89] How can I not shout for joy when I

---

[86] Psalm 92:14
[87] Psalm 17:1
[88] Psalm 34:13
[89] Psalm 63:3 & 5

sing praises to You.[90] Deliver me, Lord, from lying lips and a deceitful tongue.[91]

May my lips speak words of peace not of war, bitterness, strife or dissension. Help me, Lord, to know when to speak and when to be silent. Sometimes I speak too quickly without knowing all the facts. Sometimes I speak too hastily, not really knowing what is in another's heart. Set a guard before my mouth, Lord, and keep watch at the door of my lips.[92]

Father, I want my speech to be gracious and winsome (sensible), seasoned with salt.[93] Yet Father, even in all my longings to speak right words, I find I often stumble, fall and offend. Even when I speak with good intentions, sometimes people take offense. Will I ever reach a place in my life where I never say the wrong thing?[94]

Yet in spite of my failures and inadequacies, You say my lips are like a thread of scarlet and my speech is beautiful! I cry to You to make it so!

He said
I know that you will stumble, fall, and say the wrong thing, but I also know the intent of your heart to speak words of love and grace and encouragement and to edify those whose lives you touch. The secret is in listening for My voice before you speak. And when you do speak ill-advisedly, quickly come to Me for cleansing. To repent can seem like such an easy thing; to apologize, a demand so hard to fulfill.

"I'm so sorry" are words that will go a long way in winning another's heart! I know your heart grieves over words spoken in a way that incited anger and frustration. Then there are times when you feel misunderstood because you are misunderstood! Other times you'll be misquoted, your well-intentioned words twisted. Just remember in those times that as you need forgiveness, so others will need your forgiveness.

---

[90] Psalm 71:23
[91] Psalm 120:2
[92] Psalm 141:3
[93] Colossians 4:6
[94] James 3:2

The most important thing, dearest one, is this: do not brood on hurtful words because they will become like arrows that pierce the heart, wounding you and eventually causing huge festered sores that, if left untreated, will cause you much harm.

Learn to deflect words that hurt. Send them in My direction. I can handle them. This is a very strategic strategy you need to perfect. Because of your sensitive nature, you have suffered much from wounding words. Dear one, come here. Come once again into My arms of love. You need to come not only daily, but many times a day.

Your words of love and praise, your prayers for others mean so much to Me. Don't let the devil lie to you. He tells you your prayers are of little avail and he torments you with your failures to speak good at all times.

My dear one, you will truly fail because you are not fully perfected! You will stumble and fall as you continue to progress on your journey with Me. But tell Me, what did you do yesterday when you went cross country skiing? You fell trying to get up an icy hill, but you realized it was too steep for you, and you got up and skied back - you retraced your steps.

Sometimes you will get ahead of yourself and maybe even step into unfamiliar territory with your words. When you do, just get up, apologize, retract your words, move on and go on your way rejoicing. No use being tormented by the devil.

And dear one, this is why I say that your lips are like a thread of scarlet. Included in taking responsibility for your words is your coming to Me for cleansing when you fail. I see your words covered with My blood. Because of that the words you speak to Me are so beautiful! Your prayers are heard in the court of heaven. Everybody knows you're there because you come often to Me.

So don't be discouraged or feel your there is no meaning in your faltering words. On the contrary, your prayers are recorded and played over and over in the Heavenlies. Your tears are bottled up, residing in My presence. Remember that, as you continue to place family, friends, peoples and nations before Me.

Your prayers give Me permission and authority to act on your behalf. Even though you feel that you have prayed for some and never have seen a change, keep praying. Your words are beautiful, and trust Me that in a day when you least expect it, I will answer. My Spirit is ever faithful, working on hearts even though you may not see it.

So dear one, keep coming to Me with your love and worship, with your prayers and intercessions. You are so dear to Me. Your words are so sweet. Whether you speak them or write them, they go right to My heart! O how I love you. My heart is so ravished with your few words of love.

Verse 3B

. . . . thy temples are like a piece of pomegranate within thy locks.
...your cheeks are like halves of a pomegranate behind your veil. (Amplified)

My thoughts
There are some things others don't see. My Shepherd can tell by looking at my cheeks whether I am happy or sad. He sees me when I blush before Him. He sees my tenderness and modesty in spiritual things, and my aversion to sin.

He said
You know, My dear one, you do not need to be ashamed before Me. I see your heart and know that you have answered My call. I have seen your striving to become a good workman. [95]

When I look at you I am pleased -

- That you put effort in getting to know Me and My Word
- That your heart in tenderness before Me loathes and abhors even the smallest sin or weakness you see in yourself
- That you mourn and weep over the sins and weaknesses of others
- That you are too modest to brag about your good deeds
- That when you are commended, you blush, not wanting yourself to be put forward

[95] 2 Timothy 2:15

I commend you today, and I assure you that one day you will truly hear these words, "Well done, thou good and faithful servant, enter into the joy of your Lord".[96]

I see your cheeks in those times when you pull your veil over your face to hide the tears and the shame of your own failures and weaknesses. Today I am lifting the veil and speaking words of confirmation: do not cover your cheeks, even when you burn with shame. Do not let your imperfections mar your beautiful complexion. Let Me see your face even when you feel weak and forlorn. For there is nothing in you that can ever turn Me away from loving you and tenderly caring for you.

All you have is a gift from Me – even this tender heart I gave to you. While sin makes a heart hard and unyielding, I've given you a new heart, a heart that is tender, yielding and pliable in My hands. Cherish your tender heart. Allow My Word and My presence to keep it tender by yielding it to Me. Let Me keep your heart; I'll hold your heart in My hands and protect it.

My response
Thank You, Lord. You are so dear to me. I will not hide my face from You for I love You. Thank You for Your words of love and kindness and for Your affirmations. You are so wonderful.

Verse 4

Thy neck is like the tower of David builded for an armory, whereon there hang a thousand bucklers, all shields of mighty men.
Your neck is like the tower of David, built for an arsenal, whereon hang a thousand bucklers, all of them shields of warriors. (Amplified)

Background thoughts
The neck is what moves and supports the head, giving it a resting place. The neck unites the believer to Christ, the Head; the neck holds forth the exercise of faith and obedience.

The neck commended here is the opposite to a stiff neck of stubbornness and disobedience, or of a hanging of the head which speaks of

[96] Matthew 25:21, 23

discouragement and shame. Nor is it a neck signifying haughtiness and pride. Rather, it is a neck implying faith, holy confidence in God and in His promises. It speaks of faith - that faith by which we receive everything God has promised us.

Paul exhorted us to "lift up over all [the covering or armor] the shield of saving faith upon which you can quench the flaming missiles of the wicked one."[97] Furthermore, in Hebrews 11 we read that faith is absolutely vital, and all those who pleased God, lived their lives by faith. Anything and everything we obtain from God is obtained by faith. And every act of faith is like a warrior's shield put on display in God's armory.

I wonder if God looks at me and sees a compliant, willing, obedient, full of faith neck? I wonder how He evaluates my life? The men and women in Hebrews 11 were heroes and heroines of faith (verse 40). They won the approval of God through their faith and trust in God, even though many never lived to see the fulfillment of God's promises (verse 39).

He said
You need wonder no longer, My dear one. I see you as a woman (a man) of faith and obedience. Every act of obedience and faith, however small, is as a shield of defensive protection. I see you as a mighty warrior. You have been empowered through your union with Me. You have drawn your strength from Me.[98]

You have put on the armor I've provided, you've stood your ground against the enemy's attacks, and you've lifted up the shield of faith to quench the flying missiles the enemy sends in your direction. Don't be discouraged or intimidated. Don't look at your weakness and vulnerability. You are strong, submitted, yielded and obedient to Me, and that's all that matters. You're My warrior - My heroine (hero) - My loved one!

---

[97] Ephesians 6:16

[98] Ephesians 6:10

Verse 5

Thy two breasts are like two young roes that are twins, which feed among the lilies.

Background thoughts
What an awesome portion of scripture. He is commending the bride's beautiful figure. This is similar to Ezekiel 16:6-14 where God culminated His commendations of Israel by saying, "Your reputation was great among the nations for your beauty; it was perfect because of all the gifts I gave you, says the Lord God.

The breasts here speak of –

- Her beauty and comeliness
- Her warmth and affection[99]
- Her ability to nurture others

My prayer
Lord, You are saying I am fit to edify and nourish others and to take You to my bosom! You see no defect or imperfection in me. You say I am fit to love others and to love You. Lord, I love to feed in Your company because You, too, feed among the lilies[100] I delight in the presence and company of Your people, and I delight even more in Your company.

Your Word is my meat and drink; it is only as I feed in Your presence that I can bless and edify others. In fact, anything I have to give is only because You've given it to me. In order to maintain my ability to edify and nourish others, I must feed daily on Your Word, Your love and Your presence for You are such an awesome God!

He said
Dear one, you have embraced Me again and again, drawing Me to your heart. You have thought it was only for you to enjoy My presence, but as your Bridegroom King, I must tell you - it is I who enjoy your love, your presence! You have felt you were not fit for love, not worthy of special nearness and love but be assured that you are God's gift to Me, and I delight in you! I love My Bride, the Church, and I love you.

---

[99] Song of Solomon 1:13
[100] Song of Solomon 2:16

You are worthy, you are fit and you are ready because it is I who has made you so. There is nothing in your past that can undo this because your past is under the covering of My blood - totally forgiven, totally forgotten.

There is nothing in the present that can keep you from experiencing the depths of My love. There is nothing that will ever be able to separate you from the love I demonstrated at Calvary on the cross for all the world to see.[101]

I commend and affirm you in your desire to edify and bless others. As you delight in my presence and feed regularly at My table, I will use you for that very purpose. Not only do my people need to be edified, they need to know how to gather their own food. You are a nurturer of others, and you will bless many.

You are also My warm, loving, tender and faithful spouse, and I draw near to you to bless you and to hold you close to My heart.

My response

Hold me, precious Jesus
As a shepherd holds his lamb
Safe, serene, protected
In the hollow of his hand.

Feed me in Your pastures
Give to drink Your wine
Fill me with Your pleasures
Until the end of time.

Draw me to Your bosom
Tenderly secure
Hide me in Your presence
Safe from doubt and fear.

Let me live forever
Like the two young fawns
Feeding in the lilies
'Till the break of dawn.

Poetry written by Florli Nemeth

[101] Romans 8:38, 39

My prayer
Lord, I don't know how long You have for me to live on this earth, but as long as I do, I have two passions: to feed in the presence of Your company and daily to experience Your love in a deeper, more intimate way and to use the gifts You have given me to bless Your Body, Your Church.

There is no greater honor You could bestow than the honor of blessing and edifying that which You love! You love Your Church, gave Your very life for it, so let me be a part of Your plan. Let me love and bless at all times what You love and bless! I commit myself afresh and anew to feed among the lilies - to be nourished by You and in turn to nourish others.

O Jesus, You are so dear to me - so near! I hold You to my bosom, even as You hold me to Your bosom. Your love will never let me go and I cling to You with mine. There are no words to express the adoration of my heart toward You.

Held in arms of love divine
I am His, and He is mine.
Here among the lilies dear
Is the One I love, so near.

Fed and nourished in this place
Everything received by grace.
Held and loved in His embrace
In His presence see His face.

Blessed to bless
Loved to love
Gifts He gives to share
With His Bride,
His holy ones
Those for whom He cares.

Poetry written by Florli Nemeth

Verse 6

Until the day break, and the shadows flee away, I will get me to the mountain of myrrh and the hill of frankincense.

Isaiah 2:2

And it shall come to pass in the last days, that the mountain of the Lord's house shall be established in the top of the mountains, and shall be exalted above the hills, and all nations shall flow into it[102]*.*
Mine house shall be called an house of prayer for all people.[103]
And upon every high mountain and upon every high hill there will be brooks and streams of water . . . .[104]

He said
Dear one, until that day when shadows flee away and there is no more night, I invite you to come with Me to the mountain of myrrh and the hill of frankincense. That is where you will find Me - in the place of prayer. And that is why at times you feel such resistance in your spirit. Your flesh opposes this because it is a place of total dependency upon Me and it spells death to the flesh.

The enemy of your soul also opposes you in this. He will try to keep you from the place of prayer, and failing that, he will use distractions of all kinds to keep you from enjoying the place of prayer.

When you go to the place of prayer you will find Me there - waiting for you with open arms - desiring thus to bless you. It may seem difficult to climb this mountain, but My mountains are filled with brooks and streams of water. Feasting your eyes on the beauty of My creation, you will be refreshed as you partake of the refreshing streams of water.

Drink, My lovely Bride, My Spouse, My Love! Though many cannot understand this, you know that it is in the place of prayer that you find My strength, encouragement and blessings because it is there that you will find Me. So come with Me, My friend, My beloved one.

---

[102] See also Micah 4:1
[103] Isaiah 56:7
[104] Isaiah 30:25

I said
There are times when it has been so difficult for me but I hear You, My Lord, and I am coming. With everything that is within me I give myself to being faithful to Your house of prayer because, Jesus, You are here! Forgive me for doubting You. Lord, I will get me to the mountain, to Him whom my soul adores.

Verse 7

Thou art all fair, My love; there is no spot in thee.
You are so beautiful, My love, in every part of you. (Living Bible)
O My love! How beautiful you are! There is no flaw in you. (Amplified)

"Jesus, Thy blood and righteousness
My beauty are, my glorious dress
Midst flaming worlds in these arrayed
With joy shall I lift up my head.

"Bold shall I stand in that great day
For who ought to my charge shall lay
Fully by Thee absolved I am
From sin and fear, from guilt and shame.

"Thou God of peace, Thou God of love
Let all the world Thy mercy prove
Their beauty this, their glorious dress,
Jesus the Lord, our Righteousness."[105]

My prayer
Lord, You know my sins, my faults, my failures, my shortcomings, my imperfections. You also know my regrets, and You hear my confessions. But overriding those things, You see my desire to be clean and to walk in holiness before You. I wonder what it will be like to stand before You one day - perfect?

He said
You are clean through the Word I have spoken - legally clean and beautiful. Because I have pardoned you, there is no sin found in you. [106] Because I put My grace upon you, you are beautiful to Me.

---

[105] Written by Count Zinzendorf
[106] John 13:10/Jeremiah 50:20

Deuteronomy 32:12
My words shall fall upon you like the gentle rain and dew, like rain upon the tender grass, like showers on the hillside.

I said
So Lord, Your words drop like gentle dew, refreshing my heart and my soul; because You accept me, I am showered with Your love. In Your love You have forgiven me. You can do so because in taking my place your death paid for my redemption from sin, my salvation. O Jesus, how my heart loves You. Even You cannot see my sins and failures because they have been covered with Your blood. Thank You for cleansing me wholly.

Lord, help me to be more like You in this respect. When others fail, help me to see beyond their faults. Make my words to others like gentle dew and refreshing raindrops. May my words bring healing into people's lives rather than further hurt and condemnation.

Lord, others may speak harshly or unkindly, but may I speak to them only as You would speak to me.

He said
Dear one, you have My heart when you speak words of peace, reconciliation, acceptance and love. Remember, it takes no prophetic voice to find fault! Nothing less than a deep understanding of My love will allow you to speak prophetically into the lives of others. There is no other way in which to speak love, acceptance and forgiveness.

I need you to speak good things over My people even in the midst of their failings. There are so many of My chosen ones who live in lack or in condemnation and lack of acceptance. I need you to speak My love and acceptance over them.

I accept My people on the basis of what I have done at Calvary, what I continue to do, and what I will one day do in eradicating sin and evil forever, totally triumphing over it.

Yes, My dear one, you are all fair, and there is no flaw in you. That is how I see you, and that is how you need to see My people. See them through My eyes. See *yourself* through My eyes! I will anoint your eyes with eye salve so you *can* see as I see.

My eyes shall look with favor upon the faithful of the land, that they may dwell with Me; he who walks blamelessly, he shall minister to Me.[107]

I said
Lord, it's interesting to note that the King began his commendations with the words, "*Thou art fair*"[108] then he ends his commendations with the same words, "*Thou art all fair, My love . . .*". In grace and love He adds, "*there is no spot (flaw) in thee.*" Is it because the bride needed to hear this that he spoke to her thus?

He said
You are so beautiful, My love, in every part. O that you could see this clearly. If My people could see their beauty in Me they would rise up and be who they are. They would not be impoverished as Israel was by the Midianites[109], no longer stripped and devastated by the enemy, nor living in abject poverty and fear. They would not be threshing wheat in the bottom of a wine press as Gideon did.

As they come to understand that I am with them, that I am their God, that I work miracles among them, then they will learn to know *Me.* That is My desire for you and for all My people. Come - come into My presence. Know Me - know My love - know My wonderful provision over your life. Live in My love, live in My provision, My protection and in My glory over you.

Lift up your head with joy
    Be not bowed down with shame
For I the sovereign Lord declare
    Your beauty and your fame.

Lift up your voice and sing
    Redemption draweth nigh
The battle's done, the victory's won
    And you are set on high.

---

[107] Psalm 101:6
[108] Song of Solomon 4:1
[109] Judges 6:6

Lift up your hands and praise
Jehovah God, your King
The everlasting, great I AM
To Him your worship bring.

Poetry written by Florli Nemeth

Verse 8

Come with Me from Lebanon, My spouse, with Me from Lebanon; look from the top of Amana, from the top of Shinar and Herman, from the lion's den, from the mountains of the leopards.

My thoughts
Calling me His spouse, His bride, He calls me to Himself. He wants me with Him and He wants me to see the world from His perspective. In quoting the Word during a time of temptation from the devil, Jesus defeated the enemy's intent to elicit His worship and thus destroy Him.

He saw a higher kingdom than the kingdoms of this world. He had a higher perspective and it is to those kingdoms and that perspective that He is calling me. There He can show me the glory of His Father's kingdom - a glory that cannot be compared with earth's greatest glory. O Jesus, I take Your hand. I come. Here, from the mountains of wild beasts, show me Your kingdom, Your glory and Your perspective of things here on earth.

I have put my hand in the hand of the Conqueror, the King, the Lord of heaven and earth – and yet He is my Friend, my Spouse, my Love! Show me Your glory, manifest Your beauty and display to me Your power, You who are awesome in Your love and majesty.

He said
You cannot have Me *and* the world, My child
There's only one choice to make
Relinquish your pride and let go of its charms
Leave all for yours and My sake.

Respond to the call you are hearing today
Lift up your eyes and see
There's only one kingdom and only one Lord
That will last for eternity.

My voice has gone out like the blast of a horn
I'm calling you now to come
To come with Me, My lover, My spouse
To make Me your choice and your home!
Poetry written by Florli Nemeth

These are days when I am calling My people to a higher level of commitment and life. It is no longer possible to survive among the dens of lions and mountains of leopards without a deep covenantal relationship with Me.

So in the midst of the warfare and in the midst of surrounding beauty and plenty, I call My people, My chosen ones, to come and be with Me. You are light, you are salt, you are called out ones - loved by Me.

When you answer the call to come, you come to My presence, to My heart, to My love, to My arms of protection, to your home in Me. My heart is your home, My child. No longer can My people roam this earth and be at rest for true rest is found only in Me. Thank you for coming to Me today, for resting in the promise that I will always care for you.

The Ravished Heart of the Bridegroom for the Bride

Verse 9A

Thou hast ravished my heart, my sister, my spouse . . . .
You have ravished my heart, my bride...(Living Bible)

My thoughts and prayer
He became like me. Like you. Like us. Our Brother and our Friend became our merciful and faithful High Priest. Lord, You are my Brother, my Friend; I am Your sister, Your friend! High Priest, You are merciful to me and faithful to God in dealing with my sins.[110] Jesus, You are awesome.

The fact that You call me "sister" shows five things:-

1. You condescended to be made like me, and we have the same Father[111]
2. I've been adopted and made an heir with You[112]
3. You gave me a change of nature - You made me holy; therefore, I am one with You, because we have the same Father[113]
4. You give a family connection, family ties, and You are proud to call us brother, sister, mother.[114]
5. Because you are not ashamed of Your family You unashamedly admit to that connection with us.

He said
Yes, My Sister, My Brother, My Friend, I call you this because My Father is now your Father. My inheritance, like the family name and our traits and traditions are yours. The bond of love for My church comes because My sons and daughters are your brothers and sisters. My Father loves you because you love Me. You believed that I came from the Father; therefore, He loves you dearly. My father loves you *as He loves me.* [115]

---

[110] Hebrews 2:17
[111] Hebrews 2:9,11
[112] Ephesians 1:5/Romans 8:15-17
[113] Hebrews 2:11
[114] Matthew 12:46-50
[115] John 16:27/John 17:8, 23, 24

My Father loved Me before the foundation of the world, even as He chose you and loved you before the foundation of the world.[116] My prayer for you is that the love My Father has for Me may be in you and I in you.[117]

I have made you holy. You stand before Me without a single fault because you are covered with My love.[118]

You belong to Me! I am My father's dearly loved Son, and you are Mine. There is nothing I would not do for you. I shower down upon you today all the riches of My grace.[119] Holding you close to My heart, I cover you with My love.

I long for that day when all My loved ones will be gathered together with Me. But until that day, I give you My presence and My love, My Sister, My Brother, My Spouse, My Bride. You are so very beautiful, and I love you!

My response
Lord, I don't know what I would do without Your love. Life is so meaningless without You and yet so many live purposeless, meaningless, hopeless lives because they don't know how much You love them.

There are others who may have known You at one time, but who have been off track for so long it's easy to question if they ever were acquainted with You. How can they walk so far from you, live their entire life without You? What depth of despair, to be without Your love! Lord, I'm so happy, so secure in Your love, and my heart worships You and praises you for Your goodness to me.

But what about my brothers? My sisters? My neighbors? My friends who do not know Your love? How can we touch their hearts? God, my heart aches for them. O when will they come and appear before You?

---

[116] Ephesians 1:4
[117] John 17:26
[118] Ephesians 1:4
[119] Ephesians 1:6

Hear my cry for them - for all those who do not know or grasp how much they need You.

He said
My child, you feel My heart and My pain because you are one with Me. I have called again and again, but there has been no response. With Me there is no despair because I do not give up. I call to them again and again. I will use you to have a part in this recovery as you pray and as you declare My Word, My love, My purpose and My destiny to the nations.

You will yet go to the nations, of people you have not known and you will declare My love and My goodness. <u>And as you do what I have called you to do, I will do what you cannot do.</u> I know those for whom you are praying so never forget that I am the great High Priest - merciful to those who cry out to Me and faithful to them and to My Father.

Time is irrelevant to My Father. Those He chose before the foundation of the world will truly become His even if it takes an earthly lifetime. Some may resist you, but they cannot resist Me. My love will break down every resistance that has kept them off track for so many years; My love will melt hardness as I reach down to save and embrace them. My love changes hearts and makes new persons.

Speak to them of My love, that is My desire for you. Be among those I chose in order to share My love. The time is ripe - the time is NOW! My call is urgent for today is the day of salvation. Hear the word of the Lord!

Verse 9B

Thou hast ravished my heart with one of thine eyes, with one chain of thy neck. I am overcome by one glance of your eyes, by a single bead of your necklace. (Living Bible)

My thoughts
His heart is moved and conquered just by one look of my eyes, just by one act of surrender or obedience. He is captivated and so easily conquered by my response to Him.

There is no demand that I attain a certain level of maturity in prayer before He pays attention to me or accepts me into His presence. Even when I'm too weak to do more than give Him a glance, He condescends to my weakness, overcome by my reaching out in love for Him.

My prayer

In my weakness, Lord, I look to You
Knowing full well what You'll do!
In Your love, Lord, You will run to me
Coming with a heart of love and acceptance.

Some days I feel so weak, Lord. There are times when I can do no more than look with one eye, as it were. It is then that I am overcome by Your unconditional love. There are no demands, no set of regulations, no series of expectations I am unable to satisfy. You simply call me to come.

And when I come, no matter how low I may feel, You lift me up. Lord, You are so gracious and kind. You call me to Your heart, and even when I take just one step of obedience toward You, You are totally ravished with my love. My mind says, "How can this be?" Yet my heart calls You to me again and again, and my arms embrace You and say, "Please do not leave me."

He said

Yes, I see your heart, My Child. Do not fear. You can never come too often, look too much, obey too fervently. You can never hunger and thirst for My presence too much. My heart is ravished with your love, with your obedience and with your desire to give yourself to prayer. You are totally accepted where you are today.

I am aware of those times when your desires are thwarted by distractions or immaturity, but I see every single act of obedience, even the small ones like getting up early in the wee morning hours to pray. You may not be aware of My presence, but I see, I hear, I know, I love, I draw you to My heart even in your weakness.

Today, dear one, you feel weak and tired. My heart is overcome that you would sit and visit with Me when your head is pounding and your heart is so low. Let me lift you up even as I encourage you by My grace. My love is unchanged and unchangeable! I accept you, embrace you and I love you as you are right now.

Dearest child, you ravish My heart! You are so dear, so important, so vital to My heart! Do not belittle yourself, My lovely bride! You have been thinking harshly and unkindly of yourself. You've been trampling on your beauty! Don't do this to yourself!

Every negative thought you entertain about yourself is like throwing dirt or mud on a work of exquisite art! You are My bride! When you think less of yourself than you should, you are throwing mud at My bride, smearing it into her dress. I do not take kindly to that kind of behavior. As you bring your thoughts into line with Mine, once more you will see yourself as I see you.

I see you without spot or wrinkle, and you stand before Me holy, covered with My robe of righteousness and cleansed by My blood. I paid for your beauty with My blood, indeed My very life. I am not honored by your devaluing and diminishing thoughts of yourself.

O My love, you are so beautiful to Me. My eyes are for only you! Spend more time in My presence so I can assuredly convey to you the beauty I see in you - the beauty I've placed within you and without, or upon you.

Glory in My love. Revel in My presence. Bask in My love so that My love can take effect in you and continue to transform you.

Verse 10A

How fair is Thy love, My sister, My spouse! How much better is thy love than wine! And the smell of thine ointments than all spices!
How sweet is your love, My darling, My bride. How much better it is than mere wine. The perfume of your love is more fragrant than all the richest spices. (Living Bible)

My prayer
Lord, I make the prayer of the Apostle Paul for all believers, mine. I know this is Your desire for me and for all Your loved ones that our

roots, the very core of our being, would go down deeply into the soil of Your love. [120]

You want me to be so rooted and established in love that nothing can ever move me from that position for it is there that I can grow and mature and bear fruit. O Lord, You want me to know and to experience Your love, not just read or study about it nor just understand it mentally. Love is a matter of the heart. Love can be watered and grow, or neglected and die.

You want me to feel how long, how wide, how deep, how high Your love really is. You want me to experience Your love, though it is so great I will never see the end of it or fully know and experience it. This love is for all Your children - not just a few.

O Lord, be at home in my heart today. Reveal Your love to me and let me experience it afresh today.

He said
You are fair, and you are beautiful. Your heart breathes after Me, delights in Me, loves to be with Me. Even as your heart desires to please Me alone, I love to be with you. How I cherish the way My people respond to Me and My love. You see, dear one, it is I who loved you first, planting My love within you.[121]

Because I love you perfectly, you need never fear what I might do to you. I showed you My love when I died to bring you eternal life. I, the One who is perfect love, live in you. My love lives in you, growing stronger and stronger each day. You have believed Me, and you believe Me now when I tell you that I love you dearly. Yes, I take special note of those who love Me, and I have taken special note of you. Your beauty causes Me to smile!

Let My words sink deeply into your heart; let them bring transformation, beauty, growth and fruitfulness into your life. Never forget that I look first for love, not work. Yes, you will work for Me and My kingdom, but I desire your love above all else. Spend time with Me. Allow My

[120] Ephesians 3:17-19
[121] 1 John 4:10-19

love to penetrate your heart and transform your life. Bask in My love, the love that enables you to go out and call My people to love Me, too. This is a time for you to soak and bask.

Even now you are feeling you're spending too much time in this book and maybe you should go on to something else. I say to you, Stay in love, stay in this book, soak in it, bask in it, rejoice in it! One day you will share this book with others as I have called you to do. Let your heart rest and rejoice in Me. Soak and bask in My love.

Verse 10B

How much better is thy love than wine!

My thoughts
She said this to the King[122] and now He is saying it to her. His love is so much better than mine, yet He says my love is better than wine. My love refreshes Him and brings Him great joy. He said of the woman who washed His feet, "she loved Me much".[123]

The significance of wine that was used in ceremonial drink offerings is important as He assures her that her love is preferred above outward performances and sacrifices. He chooses my love over duty, although He encourages me to be faithful in both. Given the choice of duty without love, though, He always longs for my love![124]

Your messenger, Paul, reminded us that the greatest thing is love. Greater than tongues, prophetic gifts and powers, even greater than faith that moves mountains, or that act of giving all I possess - better even than martyrdom – it is love that moves hearts and mountains.[125]

He said
Your love refreshes Me and brings great joy to My heart. You are one who, over the years and indeed, over much of your life, has loved Me much. Your love has not lessened over the years and today is deeper, stronger, more beautiful than ever before. Time has produced a love

---

[122] Chapters 1:2 and 4
[123] Luke 7:47
[124] Leviticus 23:13
[125] 1 Corinthians 13

that has grown and deepened and matured. Your love is so precious to Me and remember that as you love Me much, I love you more.

Low at My feet you have laid your burdens of carefulness, and you have wept your tears of love. Such love moves My heart. It is not your work that moves Me, or your career or good deeds - it is your love - your fellowship with Me that intoxicates my heart and refreshes My spirit. When My people bow low before Me, anointing My feet with their tears, I am moved with love.

O dear one, your love is all I need - your fellowship. Keep coming to Me, keep loving Me, for you are the apple of My eye!

Verse 10C

...the smell of thine ointments than all spices...
...the perfume of your love is more fragrant than all the richest spices. (Living Bible)

He said

You have been anointed by the Holy One
His grace placed on you
The unction of the Holy Ghost
Has come upon you too.
You've been anointed with the oil
Of gladness that I give
Your garments smell of fragrant myrrh
Each moment that you live.

Poetry written by Florli Nemeth

Dear one, your love is more precious to Me than earth's rarest spices and perfumes. I have poured out My love on you and now, as you pour out your love on Me, My heart is overwhelmed with desire for your love above all else. It is not that I don't need or desire your sacrifices and your service; it is just that your love perfumes your service with a delightful fragrance. There is no substitute for love, for spending time in My presence because you love Me; there is no service you offer that is more acceptable to me than your love!

My prayer
O Jesus, I know any fragrance I claim comes because You have poured it on me. Through Your Spirit which You have given, I am blessed to

be the recipient of Your love, Your graces and Your gifts. As You came out of the desert with Your bride at Your side You were perfumed with every spice that can be bought.[126] No wonder my life is a sweet smelling perfume to You for it is in nearness to You that I become like You. It is Your sweetness, Your love and Your beauty that affect my life.

O Lord, let me be near You; draw me nearer, closer, to You. Let me love You nearly, dearly, and ONLY on this day and every day of my life.

O Lord, may others see the beauty of Your love and grace in me that removes the stench of my old self life! May those close to me today be blessed by the fragrance of Your life and love in Me. I love You so much, Jesus.

Verse 11A

Thy lips drop as the honeycomb.

My thoughts
He says my speech is compared to honey. Like the sweet tasting, nourishing, very healthy and pleasant food it is, "*Pleasant (kind) words are as an honeycomb; sweet to the soul and health to the bones.*"[127]

Canaan flowed with milk and honey, a picture of her words that drop, or flow, as the honeycomb and like the dew that gently soaks into the earth. He's saying her words are gentle and kind and edify and encourage others.

"*My words shall fall upon you like the gentle rain and dew, like rain upon the tender grass, like showers on the hillside,*" says God.[128] And I have found that to be true. He is so gentle and kind.

Job spoke of the satisfying presence of His words:"*his counsel satisfied them*". And "*My speech dropped upon them like a refreshing shower*"[129]. Solomon wrote, "*The lips of the righteous feed and guide many*"[130].

---

[126] Song of Solomon 3:6
[127] Proverbs 16:24
[128] Deuteronomy 32:2 Living Bible
[129] Job 29:22 Living Bible and Amplified Bible
[130] Proverbs 10:21 Amplified Bible

My prayer
I do so desire that my words bring healing to others. May they drop like dew and settle like refreshing showers upon the dry ground. As I grow older, help me to grow sweeter and wiser; let my mouth pour forth speech that is sweet and kind and loving. May encouraging words drop from my mouth today, let them flow gently over the soul of every person I meet.

Especially may my mouth drop healing, helping words in my own home with my own family. Set a watch over the door of my mouth O Lord. May kind words only be spoken. And Lord, at times when I need to give counsel and direction, may my words of counsel bring peace and satisfaction, hope and healing. And may they not fall, meaningless, to the ground.

He said
O My child, My Bride, your lips drop as the honeycomb; your words are sweet to My heart. Your love and praise bring Me joy. Be encouraged today in the knowledge that My Spirit springs as an artesian well within you. As you live and walk in the Spirit, the words that flow out of you will be kind words, healing words, hopeful words.

In a world that cries for hope and healing, your words, like the balm of Gilead, bring healing. They are My words spoken through you, they drop as dew and taste like honey. It's not your words, but My words that bring healing and refreshing to people. No time spent in my presence is wasted time for it is in this place that My Word drops on you. My Word is Spirit and life and as you are refreshed and healed and filled with My Word, you are able to go out and speak as I would speak. You become My mouthpiece.

I need you to speak for Me. This is how I work and this is how I want to use you. As your life touches even strangers with gentleness and kindness, you are actually speaking My words of encouragement and counsel to others. As you write My words (and you will write!) you declare My kindness and love to future generations.

Yes, dear one, your words drop as honey on My heart, the voicing of your worship and praise and adoration as gentle rain in My presence.

Your words of love cannot fall to the ground since they are precious to Me.

My response
Thank You, Lord. You know that I long for Your words of love, too. I'm reminded that You do not drop on me like a flood or a tsunami that brings destruction. Your words don't destroy me - they come gently, building up and refreshing me. Make my words like that - gently washing over others with Your love. Let them never be accompanied by the works of the flesh: pushing, overwhelming, marked with destructive tones of anger or impatience.

He said
Yes, words of anger and hate, clamor and deceitfulness have the same effect as a flood or a tsunami. They destroy and tear down, leaving disaster in their pathway. Guard against this diligently. Never allow your anger or impatience to vent itself in a flood of destructive words because once the damage is done, it may take years to recover the ground lost, if ever.

So My beautiful child, guard your heart, for out of it are the issues of life. [131] The mouth speaks out of the abundance of your heart. So guard your heart. Do not allow evil of any kind to find its way into your heart. Get rid of bitterness and unforgiveness, hurt and woundedness. For when you speak out of your hurt, your words will always be hurtful words.

Speak only out of My deep well of love within you and let My love heal any brokenness or pain that would cause you to react with wrong words. O My dove, I love you! I love your voice. It is so sweet to My heart!

Verse 11B

. . . . honey and milk are under thy tongue...

He said
My child, the reason I could say to you what I did about the words you speak is that I know your heart is in agreement with what you say. You

---

[131] Proverbs 4:23

do not speak "honeyed" words with a heart full of hate and negativity. You are one who realizes the importance of feeding your heart with My Word and with good, positive and healing thoughts. You are sincere - not saying one thing and doing another.

You see, dear one, I take note of your inner being - your heart - not just your words. I always look deeper because I know it is out of the abundance of the heart you speak! And you will always feed others best with nourishing words when you yourself are fed and edified with My words. Your heart is the fountain from which flow your words. Keep the inner fountain flourishing, and the words you speak will be nourishing both for yourself and for others.

My response
Is this true also of the thoughts I think? Sometimes I struggle with thoughts; in fact, My thoughts can be heard as clearly as words. I seem to be in constant conversation with myself in My thoughts. I confess to You that many thoughts concerning myself and others do not line up with Your Word.

Help me, Lord, for it is here I struggle mightily. Come swiftly to my aid as I contend with a host of negative and depleting, diminishing thoughts about myself. By Your grace they cannot rule my life because I will not allow negativity to rule me. And yet I struggle in a seemingly never-ending battle to conquer with a host of negative thoughts about my weight and about my abilities in general. Other people are always more beautiful, more intelligent, more likeable than I. Would You speak to me about this?

He said
My dearest Child, your love is better than wine. One look at you and I am overcome, you ravish my heart with your beauty. Do not be overly concerned about these negative thoughts. They are the work of the enemy; they bombard you from outside yourself since they have no power over the inward man. These thoughts come from the enemy, not from Me nor from you, my Bride.

Continue to war against these attacks through the Word even as you remember that there is a difference between the thoughts of your heart and the thoughts of your mind. Though Satan, the enemy of our souls, strives to set up a stronghold, a pattern, of negative thought, that will in time affect and infect your heart, you are protected by the helmet of salvation - it is My provision designed to guard your mind.

Dear one, there are patterns of thoughts in your mind that need to be broken - patterns of thought that have been there from your childhood. Be encouraged in remembering that nothing is beyond My power to destroy as you enter into prayer and fasting.

My response
So what would You like me to do, my Love?

He said
Simply continue to fill your mind and heart with My Word. Let the words that I think about you and the descriptions of how I see you *replace* the accusations of the enemy. As you continue in My word, a new picture of yourself will emerge. As you allow My Spirit to flood your heart, a divine re-programming of your mind takes place until you will have no choice but to see yourself as I see you.

You are not alone in this struggle. It is the imperfection of humanity that threatens you. While you see the flaws in your physical body, I see your "spirit man" and I see you as perfect and mature. I see only your beauty and loveliness, a fountain of milk and honey that comes from your heart and is under your tongue!

Nor are you yet perfected in the inner man – it is My blood and My love that covers every imperfection even as you are led through the process of being conformed into My image. I work unceasingly in your life as you open your heart to My Word. The more you are with Me, the more like Me you will become. My promise is sure: one day you will stand before Me and you will be perfect - in body and in spirit, inside and out. I long for that day when I see My work completed and perfected in you. Together we long for that day when I look into your eyes and see a perfect reflection of Myself. O dear one, I draw you into My arms today and I hold you close. One day I will literally hold you and never let you go.

Prayer
May my spoken words and unspoken thoughts, be pleasing even to You, O Lord, my Rock and my Redeemer.[132]

Verse 11C

...the smell of thy garments is like the smell of Lebanon.
...the scent of your garments is like the scent of the mountains and cedars of Lebanon. (Living Bible)

Other Scriptures to consider
...as many of you as have been baptized into Christ have put on Christ.
...we who have been baptized into union with Christ are enveloped by Him. (Living Bible)[133]

I put on righteousness, and it clothed me.
Righteousness was my clothing (Living Bible)[134]

My thoughts
He says I am clothed, adorned, with His righteousness. Clothing speaks of outward things people see, and clothing makes us look good because it hides our nakedness and flaws. He says my good works are pleasing to Him so therefore the practice of clothing myself with Christ's righteousness pleases God. When my words are edifying, my heart answerable, in line with my words, and my outward walk adorned with righteousness and holiness, my life is adorned with garments of beauty.

He said
You love the mountains, dearest one, because you have experienced the sense of refreshment that comes with air that is clean and pure. Remember the pristine aroma of lofty heights; recall the glorious freshness of mountain peaks like Assiniboine, Lake O'Hara and Wentchemna Pass in the Canadian Rockies. You feel like you could live there forever.

That's how I feel about you today. You look at yourself and your circumstances and you wonder how you can lift your heart up to be

---

[132] Psalm 19:14 Living Bible
[133] Galatians 3:27
[134] Job 29:14

free and to sing praises to Me. I invite you to look, My child for behold, you are beautifully clothed. You've put on My garments, and you are stunning – handsome, indeed for you are clothed in heaven's attire, outfitted in garments perfectly suited for My child.

See! Look into the mirror of My Word and into the deep pool of My eyes. Just as your eyes reveal a lot of things about you, so Mine reveal My love and deep compassion - My acceptance and My approbation - My approval – toward you. Trust Me when I tell you that in My eyes you are perfect. Your garments smell like the scent of the mountains - you smell like Me!

My response
I feel so fragile and vulnerable, Jesus. I know You see me as beautiful, but I am struggling through some things in my life right now, and I don't feel very beautiful.

He said
You will always have issues and problems to work through. Those things do not change your beauty in My estimation. As I remind you of how I truly see you, adorn yourself. Dress up - put on some of the clothing I've given you and let My fragrance be over you today.

I am very close to you, you know! I haven't sent My angels to minister to you - I came Myself to stand beside you and walk with you wherever you go this day. I'm here, at your side, encouraging and enabling you in everything you do. O how I love you.

My thoughts

Encouraging, enabling
And edifying too
His presence not a breath away
In everything I do.

His righteousness, His holiness
My beauty and my dress
The King and Lover of my soul
The Lord my righteousness.

He looks at me, His gaze is love
        His eyes a pool of tears
He sees the beauty I can't see
        And calls me to draw near.

He whispers words I need to hear
        As tenderly He holds
The one who weeps and longs for Him
        Who feels her heart so cold.

He speaks His peace, His love, His strength
        Into her very soul
He clothes her in His righteousness
        And makes her spirit whole.

Poetry written by Florli Nemeth

He said

You'll smile again, you'll sing once more
        You'll worship and adore
My love, you are so beautiful
        My heart, it longs for more!

Be not dismayed, be not afraid
        For I the Lord, your King
Rejoice in that which I have made
        Delightfully I sing.

You're not alone, nor will you be
        I'm here to hold your hand
To strengthen you for prayer today
        To help you just to stand.

It is not wasted time, My child
        To spend your day with Me
I've so much yet to show and tell
        It'll take eternity!

You are okay - you're strong in Me
        And beautifully adorned
My love your home, your resting place
        Protection from the storm.

Poetry written by Florli Nemeth

No matter what storms you face in your life, My heart is your refuge and your hiding place. There you are totally loved and protected. I want you to learn to live your life in my heart, in My love. All of life will be changed and transformed as you live in total and complete union with Me.

My prayer
Father, I am presently being bombarded by wind and rain, and I feel I may not make it to safety. The storm around me is raging without abatement, and I see no light in the darkness ahead.

Precious Father, dearest Friend
Waters overwhelm me
In my plight I see no end
Darkness overtakes me.
If I could, I would, I know
But my heart, it fails me
Knowing not which way to go
Blackness all I see.

Jesus, Savior, precious Friend
None there is like Thee
You are with me to the end
Though I cannot see.
Touch me, kiss me, hold me close
How I need Your touch
You're the One I love the most
Love You very much!

Let me through my tears behold
Face of Love so dear
In my desperation hold
Him I love so near.

Poetry written by Florli Nemeth

Verse 12A

A garden enclosed is my Sister, my Spouse, ...
My darling bride is like a private garden, ... (Living Bible)

He said
You are My beautiful garden planted for My enjoyment alone.[135]

I have planted in you the most exquisite varieties of trees and flowers. Each of My gardens is unique and special to Me for I have always loved gardens. Your heart is My garden.[136]

I love to come into your garden just to be with you and to watch you grow. Because I'm very protective of My gardens I tend it carefully, watering you daily as I come to you. I speak with you there, I enclose you with Myself, your unfailing wall of protection. Defending you from storms and from those who would exploit or destroy you, I keep you safe both night and day. You are a well-watered garden - satisfied, healthy, and growing strong.[137]

Yes, dear one, your life is like a well-watered garden because I care about you; I watch over you day and night to see that you have everything you need.

I deal very harshly with weeds and you help Me do this. If they are not dealt with severely, they will take over your garden and totally destroy it. Sometimes you are not aware of weeds growing, or you may mistake a weed for a flower or plant. But I will point out such things to you, for I have promised to keep your garden night and day.

You also care for your garden when you rule your own spirit and guard against anger. Self-control is like walls around a city.[138] A person without self-control is defenseless against the enemy.

It takes a lot of self-control to hold your tongue and to hold back angry words when you are upset or provoked. The rule you have over your

---

[135] Isaiah 58:11
[136] Jeremiah 31:12
[137] Isaiah 27:3
[138] Proverbs 25:28

own heart is as strong walls of protection; when you submit to My protection and guard your tongue, I am able to deal with the offense or with the enemy coming against you. Conversely, when you yield to angry words, you are tearing down your walls of protection, leaving you defenseless before your enemies. Self-control is a fruit of the Spirit - a work which My presence within you accomplishes. Self-control is really self-restraint, or continence.[139]

It is the presence of the Holy Spirit within you that produces in you the ability to exercise power and control over your own emotions and words.

Verse 12B

...a spring shut up, a fountain sealed.
...a spring that no one else can have, a fountain of My own. (Living Bible)

My thoughts
This speaks of how He has put within me a spring of living water, bubbling up continually.[140] We also read in Genesis that stones were placed over the well in order to protect it from animals that would pollute the water.

Jesus spoke of springs, as well[141], declaring that rivers or springs of living water would flow from the innermost being of those who believed in Him.

Thank You Jesus for placing a spring of clear, clean water within me. It nourishes me daily, continually, and it nourishes all who come near me and touch my life. I need to guard the flow of this water lest anything evil pollute it.

He said
My Spirit within you is like a spring of living water. I said in My Word that rivers, or springs of living water, would flow from your innermost being. Rejoice in knowing that this is not just one spring or one river but springs and rivers in abundance! This is what brings fruitfulness

---

139 Galatians 6:32
140 John 4:14
141 John 7:38,39

in your life. You are a well-watered garden, My dear one. The water I give you nourishes your soul morning by morning.

My response
I need You to watch over me, to keep me, to nurture and nourish me. I need You to determine the flow of my springs and to keep guard over me.

He said
My Word says that I will keep My vineyard night and day. I water it every moment.[142]

You are My vineyard, a garden enclosed for My pleasure alone. Because I am your Keeper. I guard your garden and springs night and day lest anyone would harm it. It is My care of you that causes you to be fruitful. Hand in hand with My care is your willingness to surrender to My care, to take hold of My strength and to trust Me totally.

You have done this! You have chosen to draw from My strength, and you have surrendered to My protection and care.[143]

You see, there are those who do not want My care and protection. They feel they can do it on their own. But you have come to Me again and again in your weakness and desperation, crying for help, reaching for help, claiming My help and strength as your portion. This pleases Me. Be assured that when you come into My presence, I spread My covering over you, protecting you and sheltering you.[144]

I am your Shepherd, your Guide, the One who leads you to the springs of life…for it is life that I have placed within you and sealed for Myself. I come daily to your garden to fellowship with you and to strengthen and encourage you.

My response
Jesus, my mind is so distracted this morning. I can hardly take this in. I want my springs, my fountain, my garden, to be available for You alone.

---

[142] Isaiah 27:3
[143] Isaiah 27:5 Amplified
[144] Revelation 7:15, 16

He said
Do not trouble yourself because I am your Shepherd. As I lead you beside still, restful waters it is my purpose to guide you to springs of water - I lead you there because of My love for you and because of My mercy toward you.[145]

I treasure the moments you spend daily with Me. I love your reliance on Me, love that you feel you cannot face your day without spending time with Me in prayer and in My Word. I, too, look forward to these moments we share because the truth is, I cannot do without you. You are a fountain that brings Me great joy.

My prayer
God, I need Your protection. Come spread Your tabernacle - Your presence - over me. I cry to you as Ruth cried to Boaz, "Spread your wing of protection over your maidservant, for you are a next of kin"[146]

(Ruth could have gone after younger, more eligible men, but she chose to belong to Boaz because he had a claim on her - and she placed her claim on him.)

Jesus, You have a claim on Me, and I choose to put my claim on You. I want You alone. The garden of my heart is for You alone. The springs You have placed within me are for You alone. Spread Your tabernacle over me as I yield to Your presence, Your protection, Your peace and Your prosperity. I belong to You alone.

He said
You are My Bride, the Lamb's wife and you are Mine. Yes, I will protect you and provide for you, and I will make you a blessing to the nations. The springs within you will be released to bring healing to the nations. When you pray, the springs are released but they are kept for Me alone.

How I love you, My spouse, My beloved bride. One day you will stand before Me in white - in My imparted beauty - and I will wipe

[145] Psalm 23:2/Isaiah 49:10
[146] Ruth 3:9

away all your tears, all your confusions and misunderstandings, all your misinterpretations. You will stand before Me, perfect, mature, beautiful.

O how I long for that day. It will be soon, but only My Father knows the exact day and hour. In the meantime, I want you to live as My bride - as one would expect the bride of Christ to live. Do not be led off track by how you feel or even how you look to yourself.

As Boaz did what needed to be done to make Ruth his wife, so I am working to make you My wife. Be patient for the day is coming when you will stand before Me, the great wedding day I long for. In the meantime, I come to you and shelter you with My presence, and I nourish you, watering your garden and protecting your garden night and day. So rejoice in the shadow of My wings and look up - your redemption draws near!

My response

Lamb of God, Eternal Son
Draw me close - Make us one.

Lamb of God, My Shepherd dear
Come to me - Draw me near.

Lamb of God, Your sheltering wings
Hover over me - Make me sing.

Lamb of God, My Lord and King
Lead me to the Rock - The springs.

Lamb of God, Within - above
Shelter me - Within Your love.
Lamb of God, Your dear child speaks
Guard me now - Your garden keep.

Lamb of God, And fount of life
Guard my springs - From fear and strife.

Lamb of God, Your bride awaits
Glorious day - Her glorious fate!

Poetry written by Florli Nemeth

Verses 13 & 14

13 - Thy plants are an orchard of pomegranates, with pleasant fruits; camphire, with spikenard,
14 - Spikenard and saffron; calamus and cinnamon, with all trees of frankincense; myrrh and aloes, with all the chief spices.

13 - You are a lovely orchard bearing precious fruit, with the rarest of perfumes;
14 - Nard and saffron, calamous and cinnamon, and perfume from every other incense tree, as well as myrrh and aloes, and every other lovely spice. (Living Bible)

My thoughts & prayer
A glorious wonder, Christ wants to feed His church with what I possess in secret. He wants my heart to feed others.

Lord, You have given me so many gifts and graces and You want those blessings, now hidden in my heart, to feed and bless my family and my extended family, Your church. Sometimes I keep these things hidden, just between You and me, and there is a place where that needs to happen. But there is a time when You want Your graces in me to flow out in order to bless others. You have declared me an orchard with pleasant fruits and with trees of spices.

Just as it takes time for an orchard to develop, so You have been working in my life over many years to produce the fruit of the Spirit in my life. And there is fruit in abundance, not the produce of just one tree, for You have called me "an orchard", a title representative of many fruits and spices, many gifts and graces.

Lord, it's a huge responsibility to care for an orchard. But then I have to remind myself that You are the Gardener and the fruit is Yours.

He said
Yes, My child, over many years these trees and plants, spices and flowers have been produced in your garden, planted and nourished by Me. And now is a time in your life where you have so much to share. Do not hold back or draw away from the opportunities I give you - whether they be on a one-to-one level or on a larger scale.

Be faithful to share on an individual level and be assured that I will bring people into your life and send you to others. Sometimes you will meet people almost by accident, but it will prove to be a divine appointment.

Your ministry is sweet to Me; your desire to be a blessing, a pleasant offering to Me. I take great pleasure when I see you reaching out to others to bless them. Sometimes you do so at great cost to yourself, physically or emotionally. In those times it is the wondrous fragrance of myrrh and aloes that emanates from you.

Other times you share just a small prayer with someone or over someone, and the frankincense in your life is manifested. You may never know the impact of a single prayer and what effect it will produce in someone's life.

I know, dear one, the graces in your life have not come without cost, a cost reflected in the abundance of henna and spikenard in your orchard. You have experienced things in your life that have cost you deeply in terms of time, money, relationships and even reputation. You've learned from costly mistakes that threw you off course for years at a time. You've learned invaluable lessons through costly disciplines and chastisements.

I cannot begin to tell you how proud I am of you. You've come to the cross again and again. You've prostrated yourself before Me in humility and in anguish. And you have drawn from My strength that which has enabled you to keep going, even in the face of demonic adversity.

There is not a thing in your life that is hidden from Me. I'm aware of all the little grievances, annoyances, hurts and pains you've brought to the cross, From those journeys to the cross now flow beautifully fragrant henna with spikenard, just two among the many rare and perfumed spices found within your inner life.

Am I finished? No. There are yet more spices I desire to plant in your orchard, more growth to come. But dearest one, your orchard is beautiful. Your heart is full of lovely things needing to be shared. Your ministry is pleasing to Me.

I encourage you to keep coming to Me, keep growing in Me, keep opening up your life to My workings and My graces. There is a sweet, wholesome fragrance in your life, a fragrance that I can call My own for it comes from Me.[147]

You are a life-giving perfume to many. Continue to share your life and your love with those I bring into your life. As I affirm you today, I breathe out My love to you. You have so much to give. You are not a dry, barren land. You are a beautiful and fruitful orchard in the prime of your life. Don't look to others with big ministries and feel you have nothing to give. I've given some a very large influence; most, have a smaller sphere of influence.

Too many of My people fail to remember that one is not better than the other; in fact, the one who may impact thousands of people does so only because I've given them that influence. And the greater the gifting, the higher the accountability. Don't look for large things, be faithful in what I give. That is what pleases Me most. And you do please Me, My dear child.

He said again
Where do these plants, these rare perfumes, and these fragrant spices come from?

Every time you are hurt and you forgive, a beautiful plant is placed in the garden of your heart. Every hurt, every painful word spoken to you, every bitterness, every rejection, every evil thing the enemy threw at you as well as everything you turned to praise, everything you laid at My feet, everything you've brought to the cross, I have turned into a beautifully productive plant in your garden.

You have many plants bearing perfumes and spices because you have learned to bring your grievances to Me. And life is full of such grievances and hurts. No one can escape them. You will experience them even in the closest relationships as well as in the church and in the world.

Conversely, every time you allow a grievance to remain, it will grow a bitter root in your life that will grow and grow and grow and eventually

---

[147] 2 Corinthians 2:14-16

destroy your garden for weeds need no encouragement to grow. If you would be a beautiful garden you must get rid of every weed, ruthlessly cutting down and destroying that which would otherwise destroy you. The importance of forgiveness is this: it releases the seeds of love in your garden. Have you not declared your desire for a harvest of love? Then plant forgiveness and love will flourish.

These secrets are so important for you to understand if you are to enjoy a beautiful garden, a retreat that is not only for your enjoyment, but for Mine as well. Your perfumes and spices bring Me much pleasure and joy, whereas it pains Me deeply when I come to your garden and find weeds taking over an area where you've allowed unforgiveness or bitterness to thrive.

My response
I am so amazed at this revelation. I had no idea You turned every painful thing into a beautiful plant. Search out my garden, Lord, and see if there are any weeds that need to be rooted out. I want to walk in forgiveness and love in every area of my life.

Verse 15

A fountain of gardens, a well of living waters, and streams from Lebanon.
You are a garden fountain, a well of living water, refreshing as the streams from the Lebanon mountains. (Living Bible)

My thoughts and prayer
He says I am a fountain of gardens. What He gives me is the overflow of His graces in me, and the abundance is for others, an overflow that brings encouragement and strength.

And I myself also am persuaded of you, my brethren, that ye also are full of goodness, filled with all knowledge, able also to admonish one another.[148]

"*...the Holy Spirit displays God's power through each of us as a means of helping the entire church.*"[149]

[148] Romans 15:14
[149] 1Corinthians 12:7 Living Bible

When I share what You have given me, I bless others. That is Your intention for each of us, because all have been given something to give - even if it's only one thing. Your gifts were never given to be spent only on ourselves – they are for Your body, Your garden. Lord, the fountain comes from me, but the streams come from You. Connect my heart with Your streams.

He said
I give to you a hidden, inward source of supply. I live in your heart. I am the inner spring within you, and I water you perpetually and forever. My supply is not exhausted when you have a bad day, because My fountain is a perpetual spring of water within you to refresh and strengthen you.

I see you even today drawing from that fountain, that spring - drawing from your inner experiences of the Holy Spirit. My Word says that rivers of living water would flow from your innermost being. The Holy Spirit is so awesome in your life, and I see you as one who brings blessing to others. It is the overflow of your life that ministers to others. And I want you to overflow with My blessings and anointing, and with My strength and joy.[150]

In My sight you are a well of living waters. Because you have walked with me over the years, you have stored up waters - an abundant supply to share with My people. This is how I see you, and this is how you need to see yourself.

You are not an empty vessel with nothing to give. You have so much! So do not wonder when I send empty people to you. Don't try to figure them out, just give them water. Simply share the good things I've given you. Some do not have that history and need what you have. Don't question or analyze or begrudge people. Give freely from your well, even when you may feel there is nothing more. I'll see to it that your well never runs dry. So give with joy and abandonment; with freedom and generosity.

---

[150] John 7:38

Not only do I see you as possessing inner springs of life-giving water, I see you as streams from the high mountain – one who possesses an outward source of supply, an anointing of the Holy Spirit upon you. It is not just one stream, but many streams as I anoint you again and again. I pour out My Spirit upon you and release the gifts of the Holy Spirit upon you today and every day. There are many kinds of gifts, but one Spirit. There are many ways to use these gifts, and there are also many ways that I work in people's lives but whatever My Spirit gives is meant to bring profit, edification and blessing to the church, the body of Christ.[151]

Some have one gift, others, many but the Source of all gifts is My Spirit.

Dear one, you are anointed today to pray, and the streams from your life will flow out to bless this city, this nation and the world. Your prayers are not in vain. Every prayer you and others pray has been wafted before My Throne. You are known in My Throne room because you come there often and regularly. Do not let the enemy deceive you into thinking your prayers are powerless or irrelevant. Every prayer you pray is energized by My spirit. Draw from Me today, dear one. I see your sadness and your weariness. You have stored up not just one well, but many wells! Draw water from your wells today - from My wells within you, and draw water with joy![152]

Your wells may seem to run dry, but remember the streams and connect with them. Link up with what I am doing in other parts of the body because what I do in another is for you to enjoy and what I do in you is for others to enjoy.

Don't barricade or dam up the streams but rather, let them flow freely. This is your outward source of supply - your life and strength and health.

[151] 1 Corinthians 12: 4-7

[152] Isaiah 12:3

Verse 16A

Awake O north wind, and come, thou south; blow upon my garden that the spices thereof may flow out . . . .
[You have called me a garden, she said], Oh, I pray that the [cold] north wind and the [soft] south wind may blow upon my garden, that its spices may flow out [in abundance for You in whom my soul delights]...(Amplified)

My prayer
Awake, O Spirit of God! Let me know Your quickening, Your stirrings in my heart. Come! Let me know You are here. Give me some sign of Your presence in my life.

Blow upon my garden. Breathe upon me. Stir me. Quicken me. Let the spices in my garden be beaten by the north winds and the south winds in order that the fragrance of Your beauty in me may send forth its fragrance.

Lord, I do so desire to be fruitful! I pray Your north winds of difficulty would blow upon my garden. I receive Your winds of adversity. Let them do their work to demolish whatever in me is opposing Your purposes and Your destiny. Thank You, Lord, for these north winds that uncover areas of the flesh that need to go to the cross.

Lord, I also need the south winds of Your love and comfort. I need them both. Father, my flesh prefers only the ease of gentle, comforting south winds but I rest in gratitude because You know what is best for me at every season of my life.

Father, I welcome Your dealings in my life. I long for my garden to bless others.

He said
Child of My heart, you are precious to Me. The north winds from My Spirit have blown upon you in recent days. Do not think it strange for this is how I train those I love; this is how I will always work in your life.

As there are seasons in the natural realm, you have experienced seasons in your spiritual life. You have been going through a cold, bitter, winter experience in recent months. You've had to draw very near to Me for warmth and protection, and you've cried out to Me in your desperation. This is all part of My working in your life in order to bring you to a new level of fruitfulness.

The soft winds of My Spirit are about to blow over your garden. And when they do, things you thought were dead will spring to life, and you will discover new fruitfulness and new plants in abundance. This is a continuous process in your life. So I encourage you to embrace difficulties and frustrations and confrontations. Do not try to avoid these or to prevent the north winds. Embrace them while anticipating the gentle breezes that will come.

Sometimes the harshest north winds come from your own household, your own friends or family. These winds are extremely difficult to bear, but I call you to embrace even these. Remember that I am in the winds no matter where they come from. I will never, never leave you nor forsake you.[153]

The secret? When these storms roar around you, threatening to destroy, run into My arms with confidence that nothing will be destroyed except that which is not of Me. What remains will be strengthened and invigorated by every stormy gale. I love you, dear one. I see you on your face before Me in the desperation and despair of your heart. I come to you today to quicken and empower you, to stir up the spices within you and to blow their fragrance out upon the world around you. Be encouraged for you are blessed and loved. You are a fruitful garden, set apart for Me alone.

Verse 16B

...Let my Beloved come into His garden and eat His pleasant fruits.

My prayer

Jesus, my heart is Your home and I call out to You to come, to enter my garden that is Yours, my dear Beloved. My heart belongs to You for all that is beautiful and productive is the result of Your work in my life. From the beginning of Your Church you promised that you would

[153] Hebrews 13:5

be in us and we in You[154] and that You would reveal Yourself to those who love You and keep Your words. You promised that you dwell in us and make Your abode with us.

Jesus, You have kept Your promise. You came to me, making my heart Your special dwelling place and Your own particular garden. You planted the fruits in my garden – this I know for I have nothing to offer of my own. I choose to yield my heart, the garden of my heart, to You. Even now I call out to You: Come, Lord Jesus. Enter Your garden and enjoy the fruit of Your work and love in my life.

He said
I hear your invitation. It's not as if I am far away, for I inhabit the hearts of all My people. But it is possible for you to relegate Me to one small room of your heart when really I desire to occupy each part of your heart-home. I crave the beauty of your presence and the delightfulness of your garden. I have always loved gardens and it is there that I desire to cultivate beautiful plants of love, joy, peace.

It is My presence within that produces My fruit within you. But don't be overwhelmed or discouraged when you see weeds of the flesh. Your flesh is wicked, sinful, deviant, non-complying, and it will never yield to the Spirit of God or produce My beauty within you. It will always produce death and destruction and desolation and despair. Without Me, you can do nothing.

But you see, when you invite Me into your garden, yielding to the Holy Spirit and His presence within you, beautiful fruit results. Our presence within you will do great things in your life. The more you yield to Me, the more I can work in you to create beautiful flowers and plants in you.

And note, My dear beloved one, these flowers are for Me. You are calling Me to come and to enjoy the fruit I Myself have placed within you.

My prayer
Yes, my Beloved, I see that now. It's not for me, nor even for others, although they too will benefit. It is for You. My Beloved, My garden is first for your enjoyment. O Jesus, come today and feast upon Your

[154] John 14:21, 23

choicest fruits. Take my hand and let us walk in Your garden. Show me some of the beautiful things You are doing. I want to be with You.

Jesus, I always thought of my heart as my garden and my responsibility but how releasing to comprehend that the fruit You desire comes only from You. You know I'm not a great gardener, and even if I were, it is not in me to do Your work.

I see it is not my garden; it is Yours. I am Your inheritance; I belong to you. I am Your responsibility. The only thing required of me is permission and a yielded heart. Do what You will for I desire only to please You and to bring joy to Your heart. I live for You alone.

Chapter Five

A Celebration of Love

Verse 1

I am come into My garden, My sister, My spouse, I have gathered My myrrh with My spice, I have eaten My honeycomb with My honey, I have drunk My wine with My milk. Eat, O friends! Drink, yes, drink deeply, O beloved ones.

My prayer
Jesus, You came to me this morning, knocking on the door of my heart, in answer to my call to You to come. I now open the door; enter and make Yourself at home in Your garden.

He said
I have come, My dearest friend, My spouse, to bless you and to make you a blessing. You are My inheritance, My joy, My crown. I delight to be with you, and your garden yields beautiful fruit. Today we celebrate your love for Me. Feasting on the fruit of your life, I receive strength; in turn, I give to you honey for strength and wine for refreshing. It's a day of rejoicing so sing and dance and revel in My nearness to you. I rejoice in you, in your love for Me, in your desire to be My friend. You are Mine - Mine forever!

I said
A part of me cringes at Your complete ownership. Does that mean You will lord it over me and squelch my identify, my creativity? I'm so sorry to feel this way, but a part of me wants to be independent and

self-serving, self-sufficient and self-aware. Can You own me and yet allow me to be the person You created me to be?

He said
My ownership of you is never to lord it over you or to diminish who you are as a person. My ownership of you is to ***serve*** you - to help you become the person I created you to become. I've come into your garden not to gather just for Myself, but to gather for you and for those around you. Though your garden blesses Me, providing Me with food and drink I cherish, My ultimate desire is to bless you and others. I desire My church to be blessed and influenced by your fragrance and your fruitfulness.

My dear child, My heart delights in you! I understand your reticence and I long to heal it by touching it with My love. There is no intent to hurt or cause pain in My love for I do not come to diminish but to increase your fruitfulness and your impact upon My church. I come to enlarge you and make you a voice, not just an echo. For what you have to share will bring great blessing to many people.

I said
O my Love, You have spoken of nine things here - My garden, My sister, My spouse, My myrrh, My spice, My honeycomb, My honey, My wine, My milk. I know there are nine fruits of the Spirit - actually, fruit, singular, of the Spirit.[155] And the fruit is Yours, the product of Your presence within me. Never the result of my work or self-effort, it all belongs to You.

Jesus, if You enjoy being in my garden, it is because *it is Yours*! And I am so happy to be Yours. Anything I have to give You is Yours from the beginning, the reflection of Your loving kindness and Your tenderness. My heart yearns, cries out, and aches for you. Your presence is the answer to My prayer!

Your nearness brings me such joy. I run into Your arms. I look into Your eyes and I see love, forgiveness, compassion, and a yearning that is far greater than my own - a yearning for intimacy.

---

[155] Galatians 5:22,23

He said
I long to be near you at all times, and I have promised I would never leave you nor forsake you. There are times, however, when I reveal My nearness to you more clearly. These are times of feasting. Today is such a day for you. There are other times when I hide My face so My people will seek Me more clearly. Other times My presence is not so easily discerned because you have pushed Me away, or you have grieved Me by your sin or disobedience.

But always I will come when you call to Me. And when I come I will do for you exceedingly abundantly, above all you ask - far above all you dare to ask or think, infinitely beyond your highest prayers, desires, thoughts, hopes or dreams![156] My sister, My spouse, My friend, you bring Me such joy!

I said
O Jesus, reveal Yourself even more clearly to me. Stay! Eat! Drink! I receive – Your blessings and Your love. Release Your love through me to others. Anoint me to speak Your Word. How I love Your Word.

The Test of Maturity

Verse 2

I sleep, but my heart waketh: it is the voice of my Beloved that knocketh, saying, Open to Me, My sister, My love, My dove, My undefiled: for My head is filled with dew, and My locks with the drops of the night.

I said

> I hear His voice awakening me
> He's calling to me now
> His voice is saying, Open up
> The door is shut - The night is cold - The dew is wet
> I'm calling you to grow in love
> To experience My suffering
> In Gethsemene.

Poetry written by Florli Nemeth

[156] Ephesians 3:20, Amplified

Are You calling me to experience Your love in the midst of testing? In the midst of intense suffering where nothing makes sense? If so, help me to hold on to You, Lord, to trust You in the darkness, in the storm, in the uncertainty of life. I've trusted You in the day, and I'm sure I can trust You in the dark night of the soul. I'll be okay as long as I know You are near.

Because I know You are near, I am able to sleep in the night season, totally at rest in my God. I'm at peace whatever may happen in my life because I know You are good. There is safety in Who You are. You are with me even when I cannot see You. O my Lord, even when the north winds blow I can lay me down and sleep, resting in Your arms of love, resting in Your covering and Your protection. Because You slept in the boat in the middle of Galilee's storm, I am able to sleep in my storms.

Let me know and experience this rest of faith, and let me hear Your knock at the door of my heart, drawing me to a new day, to a new season in my life. I don't want to miss hearing Your knock and Your voice.

He said
My precious one, My love, My dove, My perfect one - you are My sister, My bride, and I love you! I am acquainted with your weaknesses and your inabilities for I have known the sufferings of humankind. Not only am I your God, I too was once a man, your Brother and a participant in the pain of all humanity.

But while you are My sister, you will always be My love, My dove, My perfect one because of what I endured in Gethsemane and at the cross. I am well acquainted with your heart of obedience and loyalty to Me, even in those times when you do not understand My dealings with you.

I see your heart is perfect in your desire to obey Me without compromise. You are not yet without fault - you know that because you see your weaknesses and imperfections. But I see you as perfect, My dear and precious dove, the love of My heart. Looking upon you, I am satisfied that My pain and suffering were not in vain.

I said

I open to You, Lord,
I rise up from my bed
I open up the door for You
With dew upon Your head.

Wherever You may lead
Whatever You may do
I'm ready, Lord, to run with You
To share the night and dew.

I trust You with my life
You've never failed me yet
You've promised to protect and keep
Me safe from Satan's net.

No matter dark the night
Or stormy gale may be
I'm safe within the arms of love
The One who shelters me.

The seasons come and go
The storms may rise and fall
But loved, secure and safe am I
Whatever may befall.

My Lover's voice I hear
His knock - His touch so dear
My heart responds - my heart and soul
And draws Him to me near.

Poetry Written by Florli Nemeth

Verse 2, Continued-

I sleep, but my heart waketh

My thoughts

I want to look at this verse again from another point of view. There seems to be some conflicting things in this verse. Do we see here the two natures within as Paul described in Romans 7 - the flesh lusting, or striving against the spirit?

"*My heart*" speaks of the renewed part, the circumcised heart that Paul spoke of. In Ezekiel we read God's promise to give us a new heart and to put a new spirit within us. Ezekiel 36:26

God wants our hearts because He wants to -
- cleanse (verse 25)
- empower (verse 27)
- establish (verse 28)
- enrich (verse 28)
- and increase us! (verses 29 & 30)

My prayer
Lord, I know I do have two natures within me - two principles at work and in conflict with each other. While one sleeps, the other is wide awake. If I see only my old nature I can forget and even disclaim Your graces within me. Help me not to condemn myself when I see my sinful nature but rather to run to You and yield myself to You afresh.

Contrariwise, if I see only my new nature, I am liable to forget my unrenewed nature and the tendency there is always to fall back into the deeds of the flesh. Help me not to absolve myself as delighting in Your law, seeing only my new nature and Your graces within me.

He said

I am knocking, I am calling
I am trusting you will rise
I am speaking, I am asking
That you look into My eyes.

My work in you goes on for there are areas of your heart not yet opened to Me, areas of your life where I do not feel welcome. Dear one, I desire to remove everything that would mar and hinder your fellowship with Me. I cannot abide separation of any kind between us because you are My sister, My love, My dove, My undefiled one and precious to Me.

When I suffered in the garden of Gethsemane before going to the cross, I thought of you. I saw your face and discerned your need for a Redeemer and a Saviour. I am He, the One who died for you and rose again, your Saviour, Your Redeemer and the One who knocks insistently at the door of your heart. My call to you is simply to open every area of your heart to Me.

I said
Now I understand! This is grace! Your love for me has nothing to do with what I have done or what I can do; You simply love me for who I am. I'm Your sister (Your brother). I'm related to You by my new birth. I'm Your love, your dove. I'm brought into a loving bridal relationship because You desire nearness to me. By Your grace I now stand as undefiled, Your pure one because You have put Your Spirit within me and clothed me with Your beauty.

Set free from slumber and drowsiness, You have filled me with Your Spirit and called me to a walk dependent on Your Spirit. It is in that place that I am enabled to resist the lusts of the flesh. None but you can set me free from the power of my lower, sinful nature. Responding to You, I open the door, rising up to greet You, I am set free from slavery to my lower nature. There is such a wonderful truth here. Lord, teach me more.[157]

He said
You have grasped the great secret to living your life on a higher plane. It is so simple that many of My lovers miss it. Your flesh cannot rise and operate or dominate when your heart rises and opens to Me, when your heart responds to My knock and My voice.

Then, as you act in response to My call, My Word will keep you from sin for it is a powerful force within you. As you heed My knock, the nudging of My promptings within you, you will become even more sensitive to My call to you. As your heart continues to hear Mine, you will not miss the beat of My heart.

My response

Come Lord Jesus, take possession
All my heart and all my life
Not one room be left in darkness
Not a thing that causes strife.
Come and take full ownership
Rightful Owner, Lord and King
Gladly to You I surrender
Master, Lord of everything.

[157] Romans 7:25

Glad surrender, blissful gain
You my Father, I Your child
Yours the promise, mine the blessing
I Your dove, Your undefiled.

Poetry written by Florli Nemeth

Verse 3

I have put off my coat, how shall I put it on? I have washed my feet, how shall I defile them?

My thoughts
Lord, some commentators feel that she is compromising here and disobedient in not rising to answer the door. Others feel this was not a refusal to obey, but a commitment to avoid defilement and a desire to walk clean before God. So is she compromising here? Or is she in the place of mature obedience? Help me understand, Lord.

He said to me
I see the weariness you feel today, My dear one, My dove. I see that you have removed your coat, that is, your way of doing things, your own merits. And you have put on My robe of righteousness. You are saying, "How can I put on *my* defiled garments again? How can I go back to the sin and compromise of doing my own thing?"

This is what I hear your heart saying. And you have committed yourself to My daily washing of your feet. Your heart desires to be cleansed by Me daily. You no longer want to go your own way and do your own thing. I see your commitment to Me, My dear one, and it rejoices My heart to see you thus walking in My provision for you in My daily cleansing.

My response
So why are You knocking, Lord? Are You calling me to further obedience? To a new obedience - a new calling?

He said
I am always calling you to new levels of obedience and prayer. It is good for you to remember you are clothed in My robes of righteousness, otherwise you might try to go about establishing your own righteousness.

You see, dear one, even your obedience to Me must be based on what I am doing in your life and not on your own merits or good works.

Obedience to prove your maturity or your merit is really disobedience for true obedience comes from a heart prompted by love and covered with My robe of righteousness, not from trying to gain merit. The obedience that I recognize comes only from the place of merit I have given you.

As we journey together, I teach you new truths – truths that are impossible to grasp apart from My spirit.[158] You see, I'm not asking you to put on your coat, but Mine; I'm not requiring you to wash your own feet because it is I who wash your feet in the place of prayer and by My Word.

It is to a new level in prayer and My Word that I am calling you because I see in you a heart that is obedient and submitted to Me.

Verse 4

My Beloved put His hand by the hole of the door, and my bowels were moved for Him.
My Beloved tried to unlatch the door and my heart was thrilled within me. (Living Bible)

My prayer
Lord, there are days when I am like that maiden. In response to her call to You, You came.[159] She invited You to come to her garden and in answer to her prayer, You came. But here's my dilemma, Lord: now that I find You knocking, asking to be admitted – why are You outside?

Your call invokes so many questions, Lord: why is the latch of her heart locked? Why does she refuse Your call? Is it because she is too weary? Because Your call is an inconvenience to her?

Now here[160] I find You trying to unlatch the door to her heart when all the while You have the key to her heart that opens the door.

---

[158] Romans 11:33,34

[159] Compare Song of Solomon 5:4 with 4:16

[160] Song of Solomon 5:4

He said
You will always need My presence, My Spirit, My working in your life. My call may come to you at the most inconvenient times, but My hand upon the door of your heart will always move you to rise and do what I am asking you to do. In this case, I did not call her to do any great exploits for Me - I merely called her to open her heart to Me.

The door to her heart was locked because I answered her request. You see, she'd asked for the north and south winds to blow upon her garden so the spices could flow out and I honored her request. The cold, bitter north winds of winter had begun, and she had secluded herself, finding shelter and protection from their power. What she did not comprehend was that I wanted to be with her during the difficult time of suffering.

O My dear child, when the winds begin to blow in your life, look for Me. Never will I fail to come to you in the night of your soul, announcing my arrival by My gentle knock upon your heart. My hand will rest upon your heart, placed there to help you endure the storms. Never will I leave you alone. I will always come to you.

I will be there in those darkest moments and the stormiest times of your life. I am never offended, even by your lack of response. I am persistent in My love, undeterred in my pursuit of My beloved, and ever aware of those times when you are weary, frightened or too exhausted to pursue Me. It is My hand that will bring comfort and strength and grace for every storm in your life.

My response
My heart thrills within me at Your touch, Oh, Lord. I long to feel Your hand, the knowledge of Your gentle touch upon my life. I thrill to know that it is when I need You most that You are nearest to me.

"Not so," the enemy tells me. He tells me that the storm is a sign of Your anger, a sign that I have failed in some way to please You. He accuses You of deserting me, tells me that's why the storm winds blow.

But You remind me that You use the winds to waft the beautiful perfumes of my garden. You tell me once again that You will come to me and touch me with Your hand when I feel most alone. In my sense of desolation You are my Comforter, my Beloved Lord. My heart yearns to feel Your touch and hear Your voice. Thank You for coming to me this morning and touching my heart with Your love!

He said
The winds may come to you from the hand of the enemy as they did with Job, or they may come as the result of your faith in Me and obedience to Me. Whatever the case, they come with My knowledge and permission, and I will be with you.

When you hide yourself in your shelter and think all is lost, I will come to you and touch you because I want to be with you. When you share My sufferings I am always there with you, My head wet with dew, in My desire to strengthen and encourage you in every time of storm and testing. Be assured of this: never will you face life's storms alone for I will never leave you or forsake you.[161]

Verse 5

I rose up to open to my Beloved, and my hands dropped with myrrh, and my fingers with a sweet-smelling myrrh upon the handles of the lock.
I jumped up to open it, and my hands dripped with perfume, my fingers with a lovely myrrh as I pulled back the bolt. (Living Bible)
My hands dripped with myrrh, and my fingers with liquid [sweet-scented] myrrh [which He had left] upon the handles of the bolt. (Amplified)

He said
Dearest Child, lover of My heart, I pour out My grace upon you today. Rise and follow Me to the place of intercession and death, yes even to Gethsemane. Just as you followed Me to the mountain of myrrh, and as you opened your heart to the north winds, so now by your "yes" you have opened your heart to meet me in that Garden. Join Me, My beloved in the place of intercession for you and for the whole world.

My response
Thank You, my Lord, for the abundance of Your grace in my life. It overflows, dripping over me and out of all proportion to my failures and my sins. Your grace surpasses the failures and weaknesses in my life.[162]

---

[161] Hebrews 13:5

[162] Romans 5:15, 20

Your grace given me in proportion to my need and my tasks, is a special endowment that enables me to do and be what You have called me to do and be. Not only is Your grace enough for me, You have given *more* than enough! [163]

He said
Yes, dear one, you have received My favor and love and mercy in abundance . . . You will always have it in abundance, for it is My strength and it is shown most effectively in your weakness. Your heart clearly responds with a "*Yes*" to My call, but sometimes the weakness of your flesh draws you back or tempts you to cling to what is familiar because you fear the unknown.

But even in your weakness, I pour out My grace upon you, enabling you to do what you thought you could not do. Like oil applied to the hinges of the door, My grace makes it possible to open easily and noiselessly when I call. My grace, My favor and the power of My strength are upon you.

My prayer

Jesus, in my weakness
How I need Your grace
In my sorrow and my pain
Need to see Your face.

Thoughts of failure and defeat
Often plague my mind
I just need to think Your thoughts
And Your mercy find.

Where You are, You leave behind
Myrrh and perfume sweet
Grace poured out with favor, love
All my needs to meet.

Precious Jesus, Saviour, Friend
There is none like Thee
Here's my heart, my life, my love
Yours alone to be.

Poetry written by Florli Nemeth

[163] 1 Corinthians 3:10 & 12:9

Verse 6A

I opened to my Beloved, but my Beloved had withdrawn himself and was gone; my soul failed when He spoke; I sought him, but I could not find him, I called him, but he gave me no answer.

I said
O Lord, at different times in my life I have experienced the loss of Your manifest presence in my life. I have to confess I don't always *feel* Your presence and Your love but I have learned that even when the feelings are gone, remembering Your faithfulness and love sustains me.

But this I long to know: why do You withdraw Yourself from me? Is it to cause me to pursue You more intensely? Is it to draw me deeper? Is it to reveal the greatness of Your grace and strength in me?

He said
O My lovely bride, to answer your question - it is only the *sense* of My presence you fail to discern. It is not My actual presence, for I have promised never to leave you nor forsake you. My word to you is that I will be with you even when you pass through the waters of affliction and the flames of persecution.

As a father teaches his child to swim by removing his hold, showing him that he can paddle on his own, so I withhold human emotions to let you know that you can overcome. Or as a father encourages his child to go out deeper, while all the time calling him to follow, so I allow circumstances to come that make you realize that you can safely conquer every challenge.

Like a father teaching his child to ride a bike, picture how he runs beside. He holds him up, secures the two-wheeled bike to keep his precious little one safe. Yet there comes the point where father withdraws his hold, knowing that his child can do it on his own. Though the child may wobble or even fall, the father is confident that his child has mastered the skill.

These are imperfect illustrations to be sure, but it is the lesson I want to teach you. In all My dealings, I call you into a deeper intimacy, a closer walk – a "deep calling unto deep". My purpose in all this is that you will experience more of Me. In those places where you feel I have withdrawn, I am there, seeking to draw out the yearnings of your heart. At other times it is to show you how strong you really are in My strength and with My graces upon you. Often you have cried to Me and I have poured My strength into you; other times your heart has thirsted for Me in a desert place where you have felt desolate and alone. There, too, you called out to Me.[164]

Do you not recall times when you have felt the attack of the enemy and in the absence of seeing or feeling My presence, you cried out to Me, even though you could not sense My presence.[165]

All of these experiences are meant to take you deeper into My Love and a greater realization of My love. The seeming withdrawal of My presence is not to chastise you but to show you that you *can* walk in My strength and minister in My love. O My beautiful bride, even now I see the yearning of your heart for Me. I delight in you. I love you so deeply, so intensely, so completely.

It is the work of My Spirit to draw you to My side. In response to your prayer [166]I am drawing you, for [167] as I draw you deeper and deeper into the ocean of My love you will experience the love that knows no end and no beginning. Not only will I answer every prayer you have ever prayed, whether for yourself or for another; indeed, I will act in response to the longings of your heart.

Verse 6B

My very soul failed me when he spoke.
My heart stopped. (Living Bible)
My soul went forth to Him when He spoke, but it failed me [and now He was gone]! (Amplified)

> In the dark of the night
>   I feel so alone
> I'd opened up for Him I love
>   And found that He had gone.

---

[164] Psalm 138:3 and 143:4-7

[165] Psalm 42

[166] Song of Solomon 1:4

[167] Song of Solomon 1:4

His presence now is gone
His face is hidden from view
My heart cries out, My Lover dear,
What am I now to do?
Your voice I still recall
Inviting me to arise
To open and unlock the door
Your voice no mean disguise.

Poetry written by Florli Nemeth

Prayer
Lord, am I overstepping myself? Am I going beyond what I am capable of doing here in the Song of Solomon? Am I going beyond my experience?

He said
No, you are not going beyond your experience, you are gaining. But as you gain a new perspective concerning the things you are going through, and at the same time with perspective on my dealings in your life, you are learning how to verbalize what I am doing *in* and *for* and *through* you. This is not presumption since it was I Who led you to learn the secrets of this book. I have many things yet to say to you, things I would have you share with My Body.

You are neither moving in impudence nor moving ahead of Me. Listen for Me - watch for Me for I will come again to you. My anointing continues upon you, anointing bestowed for understanding and skillfulness in writing down the vision. It is I who am calling you to do this. As I continue to anoint your understanding, I am calling you to write the vision down. This is not the work of your own initiative but rather a vision that I have birthed in you. Stay close to Me and close to My Word as I fulfill My vision in you.

Write the vision plainly so that it can be read by many, easily and quickly. Never forget that My callings are set for an appointed time so though it will not come to pass immediately, the fulfillment will come. It may not happen right away. Wait patiently before Me. As you wait in patience for My fulfillment, do not despair. Be patient - My work is never overdue by a single day.

I spoke to the Lord further
Lord, have I slighted Your call? Have I failed to open my heart to You? My feelings of desolation and emptiness threaten to overwhelm. I feel I cannot hear Your voice today because You have withdrawn the presence I love to feel.

He said
Dear one, I am drawing you away from pleasures that are not wrong but that do not satisfy your longing for deeper intimacy with Me. I have treasures for you in My place of prayer that far exceed TV programs and books, treasures that await you as you worship. You feel your experience is shallow? Let Me draw you out into the deep.

I responded to the Lord
As I look into the mirror of Your Word, I see weaknesses You also see in Me. I see what You see and I confess that my inability to change anything about my own person, let alone change the world, causes me deep despair. It is then I am reminded that the weaknesses you see in me are healed by the power of Your love.

But how can the power of Your love work in my life if You've withdrawn Yourself? Please do not withdraw Your presence for any reason.

He said
Dear one, why are you seeking Me? For your enjoyment alone? Do you love Me because I make you happy or does your love for me come from an understanding of Who I am? Do you love Me for My gifts or for My person? Will you obey Me only when circumstances are right and conducive to your obedience or will you obey Me, come hell or high water?

As you search your heart by looking through the mirror of My Word, allow My Holy Spirit to show you what's in your heart. I want you to walk with Me as an equal partner, yoked together with Me. It is only as we walk in partnership and intimate relationship that, you will be able to reach out to those who are lost and do not yet know Me. I'm calling you to the fellowship of My sufferings and to the power of My resurrection.[168]

---

[168] Philippians 3:10

It is by sharing My sufferings that you are transformed; it is in the place of death you are made more like Me. Embracing your cross, you become like Me. As My resurrection power flows to you, the power that overflows from My resurrection will overflow to you. I am free to exert the power of My resurrection life over your life today so rest in My love and in my presence. Search for Me with all your heart in prayer, in worship and in the Word. I am your God and your King. I love you, My Bride.

I replied
Lord, sometimes the storm seems to prevent me from finding You or hearing Your voice. It is in those times the enemy stirs things up, making it seemingly impossible to hear Your voice above the winds. You could be a few feet away and I would not see or hear You. But it is also at such times that I continue reaching out to You, relying on the Word You have spoken in the past. Your Word is always alive in my heart and speaks to me there.

He said
There are different kinds of storms that come to My people but perhaps the most difficult are those times when it is the storm of broken relationships. The Psalmist David knew the pain that comes with having a friend, a companion, an equal, who become an enemy".[169] Distracted at the noise of the enemy, persecuted and threatened with death, [170] he chose to believe God. His confidence was in knowing that even though the tide of battle might run strongly against him, I, the Lord, would rescue him. Throughout it all he consistently leaned on Me and encouraged others to do so.[171] That is My encouragement to you today. When you cannot see Me, when you cannot hear Me, lean your heart upon My Word, trust and do not fear.

> When the storm clouds overhead
> The gathering clouds engulf your soul
> Know that I the Lord your God
> Will never let you go.
> So cast your burden on Me now

[169] Psalm 55:12-14

[170] Psalm 55:18

[171] Psalm 55:3, 18,22, 23

And know that I am near
I will bear your grief and pain
And take away your fear.
I'm very near - you need not fear
I'd never leave alone
The Bride who gives Me so much joy
My heart is now your home.
A shade by day, a fire by night
A shelter from the storm
A canopy, defense of love
Protection from all harm.[172]

Poetry written by Florli Nemeth

The storm clouds, be they rainstorms beating against the wall, or the wrath of cyclones or tornadoes - they are all dust beneath My feet. [173].

I can dispel the storm clouds as easily as a vacuum or broom gets rid of dust and dirt. It is in the storm that I demonstrate My power that is well able to shelter and protect you. Storms are reduced to a whisper by My power. When you cannot see My face, trust My heart; when you cannot hear My voice, trust My love.

Nestle into My shelter today and rest in My love.
So when you cannot see My face, Or hear My loving call
Just rest within My arms of love, And yield to Me your all!

Poetry written by Florli Nemeth

Verse 7

The watchmen that went about the city found me, they smote me, they wounded me; the keepers of the walls took away my veil from me.

My thoughts

Who could have anticipated this north wind? Who would have foreseen that the watchmen, her spiritual authorities, would leave no stone unturned in seeking her out? And as if the storm did not rage with sufficient strength, when they found her it was to bring her hurt.

[172] Isaiah 4:5,6 and 25:4

[173] Nahum 1:3

Perhaps they had heard things about her ministry and they wanted to discredit her?

Instead of the protection she should have known from these spiritual authorities, they rose up against her and spread lies about her. Their publishing of false accusations deeply wounded her because these were her friends, her pastors, the ones she highly trusted and esteemed. In taking her veil, they deprived her of any place of ministry. Stripped of her reputation and ministry opportunities, she feels bereft of the very presence of God, naked as it were before God and the world.

I said
These words bring me so much pain. Along with feeling that You have left me I have been mistreated by one I love and respect, by one who is supposed to protect and cover me. The wounding of words is so painful to my heart. Yet here I stand, deprived of what I need and long for the most - Your presence and my place of ministry. Lord, I will not be bitter against the one who hurt me thus; and I will be faithful to You. I will forgive.

I will continue my search for You, never ceasing to worship You. I will draw near to You. I will be Yours alone, even when misunderstood, mistreated, mishandled.

He said
When you feel alone and rejected, think of Me. I suffered mistreatment, rejection, persecution and death so you could go free. That was the cost of setting you free and making you My bride.

The embracing of your suffering releases the spices of your garden because death always results in life. As you humbly submit and lay down your life My beauty and sweetness flow freely from you.

Every life that I use for My purposes experiences the north winds at some point in their lives. No one I use for My purposes is exempted. The key is to learn what to do with failure, rejection, criticism and personal attacks. These all come as battering rams against your soul. But as you allow what I allow, embracing every blow, falling at My feet in humility, I reveal Myself to you in that very place. It is there that you will rise from the pain to walk in new strength and power.

The watchmen had no trouble finding her. Not only did they see the immaturity and imperfections in her but the state of their own hearts that denied her the covering and encouragement she needed.

I could have protected her from their unjust criticism, but I allowed this to happen to her. I saw the pride and self-sufficiency that was in her. These winds will deal with that by scattering and blowing away what should not be in her garden, spreading abroad and dispersing the beautiful spices of her garden. The winds that seem so contrary thus serve a two-fold purpose within the heart of My bride.

So dear one, when you are confronted with a test such as this, don't let the words wound you and destroy you. Let them cause you to fall at My feet, giving all to Me as once again you lay your life at the foot of My cross. As you surrender to the winds to do their work, you will know what it means to be left with Me alone.

Verse 8

I charge you, O daughters of Jerusalem, if ye find my beloved, that ye tell him, that I am sick of love.
...[simply sick to be with him] Amplified

My thoughts
Here I see the intensity of her distress increased. No longer able to be sustained with raisins and refreshed with apples[174] her pain becomes like that of a woman in travail.[175] Where once earlier[176] her sickness was weakness or pain that merely required food, her words imply deep travail. These are sharp pangs and vehement desire which cannot be satisfied apart from Christ's presence.

My prayer
O my Beloved, I cannot bring forth fruit without Your presence. I languish in despair; my soul consumed in sickness without You. I *must* find You. I *must* sense Your presence.

---

[174] Song of Solomon 2:5
[175] Song of Solomon 5:8
[176] Song of Solomon 2:5

My thoughts
I see here that the bride goes out and speaks with the daughters of Jerusalem. Rather than isolating herself from the body of Christ, she opens her heart and asks prayer of those who are weaker and less mature than herself. It shows me that praying for ourselves and asking prayer of others go together. And sometimes it is appropriate to ask those less mature than ourselves to pray with us and for us.

I see also here that she did not bring up the faults of the watchmen! It was for *herself* she requested prayer. This speaks deeply to my heart. She neither forsook the body of Christ in her pain nor did she expose the watchmen, the cause of her pain. In it all, she knew the answer or solution to her problem was found in Your presence.

My prayer
O Lord, under excruciating circumstances over which she had no control, she did not allow herself to become offended but rather even as the enemy used such circumstances in an attempt to destroy her, she called out to You, driven by her pain to a deeper hunger and passion for Your presence. Help me Jesus, to respond in similar circumstances as she did.

He said
You will find Me - you will *always* find Me in the company of My people. All My trusted servants have experienced times of intense testing where the temptation is to withdraw from the church and become offended. That is the natural response, and a very human response.

But notice - she did not blame the watchmen for her condition or point her finger at them, even though she could have done so with good reason. Although they were wrong to have wounded her so deeply, she did not allow the offence to destroy her relationship with My body or with Me. Instead, hiding nothing, and blaming no one she called out for more of Me. She did not blame others for her pain, but rather asked for prayer. Crying out for Me she became even more passionate in her pursuit of My presence.

Dear one, this kind of a response will always bring release and growth, expansion and destiny. So many of My servants have short-circuited their destiny in My kingdom because of offense. My heart aches for those who have been wounded in the house of their friends. [177]

Offenses are harder to resolve than armed battles.[178] It is harder to renew friendship with an offended individual than it is to capture a fortified city. Their anger not only shuts you out like iron bars but the anger shuts Me out as well. I grieve over My loved ones who have failed the test of love in the matter of offenses. The secret to passing this test? Live in love.[179]

My servant and[180] Apostle, John wrote to My church "whoever loves his brother [even a watchman who hurts you] lives in the Light, and in the Light there is no occasion for stumbling or cause for error or sin."

My servant, Solomon also wrote in wisdom: "He who covers and forgives an offense seeks love, but he who repeats or harps on a matter separates even close friends." [181]

There will always be offenses. Sooner or later, they will visit each one of My children. Be on guard, for often they will come through people closest to you. Offenses caused by those who love you and are committed to you in their role as watchmen wound deepest. Offenses may come from other sources in the body of Christ, but always the offenses that affect you the most will come from those closest to you.

You have experienced this on many occasions and I never fail to take note of your response of lovesickness for Me since nothing escapes My notice, so deeply and dearly do I love you, the object of My love.

My love also extends to those who have imprisoned themselves within those iron bars of anger and offense. When you see them, pray for them and love them. Some of them are ministering within their little cages, thinking they are being greatly used of Me, yet they cannot see the bars that limit them and prohibit their advance into their full destiny.

---

[177] Zechariah 13:6

[178] Proverbs 18:19

[179] 1 John 2:10

[180] 1 John 2:10

[181] Proverbs 17:9

You know of such and are thinking of them even at this moment. The only way for them to be set free to advance is to lay down their offence. Some will never do this. It doesn't mean I love them less, only that they will never know the fullness of My love and purpose for them.

Others can be won by love and prayer, and they will eventually lay down their offence and go free. Pray for these and love them to freedom.

Dear one, you have My heart, and I hold yours in the palm of My hands. Be encouraged in My love today for, you are My beautiful bride, My chosen one.

The Bride's Response to the Test of Maturity

Verse 9

What is thy beloved more than another beloved, O thou fairest among women? What is thy beloved more than another beloved, that thou dost so charge us? [the Living Bible calls her "a woman of rare beauty".]

My thoughts & prayers
This title, "O thou fairest among women" was given to her by the Shepherd Himself. Now the daughters of Jerusalem address her with this same title, based on the spiritual beauty they see in her. But it is Your grace and Your beauty within her. The daughters do not wound her as the watchmen did, but speak respectfully to her even as they desire to know her Beloved.

Jesus, do others see in me a lovesick heart? See a heart that responds in love no matter what the wounding? Do those less mature see Your beauty and love in me? Do they observe a humility that is willing to ask for prayer and for help? Do they see You?

What do others see in me when I am wounded or offended? Does the harshness of a bitter and critical spirit manifest itself or do they marvel at a lovesickness for You that is displayed in me?

These daughters of Jerusalem knew of her Beloved, but they did not know Him intimately nor had they knowledge of His indescribable beauty. They did not ask "Who is your Beloved", but rather, "What is your Beloved"?

I have known people throughout my life that captivated me with the love for You that I saw in their lives. I could name many who strongly influenced me in my youth. They knew God. They were lovesick with Jesus and the love I saw in their lives inspired me to seek the love of this Beloved One. I wanted to know and love Him as they did. Others impacted my life as I read their biographies.

I cannot help but ponder: What kind of an impact do I have on those younger and less mature? O Jesus, my heart's desire is that others would see Your love and Your beauty in me to such an extent that they are inspired to pursue You more intimately. My passion is to know You more and more intimately and to show forth Your love and beauty more and more, especially to those close to me. These are My thoughts, Lord, but what would You say to me?

He said
I will bring to you those who have a hunger and a desire to know Me. There are many in your life right now who respect you and desire to spend time with you. Be sensitive to those ones I bring into your life, and be open to share your life with them. You have a deep, enduring love for Me, your Beloved, the kind that no winds of trouble or persecution can put out. The love you have for Me is like a burning fire on the inside of you, destroying what is of the flesh and purifying the silver and the gold in your life.

I will give you many opportunities to share My beauty and My love with younger people. Just keep your heart open and humble before Me. Sometimes you will not see immediate results as you minister to a person, causing you to wonder if it is worthwhile to spend the time and energy. I would encourage you to persevere. If I have brought a young person into your life, it is for a reason. You may not see the results, but as you open your heart and share My love, I will impact their lives, touching and transforming them.

My time frame is not always visible to you but My purposes will be fulfilled in the lives of those to whom you minister. Don't submit to pressure from others; don't look to what others would or wouldn't do. Just do what I've called you to do and be released from expectations and demands placed by others upon your life.

When you open up your heart to share My love with someone else, you open up to Me! I love you so very much. You call Me your Beloved, but I call you My beloved, My beautiful one. I adore you.

You may find that difficult to accept, but dearest one, if it is right for you to adore Me, is it not My right and privilege to adore you? I adore all my precious ones, and I adore you as I adore My precious ones, those who are called My chosen ones. Don't be confused; when others are drawn to you, they are really drawn to My love displayed in you.

It is not surprising then that the more My love is released in you, the more others will be drawn to you. Your destiny, calling and life purpose is to love Me, to be loved by Me, and to be the fragrance of My love and life wherever you go. As this realization grips your life, your latter years will be the greatest, the best, the most fulfilling and the happiest years of your life. This is My will that you become a beautiful reflection of My love and that your latter years will be indeed the most glorious of all.

Verse 10

My Beloved is white and ruddy, the chiefest among ten thousand.

My prayer
Lord Jesus, You are the picture of divine perfection, of infinite perfection. It was Your purpose in making us Your own that we would display Your virtues and perfections.[182]

Your people are Your treasure, Your kingdom of priests set apart for the purpose of worshipping God. You are the Chief Cornerstone, as the Apostle Peter said, a chosen, honored, precious chief Cornerstone!

Not only are You the Chief Cornerstone, You are the carefully chosen precious Cornerstone of Your church, the Cornerstone (once rejected) has become the most honored and important part of the building, Your church.[183]

Jesus, as Husband to Your church, the Bride, You are incomparably more beautiful, more radiant, and more perfect than any thing or any person ever could be. Earth has no words to describe Your incomparable worth and beauty. Of all the loves on earth, none compares to Yours.

How can I thank You? What worship can I bring? You who became servant to all have become the sovereign over all. Rejected and condemned to death for our sins, You have been exalted as Head of the church, the chief Cornerstone, the pearl of great price, the Lover of my soul.

---

[182] Job 11:7/1 Peter 2:9

[183] Exodus 19:5,6/ Ephesians 2:20/ 1 Peter 2:6 & 7 (Living Bible)

I honor You today for Who You are - King and God. At the cost of Your very life You left the love and beauty of Your Father in heaven to become the beautiful One, the lovely One, the chief among ten thousand. King of kings, Lord of lords, Son of God and Son of man, there is none like You in heaven or in earth

And yet You are not ashamed to be called my Brother, my Husband, my Lover and Friend. In gratitude I call to You: let Your love and Your glory be displayed in me. May we, Your church, truly display Your love and beauty in a dark and dying world.

Forgive us where we have been so taken up with other loves and other things in our lives that the beauty of Your love has not shone clearly through us. Forgive us where our failure to walk in love and unity has tarnished our world's perception of Your beauty. Forgive us where we have misrepresented You!

You came to bring us life, to beautify our lives with Your love and to make us Your Bride. Jesus, You are incomparably awesome in Your love for your Bride, and in Your glorious, eternal beauty.

You are tender, You are gracious
You are loving, You are kind
You are chief among ten thousand
You are glorious - You are mine!

You the Stone that was rejected
Set aside and put to death
Hated and despised of men
Deprived of very breath.

A man of sorrows, grief and pain
A root out of dry ground.
No beauty to be seen in Him
No honor or renown.

Yet He was wounded for my sins
And bruised for all my shame[184]
The chastisement He bore for me
Was written for my name.

---

[184] Isaiah 53

Yes, He who bore the sins of all
        Who poured out all for me
He is the One who rose again
        In glorious victory!

He died my death, He lives again
        He offers life and hope
He has become the cornerstone
        The Chief, the Head of all.

His name is honored and revered
        His fame throughout the earth!
The loving Christ most beautiful
        Of incomparable worth!

Poem written by Florli Nemeth

Verse 11A

His head is as the most fine gold...
His head is as precious as the finest gold. (Amplified)
His head is purest gold... (Living Bible)

My thoughts
Christ is the Head of every man and God is the Head of Christ. The Godhead speaks of union: God dwells in Christ, and we are in Him. What an unspeakably wonderful union![185]

God is *in Christ* - Christ is *in me*!

I have everything in Christ, filled with the Godhead - Father, Son and Holy Spirit, *because, or through* my union with Christ. As Head, He is Sovereign with authority and power over every other ruler.

This union and this power are found in none other. As Head of the church, He gives life, influence and direction to the entire church. Under His direction the entire Body of Christ, the Church, is fitted together perfectly. The whole body is healthy and growing and filled with love, or *full* of love.

---

[185] 1 Corinthians 11:3/ Colossians 2:9,10 Amplified & Living Bible

Two words in the original Hebrew are used to describe "gold" in this verse. The first word signifies shining brightness and beauty. The second descriptive word for "gold" signifies solidity and firmness.

My prayer
Jesus, Head of Your church, we acknowledge the excellence of Your leadership. Under Your headship we find direction and leadership, protection and shelter. I believe that the Bride also was proclaiming that You are a beautiful, sovereign, just, kind, wonderful God and King.

No despot ruling with a rod of iron, You condescended to become one with Your loved ones; it is Your union with me that gives me everything I need. You are my glorious Head, supreme, sovereign Ruler of all. You are one with me. Your riches, the finest gold, have enriched all who possess You - just as gold enriches and empowers the owner!

Daily You enrich my life, supplying me with direction and leadership, protection and love. You have given me everything I need. I value Your Headship and Your authority in my life and in the church. I don't know if I'll ever understand with my finite mind what this all means, but my heart receives You, Jesus. I love You and crown You King and Lord of my life. You, my Beloved, are pure gold. You are my Head, the One I choose to be one with, the One I love above all others. Lord Jesus, I want to become more and more, in every way, like You. Because of You I am healthy and strong and growing and full of love. But even then I ask: How can I be full of love? The One who is full of love lives in me. How can I be strong? The Strong One is in me.

Ephesians 4:16
Under the direction of the Head, the whole body - the church - is fitted together perfectly, and each part in its own special way helps the other parts, so that the whole body is healthy and growing and full of love. (Living Bible)
Because of Him, the whole body (the church in all its various parts) closely joined and firmly knit together by the joints and ligaments with which it is supplied, when each part (with power adapted to its need) is working properly [in all its functions], grows to full maturity, building itself up in love. (Amplified)

Lord Jesus, You are indeed the Head of the church. Help us to see that we *must* understand how You see us as Your church if we are to grow and come to full maturity.

Help us see how perfectly joined and connected we are to every part of Your body. Because our eyes have been blinded, we haven't seen this, and we have suffered so much fracture. When each part of the body does their own thing, thinking they are more on fire, more on target than other parts of the body, we dishonor You. To our shame we have criticized and maligned those parts of the body that are different from us. Never let us forget that we are part of Your body.

Too often we have felt no compunction in alienating ourselves from others or bragging that we have more revelation, greater understanding or more influence than others. We've hidden behind our silence in such matters or justified ourselves in our boastfulness even as we have torn apart, joint by joint, the Church that You love.

Forgive us Lord. Forgive me. Open our eyes to see the beautiful oneness You have given us. Give us a revelation of how we are so intricately and intimately connected to one another.

Open our eyes to see that if we are not fitted together perfectly, it means we are not submitting to the direction of the Head. It doesn't matter how mature we think we are, if we are not living in loving relatedness to the whole body, we are neither healthy nor mature.

We must live and walk in this kind of connectedness to the body of Christ, there is no other way. Unity is not an option but an absolute necessity if we are to be the mature and glorious bride of Christ throughout the earth.

Lord Jesus, open our eyes. Open the eyes of Your people and Your servants to see how we must relate to you as the Head of the church. I submit to Your authority in my life, to Your leadership, to Your direction. You are the One who supplies us with everything we need, You our glorious, victorious, risen Head, our risen Lord and King.

Verse 11B

. . . .His locks are bushy and black as a raven.

You remain the same, and Your years shall have no end.[186]

[186] Psalm 102:27

You remain and continue permanently. You remain the same, and Your years will never end nor come to failure.[187]

Jesus Christ is the same yesterday, today and forever.[188]

My prayer
Lord Jesus, You are awesome in Your love for me and for Your church. We grow old and pass away; everything around us fades and dies. But You remain faithful, strong, vibrant, alive - the same from eternity to eternity. Your strength never wanes, Your love never fails and Your kindness and mercy endure to all generations.

And Jesus, You are committed to do the will of the Father - to fulfill what is written of You in the volume of the book.[189] You came to earth to lay down Your life in order to fulfill every promise and every prophecy concerning Yourself. That is why You could say at the cross, "It is finished". You completed the work required to bring redemption to mankind. Every promise was fulfilled. You are faithful to Your Word over me and over all Your church. You have begun a good work in us, and You have promised to complete it.[190]

You are helping me to grow in grace every day of my life, and one day when I stand before You, Your work in me will be perfect and complete! Thank You, Lord Jesus, for Your dedication to me and to every one of Your loved ones. You promised to build Your church, and You said the gates of hell would not prevail against it (overpower it or be strong to hold out against it). I believe You are committed to see this fulfilled in Your church.[191]

Your purpose is to sanctify the church, cleansing her by the washing of the water with the word.[192]

---

[187] Hebrews 1:10-12

[188] Hebrews 13:8

[189] Hebrews 10:7

[190] Philippians 1:6

[191] Matthew 16:18

[192] Ephesians 5:26, 27

One day You will present the church to Yourself without spot or wrinkle, holy and faultless. Since before the foundation of the world Your commitment is to beautify and adorn Your bride, the church. One day she will be presented to You - the Bride - the Lamb's wife.[193]

Thank You, my Lord, for Your dedication to me and to Your bride, the church. It is Your love that transforms my life and adorns me, Your love that never lets me go. No matter how I may fail You, You will not fail to accomplish Your work in me.

Verse 12

His eyes are as the eyes of doves by the rivers of waters, washed with milk and fitly set.
His eyes are like doves beside the water brooks, deep and quiet. (Living Bible)

My prayer
Your eyes to Your enemies are as flames of fire, and they tremble in terror before Your gaze. But to Your people, Your eyes are as the eyes of a dove - loving and lovely, pure and clean, and fitly set as stones or jewels are set with no flaw. You are exceedingly beautiful to look upon because Your eyes are penetratingly lovely and pure!

Lord Jesus, my heart is encouraged to know that You see so clearly into my life. You know everything about me, and as another once wrote[194] "You know all - what we are, what we have need of, what is good for us, and what is designed to our prejudice by any of our adversaries, and cannot mistake."

You know the secrets of my heart - my dreams, my hopes, my desires. I am comforted to know that You care so deeply, so lovingly.

You said earlier that my eyes also were as doves' eyes.[195] When I gaze on You I become like You - not all knowing as You, but I begin to see things clearly and accurately even as You do[196].

---

[193] Revelation 21:2 & 9

[194] Author, James Durham, Geneva Series of Commentaries entitled "Song of Solomon", page 301

[195] Song of Solomon 4:1

[196] 2 Corinthians 3:18

Sometimes I wonder why people cannot see Your plan or Your purpose, and I wonder how they can ridicule Your people, Your Word and Your laws with such certainty and impunity. My heart often thinks when I look at such people, how can they be so blind? So ignorant? Yet Your Word declares we are all blinded by sin, going our own way, choosing our own path. And we don't understand because as Paul said, our minds are darkened.[197]

He said
Yes, and that is why you must *hold to* the Light and *hold up* the Light! If I be lifted up, I will draw all men unto Myself. It is imperative that you understand this: You cannot beat down darkness and to come against the darkness is almost always futile because people are blind! Beating them over the head with the Bible won't change that. My servant, Paul, said to pray that peoples' hearts be flooded with light so that their eyes would be opened.[198]

You see, the eyes only reflect the heart…that is why I said you had eyes like doves. Because your heart sees Me clearly and knows Me and loves Me, I see love and a desire to please Me when I look into your eyes. I am overcome with just one look of your eyes. Your beauty draws me. Keep gazing into My eyes, for I desire your love and your beauty, and you bring Me great joy.

My response

I love You, I love You, My Master, I do
My praises, my worship, they all go to You.
You light up my darkness, You open my eyes
You flood me with light, turning darkness to day.

O Jesus, my Saviour, my heart longs for You
To gaze at Your beauty, my life be renewed.
I see in Your eyes, Lord, perfection of love
The purity, wholeness and loveliness of doves.

You see me, You know me, You love and You care
You watch o'er me daily and count every hair.
My past and my future, my faults and my sins
My dreams and desires, My thoughts deep within.

---

[197] Romans 1:21

[198] Ephesians 1:18

You see them, You know them, You don't miss a thing
You lovingly guide me, You make my heart sing!
You lift me to heaven, You give me to see
The King in His beauty, His eyes fixed on me.

I'll love You forever, my God and my King
The beauty of doves' eyes inspire me to bring,
Praise, adoration and love evermore,
Jesus the Truth and Life, Jesus my Lord!

Poetry written by Florli Nemeth

Verse 13A

His cheeks are as a bed of spices, as sweet flowers...

My prayer
To look at You, to see Your face, is to experience the fragrance and beauty of a garden abounding in spices and sweet-smelling flowers.

When I ride my bike on the trails through the beds of wild roses in June, I am intoxicated with the scent of the wild flowers. When You reveal Yourself to me, I see the sweetness of Your face and I sense the delightfulness of Your emotions. You are filled with joy and delight when we meet - I am so blessed to be in Your presence. Your Word says that in Your presence is fullness of joy.[199]

In speaking of Your presence in his great sermon after the outpouring of the Holy Spirit, Peter also referred to Psalm 16:11 when He said, "You will enrapture me [diffusing my soul with joy] with and in Your presence." [200] "You have let me experience the joys of life and the exquisite pleasures of Your own eternal presence."[201]

Jesus, Your presence is so wonderful. Morning by morning You reveal the sweetness of Your character to me. Although You are always with me, I cannot always see You but it is in our secret place that we meet.

---

[199] Psalm 16:11 KJV

[200] Psalm 16:11 and Acts 2:28 Amplified

[201] Psalm 16:11 Living Bible

It is there that You reveal Yourself and I am filled with joy, overwhelmed by the wafting fragrance of Your all-enveloping love.

I cannot see Your cheeks with my natural eyes, but with the eyes of my spirit I see Your love-filled smile of approval and joy. I don't come to a God who is angry at me for my sins or who delights in pointing out my faults (though they be many). I come to a God who actually loves me, who enjoys being with me and who blesses my every attempt to draw near to Him.

O Jesus, You are so beautiful! It's not just that I enjoy being with You - that would be reward enough - but the knowledge that You also cherish my presence fills me with joy. As Your fragrance wafts over me and fills my life, I become the fragrance of Christ wherever I go.[202]

He said
You have chosen that "better thing", My friend, My love.[203] You have chosen to sit at My feet morning by morning, and I will continue to reveal Myself to you. You have rightly discerned My emotions and My heart toward you.

There was a day in your life when you were so burdened down by your own faults and failures and by your misconceived notions of Me that you felt I was angry with you all the time. But you have learned, as you've been with Me, how much I love you and how much I joy and rejoice over you.[204] I rejoice over you to do you good.[205]

I spoke through My prophet, Zephaniah, and gave him the message: "I rejoice over you with great gladness, and I joy over you with singing."[206]

He understood the pleasure I experience in your love. Truly I rejoice over you today, indeed I rejoice over all My loved ones who take the time to sit at My feet. Each day brings a new song to sing over you; as

---

[202] 2 Corinthians 2:15

[203] Luke 10:42

[204] Isaiah 62:5

[205] Jeremiah 32:41

[206] Zephaniah 3:17, Living Bible

you write songs to me, so I love to write songs about *you*. I'm keeping them all for you. I know how meticulous *you* are in writing down your songs, and I, too, am preserving the songs I sing over you so that one day I can share them with you!

You look forward to that day when you will be with Me? Yes, I know you do but I look forward to that day even more because I long to reveal Myself to you more fully. Now you see Me only partially, or as a dim reflection in a mirror,[207] but in that day you will see Me face to face, clearly and accurately even as I see you now.

O My dear child, how I love you! The perfume of My love is upon you. Go in My strength with My joy and love upon you and My songs of deliverance and joy over you. Go and be a blessing.

Verse 13B

...his lips like lilies, dropping sweet-smelling myrrh.

My prayer

Jesus, Your lips speak of Your Word - sweet, precious, lovely grace-filled words pouring from Your lips. [208]

Your words strengthen the weak, comfort the sorrowing and bring healing to the sick and broken-hearted. Your words encourage the faint, give hope to the hopeless, and refresh the hearts of the languishing. You give me words of wisdom; morning by morning I wake to hear and to understand Your words. It is You Who open my ears to hear Your words[209].

Your words, like lilies, speak of the beauty and the grace Your words give. There are no other words with the power to heal and console, comfort and encourage like Yours.

And the fact that Your words, like lilies, drop sweet-smelling myrrh shows how precious and how lovely they are. Here on earth, lilies don't

---

[207] 1 Corinthians 13:12

[208] Psalm 138:2 and 45:2

[209] Isaiah 50:4, 5

drop myrrh, but this picture is used here by the bride in an attempt to show how truly delightful and wonderful Your words are to the heart that loves You.

This myrrh drops constantly, never dries up and it speaks of Your words in their sweetness. Day after day, year after year they continue to refresh and encourage my soul. You don't flood my heart so as to overwhelm me for You know me and my weakness. You just drop a word here and a word there - day by day dropping Your love and encouragements to me through Your Words and I am refreshed.

It is Your Word that gives me strength and hope and the desire to pursue Your love. For Your words are kind and gracious, accepting and forgiving, inviting and welcoming me to Your heart. O Jesus, let me hear the sweet words of Your lips today. My heart hungers after You.

He said
Does not My Word say that "death and life are in the power of the tongue"?[210]

And My Word also says that the words I speak are words of life - spirit and life.[211]

I know how to speak a word in season to the one who is weary. Do I not speak thus to you daily? Because you watch at My gates daily, looking and listening for Me, I don't have to go far looking for you. That pleases My heart.[212]

You see, I long to speak into the hearts of My loved ones, but so few take the time to still their hearts long enough to hear My voice. Those who listen to Me daily are blessed. Blessed with comfort and encouragement. Blessed with help and direction. Blessed with counsel and wisdom. Blessed with health and strength. Wherever I send My Word it brings health and healing, salvation and deliverance.

---

[210] Proverbs 18:21

[211] John 6:63

[212] Isaiah 50:4/Proverbs 8:34

My comments and thoughts
Your Word is tested and tried and proven true over and over again.[213]

Your Word is right, never wrong! It's always on target, hitting the mark in my life.[214]

Your Word is full of power wherever it is published and proclaimed. Your Word does what it says it will do.[215]

I treasure Your words in my heart, and Your words keep me from sin.[216]

Your Word comforts and consoles me in times of sorrow and grief, and Your Word refreshes me and gives me life.[217]

I hope in Your Word, especially when my heart faints and is weary. Your words produce hope and encouragement in my times of weakness.[218]

Your Word is light to my feet and to my path. [219] Sometimes the trail is hidden and the night foreboding but Your Word always guides me safely through the darkest night of the soul. Even when I cannot see more than a step in front of me, Your Word assures me that the steps of a good man are ordered, or directed, by the Lord. I believe that, I truly do.

The unfolding of Your Word gives understanding and discernment in every circumstance of life.[220]

The word of Your mouth stands forever.[221] I can build my life on it because it will never change.

---

[213] Proverbs 30:5; Psalm 119:140 and 18:30

[214] Psalm 33:4

[215] Psalm 68:11

[216] Psalm 119:11

[217] Psalm 119:50

[218] Psalm 119:81

[219] Psalm 119:105

[220] Psalm 119:130

[221] Isaiah 40:8

Your words do only good to those who walk uprightly before You since You speak only good things.[222]

Your words are gracious and comforting.[223]

Lord Jesus, these are only a few scriptures about Your words. I could go on and on, encompassing all of scripture, but yet never exhausting the graciousness and the love that is poured forth from Your lips. Thank You my Father for all Your love to me. Thank You for the things I feel and for the things I cannot see.

He said
Beloved one, stay close to My Word. Let it do its work in your life. As you absorb My Word, daily watching and waiting at My gates, I will pour My graciousness and My love into you. The result will be a gentle love in you that speaks My words of love and comfort to those languishing in despair and hopelessness. I need you to be My mouthpiece.

There are many who speak harsh words of condemnation. I did not come to the world to condemn it or to judge it but to bring salvation, safety and soundness.[224]

Share this good news. Let others know about My love. Let My people know of My love and of My desire to fellowship with them. This is your mandate - your calling - to share My love. Publish it far and wide.

I said
Lord, would You cause my words to drop sweet-smelling myrrh as do Your words? I am so often tempted to speak retaliating words to defend myself or to speak out against what I perceive to be unjust or abusive, cruel and wrong.

He said
Dearest child, I see your hurt and pain. But if you would drop sweet-smelling myrrh, you must embrace the cross. Only then will your lips

---

[222] Micah 2:7

[223] Zechariah 1:13

[224] John 3:17

speak words that bring healing and reconciliation. Do it for Me even when it is difficult and painful, for as you embrace My cross in your life, you will experience a breakthrough in your relationships. Let Me restore your hope. Don't dwell on the past. Look to Me. Look to what I am doing in your life and let Me bring healing to your heart.

I replied
I will do it for You, dear Lord. You are so dear to my heart. Help me to respond to harshness in an opposite spirit of love and kindness, compassion and understanding. Help me to cover the weakness, not expose it. Fill me up with Your love and grace, Lord Jesus. Help me to forgive.

Verse 14A

His hands are as gold rings set with the beryl . . . .

My observations
The beryl was a jewel used in the breastplate for the high priest, His hands speak of His work, of what he does. He always works for the good of His people.

My prayer
Lord, You hold me in Your arms. My name is engraved on Your hands. Your right hand holds me up.[225]

You hold my right hand.[226]

Your hands have made me and fashioned me.[227]

Your hand leads me and Your right hand holds me.[228]

Your hand feeds me and satisfies my every need.[229]

---

[225] Psalm 18:35
[226] Psalm 73:23
[227] Psalm 119:73
[228] Psalm 139:10
[229] Psalm 145:16

Your hand saves me and is not shortened.[230]

It is into Your hands I will one day commit my spirit, even as You committed Your spirit into the hands of Your Father.[231]

You hide me in the shadow of Your hand.[232] You have indelibly imprinted or tattooed a picture of me on the palm of each of Your hands.[233]

Your hands bring You victory in the nations, and You do such wonderful things for me. How can I ever thank You enough?

He said
Dear child of My heart, I hold you in My arms, clasped close to My heart. I don't leave you for others to look after. I care for you with My own hands. I shape your life, your future, your destiny. And your life is totally in My hands. Nothing can touch you without it touching Me first. So do not weep in dismay. One day, in love, I will carry your spirit in My hands and present you to My Father.

I am so proud of you, so deeply in love with you.

Verse 14B

His belly (body) is as bright ivory overlaid with sapphires.

My prayer
O Lord, Your love is so wonderful, so exquisite, so unique, and so powerfully strong. Like a mother, Your heart yearns over Your children. When we are afflicted You feel our pain. You lift Your people up and carry them when they can no longer walk. Your heart is full of mercy and compassion.[234]

Even when we turn away from You and You have to discipline us, You still have mercy, You still love, You still long for the love of Your

---

[230] Isaiah 59:1

[231] Psalm 31:5 and Luke 23:46

[232] Isaiah 49:2

[233] Isaiah 49:16

[234] Isaiah 63:9, 15

people. There is no other god who loves to the end as You do. Your love surpasses every other love known on earth.

You loved the church so much that You gave Your life for it; You gave Your life for me! This kind of love is rarely seen even for a friend, but Your love was given to me when I was still Your enemy and when as yet I did not even know You. Your love extends to every human being regardless of how deeply entrenched in sin and darkness they may be and regardless of what they have done. [235]

Lord Jesus, I pray You would open my heart to understand Your love in a deeper, more intimate way. Enable me to grasp and experience the breadth and length, height and depth of Your love. [236] You have rooted me in Your love and established me securely in Your love, and nothing can ever move me from that. Beautiful, awesome, magnificent - words cannot begin to describe Your love for me, for the church and for the world.

He said
Yes, dear one, and even your own misconceptions cannot move you from My love, nor will your failures ever remove My love from you. Nothing you will ever do can change the way My heart yearns over you. Many things change in life, but My love will never change. Reaching to the lowest hell and to the highest heaven, it follows you to the last day of your life, even to the halls of eternity. It began in eternity past and continues into eternity forever.

Nothing but My love for you can satisfy your deepest longings for love, for affirmation and for acceptance. My heart is so moved with your needs and with your love. And My heart is so moved with the needs of all My children. I trust you to share this love - to tell My people how deep, how high, how wide and how long My love is for them.

So many of My loved ones languish in despair and hopelessness even while I'm pouring out My love over them. But they cannot see or feel My concern because they are not looking in the right places for Me. I will use you to tell them, to show them the way by your life and example.

---

[235] Ephesians 5:25

[236] Ephesians 3:17,18

I responded

Lord, reveal Your love to me
Come and set the prisoner free
Love's unchanging quality
Jesus, give me love.

Lord, reveal Your love so wide
Stretching far from side to side
Love's embracing ocean tide
Jesus, give me love.

Lord, reveal Your love so deep
Treasure that I long to keep
Love that does not ever sleep
Jesus, give me love.

Lord, reveal Your love so high
Love that reaches to the sky
Love that ever draws me nigh
Jesus, give me love.

Lord, reveal Your love so long
Lifting up my soul in song
One day sing with that great throng
Jesus, You are love!

Poetry written by Florli Nemeth

Verse 15A

His legs are as pillars of marble set upon sockets of fine gold . . . .
His legs are like strong and steady pillars of marble set upon bases of fine gold... (Amplified)

My prayer
Lord God, Your legs speak of Your walk and the paths You have set before Your people. Your Word says You go before us, thus leaving us footprints to follow. All Your ways are just and right. You are a God of faithfulness and You do not deviate from Your ways and purposes and plans.[237]

[237] Deuteronomy 32:4

Your way is perfect[238] and Your Word says You make my way perfect.[239]

You instruct sinners in Your way, and You teach the humble Your way.[240]

Lord, I want to walk in Your Ways.

O Lord, let Your way be known in the earth and may it be known in my life. Your way is an everlasting way. It does not change with the times and seasons.

You make a pathway through the sea of life and a path through the mighty waters.[241]

No waters or rivers can overwhelm Your loved ones because You are with us in every trial, and You make a way through the trial.[242]

You bring Your purposes to pass regardless of what the enemy may throw at me to distract, discourage, or distance me from You. Because You are strong and powerful You enable me to walk and to make progress even upon my high places of trouble, suffering or responsibility.[243]

You are my Strength, my Bravery, my invincible army. No weapon formed against me will prosper because You are strong, and nothing can stand against You.

Pillars signify strength and beauty and durability, and the gold speaks of preciousness, graciousness and solidness.

O my God, Your ways are solid, settled on good ground. I'll not slip and fall when I'm with You. Nor are You like the gods of the heathen that cannot see or hear or move. You are moving in my life and in the

---

[238] Psalm 18:30

[239] Psalm 18:32

[240] Psalm 25:8, 9

[241] Isaiah 43:16

[242] Isaiah 43:2

[243] Habakkuk 3:19 Amplified

affairs of the world; what You do is good and wise and holy and just. Your purposes cannot fail or be altered by puny men!

Your ways may not always be discernible, but You are moving, and You will fulfill Your designs and purposes in my life and in the earth. All the counsels and designs of men will come to naught, but Your counsel stands forever.[244]

Yes, Lord, all Your ways are just and true and You are greatly to be praised.[245]

Your kingdom is an everlasting kingdom, and I will speak of the glory and majesty of Your kingdom and Your wonderful power.[246]

O God, You are great and greatly to be praised. As I trust in You I am safe, secure, because You can never be broken down or made to fail. You, my strong tower and my pillar of strength and beauty – I bring You praise.

He said
How rightly you discern Me, My precious, darling child. My *purposes* will forever be deployed. My *principles* of holiness, righteousness and truth will never change and by My *power* and love I will cause you to be strengthened and encouraged to make *progress* in your life as you walk hand in hand with Me.

And I *will* teach you My ways until you know them as did My servant, Moses. Others were content to follow My footsteps at a distance but he needed to know Me and desired to walk with Me closely. I see your desire to follow Me closely, to walk hand in hand with Me, even when the path may be indiscernible. I assure you I will hold your hand and I will lead you in a plain path because you love Me, because you need Me, because you long for Me to be near.

I promise to fulfill My purposes and designs for your life here on earth before I take you home to be with Me forever. And furthermore, I

---

[244] Psalm 33:11

[245] Psalm 145:17

[246] Psalm 145:11-13

pledge to fulfill My purposes and designs for your life for all eternity. My purposes do not end when your life span here on earth is complete. They only begin when you cross that line into My eternal presence.

That is why I encourage you to dream big dreams for kingdom purposes, because even though you may not see the whole picture here on earth, you may catch a glimpse of what I purpose even into eternity.

How does this happen? As I have spoken to you before, eternity is in the hearts of men. And that being so, why would you be surprised that I would give you a glimpse of My eternal purposes for your life and for My kingdom? [247]

Verse 15B

His countenance is as Lebanon, excellent as the cedars.

My Observation
The word "countenance" used in both places in Song of Songs (2:14 and 5:15) is from the Hebrew word meaning this: the act of seeing, or an appearance - like seeing the complete person, not just the face (4758 Strong's Concordance).

My prayer
Lord, I want to see You in all Your beauty. When I look upon You I see such beauty and grace, not found in any other. As I draw closer to You, the more stately and majestic I see that You are, and the more excellent I comprehend You to be.

My earthly imagination sees this truth as being in a huge stadium or indoor auditorium that seats ten to twenty thousand people. From the back and upper part of the auditorium the person viewed on the platform is very small and almost indiscernible.

But when I move closer to the platform, individuals become more discernible until I can easily distinguish their facial expressions as well as their form. Most stadiums now use media presentations, so if I look at the screens I can see the person larger than life, and they seem to

[247] See Ephesians 3:11 re God's eternal purpose; Deuteronomy 33:27 re the eternal God; and Isaiah 60:15 re what God has promised to make us.

be looking right at me. I'm able to clearly distinguish every nuance of expression.

This is much more enjoyable than just seeing a "speck" on the platform, more intimate than being unable to discern that person's expressions or the details of their physical appearance.

Lord, the closer I get to You, the more I am able to discern Your beauty, Your stately stature and Your glory. I cannot see Your physical form with these eyes because my flesh could never handle Your glorious, complete presence. But You so graciously reveal Your person to me through Your Word and through dreams and visions.

My Observation of "Lebanon" in verse 15b
Lebanon is a snow-covered mountain range in Palestine, covered with cedar trees that are tall, stately, fragrant, beautiful, durable, and in possession of tenacious roots to support the weight of the tree.

My prayer
Reveal Yourself more clearly to me. Give me eyes to discern Your glory and Your beauty. I don't want to walk through life as though blind and totally oblivious to Your beauty for You are glorious, victorious, and greatly to be praised! Impart sight, vision, and dreams to my heart.

I cry to You for impartation - fresh impartation, daily impartation. Look on me, Jesus. Behold me with Your eyes of love. Touch me with Your presence. Make my whole life shine with the glory of Your love!

Verse 16A

His mouth is most sweet . . . .

My observations
This is the communication of divine intimacy. His *mouth* differs from -

- His lips - His words
- His cheeks - His emotions
- His countenance - His beauty

This is the manifestation or application of His love in a personal, private, intimate way. He sheds abroad His love in our hearts by the Holy Ghost. The Amplified Bible says He *pours out* His love into our hearts by the Holy Spirit. [248]

My prayer
O Lord, it is wonderful to look upon You, to see Your beauty, Your sovereign leadership, Your dedication to Your Church, Your infinite knowledge and understanding, Your wonderful emotions, Your powerful, life-changing Word, Your divine activity in my life, Your tender compassions, Your divine purpose, and the impartation of Your glorious countenance.

But even *more* wonderful, satisfying and fulfilling are the kisses of Your mouth, the manifestation of Your love and nearness that brings me such joy. The gladness Your presence brings into my life is greater by far than the joy of reapers bringing in the harvest.[249]

The reality of Your love present in the kisses of Your mouth brings such sweetness to my life. There is an impartation that happens when I experience Your intimate presence. Such manifestations of Your presence and love come only as I choose to spend time with You and as I respond to Your love.

This is so difficult to explain to others because each of us experiences Your love in a unique way. Though it is difficult to put into words how wonderful it is to be touched by Your presence and kissed with Your love, I need Your kisses, Lord. I must have these intimate times with You. To have tasted and seen Your goodness and kindness has ignited a passion for more. There can never be enough or too many of Your delights. [250]

He said
You are so lovely, My Bride! I kiss you with My Word every time you come into My presence for it is there I reveal My love to you. I am committed to do this in your life because you are My bride - My wife!

---

[248] Romans 5:5

[249] Song of Songs 1:2 and Psalm 4:7

[250] Psalm 34:8/Song of Songs 2:3/1 Peter 2:3

You deserve My kisses, and you shall have them often - many times a day as you lift your heart to Me. I'm not stingy. I don't ration out My love; I pour it out in abundance over you.

So rest in My love. This is a way of life, the only sensible way to live your life, smothered with My kisses, My manifest presence and My love. I'm delighted when you enjoy My love and presence, and I am so fulfilled when I see how you have grown.

Verse 16B

...yea, He is altogether lovely . . . .

My observations
The word for "lovely" in Hebrew means -

- Object of affection
- Delightful and a delight
- Precious, beautiful, coveted
- Greatly beloved

My prayer
O Lord Jesus, how can my heart truly describe You to others? How can I worship You as You deserve to be worshipped?

Isaiah said You were Wonderful.[251]

Paul proclaimed: The fullness of God - the sum total of His perfection - dwells in You. [252]

John, the Apostle declared: You are full of grace and truth. [253]

David exclaimed, "Whom have I in heaven but You? And I have no delight or desire on earth beside You."[254]

[251] Isaiah 9:6
[252] Colossians 1:19
[253] John 1:14
[254] Psalm 73:25

Gold, lilies, ivory, silver, precious stones – nothing can adequately compare with Your beauty and loveliness. All comparisons fall short in every way. Should I gain the whole world and have nothing beside, to gain Your love and friendship is to gain everything!

You are so precious to me, my Lover, my Friend.

- Your love never fails, never grows old.
- You are gentle, caring, desirous of my love.
- You are kind, merciful, forgiving my sins and never holding them against me.
- You are faithful, wonderful, powerful and awesome in Your love for me.
- You are caring and considerate, a confidant Who loves and understands.
- You cherish me and are committed to my best interests.

My heart safely trusts in You. I know I will never be disappointed or put to shame. Jesus, You are my heart's desire, my consuming passion, my lifelong pursuit! I cry out as the apostle Paul did, "O that I might know You!" [255]

I abandon myself to Your love, Lord Jesus. All else on earth is unworthy to be compared to Your beauty, Your love and Your loveliness. I truly believe it will take the fullness of eternity in Your presence even to begin to love and worship You as You deserve to be loved and worshipped. No wonder John fell at Your feet as if dead. [256]

I, too, fall at Your feet today to worship You, to tell You that I love You. You are Alpha and Omega - the beginning and the end - the sum total of all perfection and beauty. O how I love You, Lord Jesus.

[255] Philippians 3:10

[256] Revelation 1:17

Verse 16C

. . . .this is my Beloved, and this is my Friend, O daughters of Jerusalem.

My observations

Believers may boast of Him and glory in Him. Their boasting of Him implies -

- A high estimation of Him
- Confidence in Him
- Satisfaction with Him
- Joy in Him resulting from confidence and satisfaction

We are commanded to boast in Him.[257] I think we can never boast in Him too much.

The words "My Beloved" and "My Friend" cannot be separated. Where He is my Beloved, He will also be my Friend. The more we know each other in the body of Christ, the more we see of imperfections and faults but the more we know our beloved Christ Jesus, the more we see of His worth and perfection, beauty and praise.

Knowing Christ for ourselves will compel us to desire others to know Him too. The bride doesn't shout down the idols or other loves of the daughters, she simply speaks of the incomparable beauty and love of her Beloved. She does it lovingly, tenderly, tactfully and convincingly.

We are not called to speak against things but to lift Christ up in all His beauty. It is then that people will be drawn to Him. He said Himself, "If I be lifted up, I will draw all men to Myself." [258]

The bride was never called to convert or change people, but rather, to present Christ! It is our job to speak of His love and His greatness - to boast of His faithfulness. He is well able to do the work in the lives of others. Lord, help me always be conscious that it is the work of the Holy Spirit to do the work of convicting and convincing.

---

[257] Psalm 105:3

[258] John 12:32

My prayer
Lord Jesus, You are my Beloved, my dear Husband and Friend. The more I know You, the more I love You; the longer I walk with You, the more I understand Your ways. The more I gaze on You, the more of Your beauty and perfection I see; the more time I spend with You, the more confident I become in Your love and faithfulness, Your care and provision and in Your protection and watchfulness over me. The more I obey You, the closer I come to You, and the more You open up Your heart to me.

This friendship we have is timeless, endless, totally encompassing every part of my life. And You draw me to Your heart, calling me Your bride, and wooing me to Your side. Jesus, I want the whole world to know how wonderful You are. You are incomparably wonderful! You are my Friend, my Beloved and I love You.

He said
Yes, you are My friend, even as I said to My disciples, "You are My friends if you obey Me".[259]

I also spoke with them about living in My love and keeping My commandments.[260]

When you love Me, you keep My Word because My Word does its work of purification in your life. It will keep you clean, and it will cause you to bear fruit.[261]

As you stay in the Word, your love will be ever new, enabling you to walk in obedience to My Word. Those who move away from My Word find their hearts become ensnared in the cares and pleasures of this world. It is so easy to get distracted, but it is also deadly. That is why I encourage My loved ones again and again to seek Me, to look for Me, to be much with Me, and to obey My words and walk in the light of My truth.

---

[259] John 15:14

[260] John 14:23 and 15:9,10

[261] John 15:3

There are a lot of man-made ideas proposed as truth, and to follow these is to walk in darkness. You have chosen, however, to walk in the light, hand in hand with Me. You have chosen Me, and I have chosen you. I chose you even before the foundation of the world. I knew your name before you were born. I *know* you, My dearest friend. Other friends might fail you, and indeed, some have failed you because none is perfect. But I will never leave you, never forsake you, and never fail to love you. You are My friend, My bride forever!

Chapter Six

The Daughters of Jerusalem Question the Bride

Verse 1

Whither is thy Beloved gone, O thou fairest among women? Whither is thy Beloved turned aside that we may seek Him with thee.

My thoughts

The daughters are now falling in love with the Beloved King, and they want to seek Him with the Shulamite Bride. It is always the duty of the older and more mature to instruct the younger and immature, the stronger to help the weaker, and the teacher to instruct and guide the student.[262]

It is also the responsibility of the wise student to receive instruction with a properly submitted attitude toward authority. Where a young person asks, "Who made *you* an instructor", or What right do *you* have to tell me what to do", you immediately discern that that one does *not* have a true heart of love to follow Christ. A true follower desiring to know Christ better will submit to their teacher, follow their instructor and obey those over them in the Lord.

The weak should never fear to ask questions. And always the strong need to make way for the weak without belittling or despising them. We who are older and more mature believers need to lay down our

[262] 1 Peter 5:5/Titus 2:4

own agendas in order to take time to edify and encourage the younger ones. The older and stronger need to condescend and acquiesce to the younger and weaker rather than insisting on our own edification, fueled by the desire that others truly hear from God and are edified.

The daughters called the Bride "the fairest among women" which showed the great respect they had for her. They don't yet call *Him* their beloved because they feel afraid to make such a presumptuous assumption. But as their desire to know this Beloved Shepherd for themselves grows, the Shepherd is drawing them as they watch the relationship between Him and the Bride.

My prayer
Lord, let me hear the heart cry of the immature ones who in their own way are beginning to call out to You. They want to help the Bride to find You, but in actual fact, they long to find You for themselves.

They don't know as yet how to hear Your voice or how to run with You. But they are growing and maturing in their knowledge of You as they are related to the Bride. Cover these ones, dear Lord, and draw them as You have drawn me.

Draw my grandchildren into Your presence as You have drawn me. Draw my children into a deeper love relationship with You. May I never be a stumbling block by my actions or my attitudes. May my life continue to draw and attract others into a deeper relationship with You. May my natural and spiritual children and grandchildren desire to know the God who is the love of my heart and the strength of my life!

He said
There are many who are impacted by your life, and many who desire to know Me as you know Me. The Bride in Song of Solomon was not afraid to share her struggles with the daughters, for in doing so they were encouraged to go deeper in God and to know Me for themselves.

Your life will impact many, and I am about to broaden your influence. For as you are faithful to Me in what I have given you, I am able to give you more.

The daughters see you as fair and beautiful. I see you even more so! Do not be embarrassed by the praise others give you. The beauty they see in you is the beauty I have placed upon you. So they rightly discern My beauty.

Although you are My Bride, I will always see you as My loving, beautiful daughter - My chosen one. And though I have many beautiful daughters, you will always be My most beautiful one in the sense that each child is the chosen one, the dearest one, the most favorite one to a mother or father.

The Bride's Reply to the Daughters of Jerusalem

Verse 2

My Beloved is gone down into His garden, to the beds of spices, to feed in the gardens, and to gather lilies.

Dear Jesus -
When You withdraw from where I can sense and feel You, I know where to find You. If You are not in the chamber, You are in the garden, in the assemblies of Your people, the church. Your garden is made up of beds of spices, of many garden plots and beds. *All* are different and unique, but some are more fruitful than others.

Your presence is found in every church where Your people gather together but sometimes Your presence is stronger in one place than another, depending on how people open their hearts to Your presence and respond to Your presence.

We can gather together with our own agendas without really seeking Your presence, and we can leave untouched and unchanged. But where we gather together to worship You and seek Your face and where we open our hearts to Your agenda, Your purpose and desire for our gathering, we will experience Your manifest presence, and we will leave the meeting touched and changed by that presence.

When the believers in Antioch gathered together Your Word says that "the presence of the Lord was with them in power". This resulted in a great number who believed and turned to the Lord. Jesus, My prayer is that we, in our local assembly, will experience such a powerful presence of God when we come together that *many* will turn to You and be delivered and changed forever.

He said
You will find Me today in the company of My people, in the garden of My heart. When you gather together with My chosen ones You come close to those I love; as you embrace My people you embrace Me and I embrace you.

So as you go to visit a part of My garden today, look for the beautiful spices and lilies. I will meet with you today as you walk there. As I display this part of My garden I will reveal Myself to you. I love My lilies and My beds of spices, and I love presenting them in their beauty. I love to show *you* off, too, for you are a beautiful lily. Your fragrance delights Me.

You may not feel My presence so strongly today, but beloved child, My presence goes with you wherever you go. My love for you is boundless. I am enjoying your presence this morning, and today you will be blessed with Mine as you go to My house - My garden - My beds of spices and lilies.

Dear Jesus
There is something more here that I must carefully note before going on. Why do You go down to the gardens? The answer is, *"to feed in the gardens and to gather lilies"*.

I think there are three aspects to the feeding part -

1. *You feed* on our love and worship as we gather together. Our worship brings You so much joy.
2. *You feed us with Your love and presence* when we come together. And I note that you always gather lilies. You gather Your peoplc closer to Your heart. You love to gather unbelievers, too, drawing them by Your Holy Spirit until they become believers. Your heart is ever desirous of gathering people to Yourself and to one another. The enemy scatters people so he can kill, steal and destroy but You gather to give life abundantly, to feed, and to cherish forever.
3. *You feed us with Your Word.* That is so important! We grow strong and healthy as we are fed and we become full of life and vitality. That is what You want for Your people, Your church. You are neither pleased nor honoured when we are weak and anaemic through lack of teaching or of our assembling together with the body of Christ. It is our assembling regularly with Your people and our receiving the Word of God into the soil of our hearts that brings You joy. Indeed, the Word will always bear fruit in our lives when it is planted in good soil.

He said
Yes, My gardens are very important to Me. I watch over them carefully, fencing them to protect them from things without, things that would destroy them. I plough them to remove the stones that hinder and destroy.[263]

Not only do I plant the choicest vines and spices in My gardens, I build a watchtower to watch over and protect them. In anticipation of much fruit, I build winepresses. None other is charged with the responsibility and care of those gardens. I personally watch over My Word to perform it.

My desire for you personally is that your life be like a watered garden and like a spring of water whose waters fail not.[264]

This is My promise to you when you pour out your life to sustain others. It is also My promise to My church when My people corporately pour out their resources to help the poor, the naked and the oppressed: each life shall be like a watered garden, flowing together in unity and clothed in the radiant joy that comes from imbibing of the goodness of the Lord.[265]

Never forget that I rejoice over you, rejoice over you to do you good. I rejoice over you as a Bridegroom rejoices over his Bride. I delight in you because you are married to Me, owned and protected by Me. I rejoice over you with joy; I joy over you with singing. [266]

I visit the gardens, not only to feed and protect My people, but to receive their love, their praise and their adoration.[267]

Your love brings Me such joy just as your worship and praise feed My heart. When I see the fruit and the results of My deep travail of soul, My joy is fulfilled. You will never know the depth of My suffering for

[263] Isaiah 5:1,2
[264] Isaiah 58:11
[265] Jeremiah 31:12
[266] Zephaniah 3:17
[267] Jeremiah 32:41/Isaiah 62:4 & 5

you, but when I look at you I am satisfied and content with the work that I have accomplished.

Verse 3A

I am my Beloved's, and my Beloved is mine...
I am my Beloved's [garden] and my Beloved is mine! (Amplified)

Dear Jesus
I am Yours for You love me, have a vested interest in me and have made me Your inheritance. Where once my focus was on *my* inheritance in You and on everything I have received from you, now I see my focus is changing. I understand that *You also* receive from me. It's not just that I enjoy being with You, but *You* enjoy *my* presence.[268]

You love to see my face morning by morning as I take time to be with You. You are overjoyed when I bring You even a small token of love and praise. I remember how lovingly my mother received the little May flowers we children picked for her from the woods. Though not a gift of great earthly value that we brought to her, I see now it was a gift *beyond* the highest value, a gift given with love to the one who loved us most. How much like that You are, Jesus.

I have not much to give
    And what I give is small
Yet You are pleased and filled with pride
    Because I give my all.

You gave me so much more!
    Your love alone so rare
Sustains my soul and lifts me high
    Upon the wings of prayer.

Yes, I am Yours alone
    None other's shall I be
For You I live, for You I'll die
    Your Bride eternally.

Poetry written by Florli Nemeth

[268] Song of Solomon 2:16

He said
You are My dear Child, My garden where I love to resort, the Father's gift to Me. You did not choose Me but I picked you, choosing you from before the foundation of the world. You are a gift in which I delight.

Because you belong to Me, you belong to the Father too and He keeps you in His care. In His care you are kept from evil and from the evil one as He sanctifies and cleanses you through My Word. The glory that the Father gave Me, I have given you so that you would be one with Me - perfectly united with Me and with each other, your brothers and sisters who also belong to Me.[269]

This is My inheritance in you. When the world sees the oneness – (the "unity") I have given you, they will know the Father sent Me, and they will understand that the Father loves you as much as He loves Me.[270]

Dear one, the Father entrusted your care to Me for He would trust none other. Because *you* are His gift to Me, you have become My only inheritance. I care only about the well-being of My people - of *you*! I rejoice over you, My Bride.[271]

One day the Father will present you to Me, a beautiful Bride adorned for her Husband. As My wife you will be clothed in all of the glory and radiance of God.[272]

How I look forward to that day when you will be presented to Me for all the world to see and recognize as My beautiful, precious, darling Bride. Though that is in the future, you are those things to Me now. Even as I am working in your life, preparing you and adorning you, I am rejoicing over you with joy and with singing.

---

[269] Ephesians 1:4 & 11; John 17:6, 10, 15, 17, 22
[270] John 17:23
[271] Isaiah 62:5
[272] Revelation 21:2 & 11

She said
I am His alone
I am His forever
Purchased by His blood
Nothing from Him sever.

Bold I stand, forever held
Safe within His hand
Confident, so lovingly
I'm shaped within His plan.

I am His alone
Gift from God the Father
Chosen for the Son
To be His sons and daughters

I am His alone
Bride of Christ the King
Clothed in righteousness
My beauty makes Him sing!

I am His alone
None other's will I be
My choice to live for Him
His Bride eternally.

Poetry written by Florli Nemeth

Verse 3B

...He feedeth among the lilies.

My thoughts
This is His word to me again[273] and Jesus also illustrated the care He has for His people by pointing to the common field lily and how beautifully it was adorned – even more glorious than Solomon in all his glory.

If God cares so much for little flowers that bloom today and are gone tomorrow, will He not *much more surely care for us*, His people?[274]

[273] Song of Solomon 2:16
[274] Matthew 6:28-30

In calling His people Israel to return to Him, God says, "*I will refresh Israel like the dew from heaven, she will blossom as the lily*"[275].

Here the Bride sees herself as a humble lily of the valley - just an ordinary human being crafted by His hands and content to grow in His garden.[276] *The King sees her as one of His choicest lilies lying among thorns - experiencing pain and anguish in a fallen world, yet patiently enduring and trusting the hand of the Gardener.*[277]

The Bride sees her Beloved feeding His flocks among the lilies.[278] *This is the answer to her earlier prayer*[279], *"Where do You feed Your flock?"*

Now she sees He has more than one flock. He has many flocks, and He feeds her among the lilies and among His numerous flocks. She receives her strength and nourishment among God's people.

In this passage i.e. 6:3, there are several possible interpretations:

1. *He feeds His flock* among the lilies, and she understands in a deeper way that He is faithfully feeding His flock and He will not fail her.
2. *He* feeds *Himself* among the lilies, indicating the delight and pleasure He has in His fellowship among His people as they respond to Him in love and worship.

My prayer
Lord Jesus, when anxious thoughts would crowd my mind and fear attack my heart, I remind myself of Your kindness, love, faithfulness and gentleness toward those You love. I remember that You actually come to my garden, morning by morning, to feed me and to nourish me. And not only that, You find nourishment in my love and praise and worship.

---

[275] Hosea 14:5 Living Bible
[276] Song of Solomon 2:1
[277] Song of Solomon 2:2
[278] Song of Solomon 2:16
[279] Song of Solomon 1:7

It is so difficult for me to understand how You could be blessed and fed by Me and yet I know it's true. You live in the praises of Your people[280], "*You dwell in the place where the praises of Israel are offered.*"

Lord Jesus, I abandon myself to worship You because worship draws You near to Your people, and I want to be near You.

He said
My "lilies" are pure and clean, washed in My holy blood. My "lilies" are growing beautifully together, cared for by Me, lovingly and tenderly. You are one of My lilies surrounded by other lilies who also deeply love Me. I cannot tell you how blessed I am when you praise Me in the darkness, in the midst of pain and suffering, in spite of the difficulties encountered and troubles endured.

Your commitment to love, your faithful pursuit of My presence, your abandonment to worship - even when your heart is breaking – is what feeds Me. Many who are my children worship and praise Me only when circumstances are good in their lives. When My people praise Me in the midst of crushing persecutions and brokenness, My heart is overwhelmed.

My heart is so pleased with you. When you look at yourself, you see your weaknesses and inabilities but I see you as a little lily, beautifully adorned, and sweetly singing your praises to Me. You are so handsome . . . so good looking . . . so desirous.

There are days when I know you feel alone and abandoned but I promise you that you are not alone. I am right here, feeding and nourishing you while I feed on Your love and worship. Furthermore, I call you to see My people as I see them: pure and spotless as the lily, fragile and weak, yet so very beautiful.

The devil lies to you and points out people's failures and imperfections. I call My people lilies because that is how I see them as reflections of the beauty I have placed in them. I long for you to see My people in that way, also. Look for My beauty in your brothers and sisters, even in those you consider to be exceedingly immature and imperfect.

---

[280] Psalm 22:3 Amplified

It is necessary that you see this because as long as you see only what the devil wants you to see, you can neither live in love nor be the blessing they need you to be. Because I want to use you greatly in ministry to the other lilies of my field, I invite you to come with Me today. Ask Me, and I will anoint your eyes and your heart to see as I see and feel as I feel.

My response
Forgive me, Lord, for my critical, censorious spirit. Cleanse my heart and open my eyes to see Your people as You see them; impart a measure of Your love for Your people to my heart so that I may be able to minister from a pure heart of love. If Your job is to feed Your beautiful lilies, then that's my job too! Just as You told Peter to feed Your sheep[281] You are calling me to feed Your sheep, Your people.

Help me do what You have called me to do. Help me to recognize that Your people also are beautiful lovers of God struggling to overcome sin. They are not sinners struggling to love God. Bring me with You today to the gardens; as You to feed among the lilies, take me with You.

He said
Begin with Me here in the garden where you are planted; you will see My lilies in a totally new way today. I'm going to teach you and train you to feed and nurture, tend and love My lilies in this garden. I may take you at a later time to other gardens but for now I want you here with Me.

When I do take you to other gardens, you will know You are going with Me, and you will not only view the garden as I do, you will feed and tend it as I do. This is what I require in all My ministers – nothing is done unless it is done with Me.

Many of My servants never comprehend this truth. They see ministry as their garden - *their* work, and they see *themselves working* with My help. They are successful to a degree because I bless My Word and I encourage My servants because I love them. I know they are trying so

[281] John 21:15-17

hard to please me. But I don't want you to labor *for* Me. I want you to labor *with* Me.

So many never recognize this vital difference but I think you are beginning to understand. I can do so much more for My people when they work *with* Me and allow Me to work *through* them.

The King's Expressions of Love To the Bride

Verse 4A

Thou art beautiful, O My love, as Tirzah…

My observations

The city of Tirzah whose name means "acceptable and pleasant" belonged to the tribe of Manasseh. Following the division of Solomon's kingdom it became the seat of the kings of Israel. Prior to that time it was a Canaanite city. It was a city of remarkable beauty, a place that lived up to its name.

He said

You, My daughter and My Bride, are remarkably beautiful within and without. It is written "The King's daughter is all glorious within",[282] and that is how I see you. You are loved and accepted, and I call you to stand alongside Me and to walk with Me today. I want to put even more of My beauty upon you. No city, however beautiful, can compare with you. You are to Me, My beautiful, delightful and incomparably gorgeous Bride!

You were once a city of Canaan, an unbeliever who knew not God but you are now conquered by My love and beautiful beyond compare. You are My love and My lovely one.

Verse 4B

… comely as Jerusalem.

My observations

Jerusalem was the city of God, the place where God dwelt, the city where the temple was built and where the ark of God's presence dwelt. David called it the residence of the King, therefore the most beautiful of all cities and the joy of the whole earth.[283]

---

[282] Psalm 45:13

[283] Psalm 48:2 and 87:2

He said
The company of those who have believed on Me is My Jerusalem. It is beautiful and the place where I love to dwell, the place where I am worshipped and loved. Your heart is My Jerusalem - My dwelling place - My home. My church is My beautiful Jerusalem, My home where I love to dwell.

The world will try to blame you, discredit you, persecute you and even destroy you but nothing can succeed in its concentrated effort to snuff out the light and life of My presence on the earth. Even the most magnificent temple in Jerusalem, built with stones, was destroyed because I could never contain My presence to a building made with human hands and restricted in one geographical location.

My city now is found wherever My people dwell. My temple is where My people worship Me in spirit and in truth. My presence is to be found corporately wherever My people gather together all over the earth. Truly My people are the joy of the whole earth; each group of believers is precious to Me, beauteous in My sight.

My city - My dwelling place - resides in the individual hearts of each one of My children. *Your heart is My home,* millions of "little Jerusalem's" around the world and all over the earth - each one is a glorious sight, a joy of the earth, and each, a residence of the King! I have put My glory upon My people, wrapped them in My glory. My presence is manifested in the earth because *the palace of your heart is filled with My presence.* The heart of each believer is a refuge for the oppressed simply because I dwell in your heart and I love and defend the poor.

My church is ordained to be a refuge for the broken hearted, the lame, the sick, the blind, because I dwell in My church to bring deliverance, to heal, to set people free. As My people come together to worship Me, My glory descends upon them, and the enemy has to flee, for *nothing* can stand before the presence of God. Even in her weaknesses, this is how I see My church and the ones I love.

When you worship Me you envelope yourself in My presence, and in so doing, you take on My beauty, enabling the world to see that I am your God forever and ever. I will be your God, your Guide even until death, and I have promised to be your God forever.

Verse 4C

...terrible as an army with banners.

My thoughts
An army is strong and fearful to behold. On earth, an army with banners is known as orderly and victorious. He says she is beautiful, comely (lovely) and terrible (awesome)! She has overcome the dark night of the soul, and she did not lose her faith or her love.

He said
O My love, you too have been tested and tried again and again, and each time you have come through the test with deeper faith and more love for Me. Do you know what that does to My heart when I see you wrestling with the powers of darkness and the enemies of your own soul as they attempt to drag you down and defeat you?

I said that My banner over you is love;[284] you have kept that banner and continued in love with Me and with My people. No matter what has attacked or confronted you, you have retained your standard.

Because you have walked in submission to My authority and to spiritual authorities over your life, you have been able to overthrow and destroy strongholds of the enemy in your own life and in the lives of others. You have also been enabled to help others overcome by breaking down the walls the enemy built to keep them from finding Me.[285]

You have not been corrupted or seduced or led away from your first love. You love Me more today than you have ever loved Me before.

You have overcome the world, the flesh and the devil because of the Strong One Who dwells within you. You have submitted to My love and to My life, and therefore you walk in My liberty.[286]

It is your faith, given by Me, that has enabled you to prevail over your enemies. You have "escaped the edge of the sword" by faith, you have been "made strong" over weakness and sickness by faith, and you've

[284] Song of Solomon 2:4
[285] 2 Corinthians 10:4-6
[286] 1 John 4:4

been "given great power in battle".[287] My help has enabled you to put entire armies to flight.[288]

This is how I see you, dear one. Your faith and your prayers are not weak or insignificant. My church may look insignificant to the world, but when you walk in love and in unity, under the banner of My love (under My authority), there is no demon on earth or in hell that can stand before you. You are glorious, victorious, an awesome army marching in the will and purposes of God, conquering the enemies without and within, and yet pursuing your first love. Yes, you are a Warrior–Bride, My victorious army.

Does this mean you will never struggle? No, My dear one but I see your struggles and your hand-to-hand combat at times with the enemy. I also have seen the way you have wrestled and wept and agonized in prayer. My son Jacob contended with Me, as well, weeping and wrestling because he sought My favor. It was there that I spoke to him, and was conquered by him.[289]

You too have conquered My heart, My Warrior–Bride. Never forget that you cannot successfully war in the spirit realm without first knowing and experiencing that bridal relationship with Me since nothing but My love will overcome the world. Not only that, it is impossible for you to consistently live in a bridal-love relationship without warring against the world, the flesh and the devil.

Thus you need to know that you are a Warrior - Bride, or perhaps in a better order, a Bride – Warrior. Not only do I take pride in you, you need to see yourself as I see you. You are not weak or a "nothing", you are strong, sturdy, glorious and a victorious warrior radically in love with the King of kings and Lord of lords. I see You as awesome, as My dear, dear Warrior - Bride, and you are protected and loved so dearly.

My response
O Jesus, I run into the arms of One who is wonderful, awesome, mighty, and oh, so powerful. I am strong because You have made me

---

[287] Hebrews 11:34
[288] Hebrews 11:34 Living Bible
[289] Genesis 32:28 and Hosea 12:3,4

so. I look into Your eyes and see how proud You are of me and my heart melts with love for You. My heart cries out to love You more truly and serve You more faithfully.

Thank You for calling me to capture Your heart. Overwhelmed with Your love and confidence in me, I long for that day when I will see You face to face. On that day I will fall down at Your feet in love and adoration but for now, I have no more words to tell You how much I love You.

Overcoming, glorious Lord
I bask in Your embrace
My heart, it aches to feel Your love
It longs to see Your face.

However long I walk this earth
My chief desire is this
To be Your lover, Warrior - Bride
To feel Your gentle kiss.

Abandoned to Your steadfast love
Submitted to Your cause
I love to find my life in You
To give You my applause.

Poetry written by Florli Nemeth

Verse 5A

Turn thine eyes away from Me, for they have overcome Me…

My observation
The king describes His love for the Bride, showing how her love has captured His heart.

He said
You have come through many tests and trials in your life, tenaciously clinging to Me when it seemed as though all hell had broken loose. It is as though you're out in the middle of the ocean, your boat has overturned, and you are literally hanging on for dear life while the waves continue to crash down upon you. Yet with a smile on your face, you look up to the sky through your tears and cry out to Me, knowing that I the One Who loves you, will never forsake you. You trust Me to come to your rescue.

There is nothing in earth or heaven that can stand against Me for I have created all that you see and cannot see. Yet, the one thing that never fails to move my heart is your love for Me, even when in the darkness you cannot see Me, even when in the storm you cannot feel Me, even when on the raging sea you cannot trace My paths.

You have sought Me, you have loved Me
You have spoken of My fame
You have trusted, you have rested
In the power of My name.

You have worshipped, you have fallen
At My feet and wept your tears
You have held Me, interceded,
You have conquered every fear.

You have labored in the darkness
When My face you could not see
You have kept on trusting in the storm
That I would come to thee.

With sight and sense and feelings gone
My way you could not trace
Yet love held on with strong design
Till faith revealed My face!

My heart is moved, I'm overwhelmed
Your love has captured Me
My cross - My crown, My Bride - My joy,
My Love eternally!

Poetry written by Florli Nemeth

My response

Lord, I stand in awe of You. You are so powerful, so majestic, and so strong - yet You cannot look at me without being totally overcome. I feel I will never understand the depth, the length, the height, the width of Your love. Yet Paul prayed that not only would I understand Your love, but that I would *experience* it along with *all* of Your people.[290]

[290] Ephesians 3:18, 19

Paul also stated that Your love surpasses knowledge without experience. To me this means we can't really know Your love apart from experiencing it. Your desire for Your people is that they be filled with all of Your fullness.

Fill me with Your love and Your life until I am totally flooded with God Himself. Your love, so great and wonderful, is inexhaustible, never ending. How great and awesome You are - even when Your face is turned away from me because You are overwhelmed with my love. I never knew You could be so touched by weak, broken people who love You!

Verse 5B

...thy hair is as a flock of goats that appear from Gilead.

My observations

The King spoke these words earlier,[291] and here the praise and commendations are repeated.[292] To me this is amazing. She must have needed to be reminded of His love for her and how he viewed her. Perhaps she needed to be reassured that no weakness or failure in her life will change the way He sees her or feels about her.

My prayer

O Lord Jesus, I've never realized how true this has been in my life. Over and over again, when I have failed You or failed myself, I have felt such strong recriminations, thinking that *now* You will feel differently about me - *now* You will chastise me - *now* you will throw me on the dump heap and I will become a broken vessel of no use to anyone!

NEVER have You done that for that would be contrary to Your nature. You have always picked me up, healed my heart, and shown me that You will never falter in Your love and commendations. *My* slips and altercations, sins and failures will never change the way You feel about me. I also know from my own experience that I so easily *forget* and need to be reminded again and again of Your love and of the beauty

---

[291] Song of Solomon 4:1& 2

[292] Song of Solomon 6:5-7

You see in me. O Jesus, You are such a faithful and wonderful Lover and Friend.

He said
My darling Bride, you comprehend rightly when you see Me as One who forgives and forgets your sins, your failures, your weaknesses and shortcomings. Throughout My Word I have proclaimed My faithfulness to you in that regard.[293]

Nothing you do or fail to do will ever change the way I look at you or alter the purposes I have for you; I want you to be reminded constantly of My love for you. I know how subtly the Enemy works to undermine My Word in your mind and heart. That is why I come to you today, again to remind you. I see your dedication to Me, your submission and your obedience. Now you have feasted of My love in My presence, you are totally consecrated to Me. As you spend time daily in My Word, you have been adorned with My love and grace. You are beautiful, dear one, and I love you dearly.

Verse 6

Thy teeth are as a flock of sheep which go up from the washing, whereof every one beareth twins, and there is not one barren among them.

My thoughts
Once again the Bride receives an almost identical commendation to those He gave earlier,[294] a reminder that the love of the King for His Bride is constant and unchanging. How often does she – do we need to be reassured? He knows our need to hear His words of love repeated again and again.

He said
Dear friend, I know you as one who meditates long and lovingly on My Word. Your spiritual teeth chew My Word daily as you come before Me and open your life to My Word. As you love My Word, you bring delight to My heart.

---

[293] 1 John 1:7-9/ Isaiah 44:22/ Psalm 103:3
[294] Song of Solomon 4:2

You are clean before Me because you are washed by My Word. I spoke that to My disciples, and I speak it again to your heart today. "You are cleansed and pruned already because of the Word which I have given you".[295]

You have allowed My Word to cleanse your mouth, brushing your teeth daily will give a clean, fresh, beautiful mouth. My Words in your mouth beautify you so that others around you are blessed and edified.

In My eyes you are a flock of ewes in pairs, or twins...a symbol of fruitfulness and of a double portion. You bear fruit in your life because you are connected to Me, the Vine.[296]

Because you are vitally connected to Me you bring forth *much* fruit. Yes, you are a fruitful vine as the result of having lived your life by My Word. Through Me your life has had a tremendous impact on others and will continue to do so. You may not always see the fruit of your life, but I see it, and I know. What blesses My heart so much is your adherence to the Word even in times of dryness when it seems nothing is happening. Be encouraged, dear one, to continue much in My Word since it is My Word that changes hearts. The words you speak come from your heart for out of the abundance of the heart the mouth speaks.

A heart full of the Word becomes a mouth filled with the Word, a mouth cleansed daily by the Word, fed daily by the Word, nourished daily by the Word.

My thoughts
I've got this humorous picture in my mind where on one occasion my mother took a bar of soap and washed out my mouth. I don't remember the bad words I must have spoken, but I do remember the unpleasant taste of the soap. The treatment was effective, though, because I don't remember Mother ever having to do that again.

My prayer
Lord, I invite You to do Your work of cleansing in my life. Your chastisements are not always pleasant (like the soap in the mouth), but

---

[295] John 15:3, Amplified
[296] John 15:5

they are profitable and beneficial to my growth in grace and in maturity. I thank You for Your Word, even when it brings correction in my life. I embrace Your Word, I hold it close to my heart, and I receive Your encouragement today. Thank You for making me fruitful and for making my words refreshing and edifying to others. Thank You for Your loving affirmations to my heart.

Verse 7

Your cheeks are like halves of a pomegranate behind your veil.

My observations

Here is the third repeated commendation showing me that the King never changes.[297] I am comforted by intimations of His love given in by-gone days. It shows me, too, that He knows my need to hear His affirmations of love over and over again.

This is a principle I see in the Word. For example, how many times are we told not to fear? I've not counted them myself, but I believe it's 366 times - one for every day, including leap year. So why didn't He just tell us once, "Fear not…", and leave it at that?

How often does a child need to hear the words, "I love you", or "I am proud of you"?

How many times does a wife or a husband need to express their love? Is it just one time at the altar where they vow to love 'til death parts them? Or does that need exist every day for the rest of their lives? I think that is what is happening here. Not only does He, the King, never change in His love and in His expressions of love, He also continues to imprint His love on my heart for the rest of my life. What an awesome God.

What He is saying to me -

As a pomegranate spews forth its sweetness when it is broken, your cheeks display your emotions and they are sweet to Me. Your love is so sweet to Me, My child. Your veil speaks of a life, a hidden life before Me, that loves to worship Me when no one else is near. Your love for

---

[297] Song of Solomon 4:3

Me is not just a "show" so others can see how spiritual you are. What you do in secret is so special to My heart!

If I were to summarize My words to you today I would say these things to you -

1. You are so very dedicated to Me and to My purposes in the earth
2. You live by the meat of My Word and are nurtured, cleansed, and comforted by it
3. And your love (your emotions) has grown and matured as you have embraced My Word, and you have been strengthened and encouraged by My Word.
4. You are so beautiful, My child!

My prayer
Lord Jesus, when You speak these words to me I long to fall before Your feet, weeping in worship. My heart cries out, "Holy, holy, holy is the Lord God Almighty" for You are worthy. I do not deserve commendations like these. I give You so little, express my love to You so seldom, and even what I do give is so small compared to what You are truly worth and what You truly deserve.

How can I say "Thanks" for *all* You do for me not only daily, but *many* times a day? My heart cannot help but respond in love to the One who is such a wonderful, faithful, understanding God.

I give myself to Your purposes in my life and in the world. I choose to live by every word that You have spoken in Your Word. I embrace You, the love of my life, even as I choose to live in Your love, the love that strengthens and encourages me day by day.

He said
Because you are Mine, I cover you with the mantle of My love. I *chose* you even before I made this world and you are Mine. My heart receives your expressions of dedication and love, and I promise to be with you until the very end of the age.[298]

---

[298] Matthew 28:20

My promise extends even to the age to come where My Bride will experience the consummation of My love and live in My home forever and ever. You are Mine for eternity. I love My Bride, the church, and I love you because you are My Bride. I look forward to that great wedding feast where the veil will be lifted and you will see Me clearly, know Me dearly, and live with Me forever.

My heart is overwhelmed with your love; I cannot refrain from speaking My desire over you. I bless you today, dear one, and I assure you of My faithfulness, My love, My everlasting strength. It is all yours today and every day of your life for you are loved by Me.[299]

Verse 8

There are sixty queens and eighty concubines, and virgins without number.

My thoughts
There are varying interpretations of this verse. James Durham suggests the daughters, virgins, queens and concubines are the same Bride - the church visible, for she is the mother that bears the daughters. [300]

It speaks also of the church invisible and the real believers who are members of that invisible church. The queens, concubines and virgins represent believers of different growth and degrees. And although there may be many believers of different growths and degrees of glory, there is but *one Bride.* In other words He is saying, My Bride is worth all the queens, concubines and virgins combined into one.

Father Juan G. Arintero[301] in his book, "*The Song of Songs*" agrees more or less with Durham's view.

---

[299] Lamentations 3:22,23

[300] "*The Song of Solomon*" by James Durham [Geneva Series of Commentaries published by The Banner of Truth Trust], page 346

[301] "*The Song of Songs*" by Father Juan G. Arintero, O.P. [the English edition first published by The Dominican Nuns, formerly of the Monastery of the Holy Name, Cincinnati, Ohio in 1974 and republished by Tan Books & Publishers, Inc. with their permission], pages 455, 456

Pastor Mike Bickle,[302] on the other hand, states that "this truth is set forth using the metaphor of a king's court without in any way suggesting an actual corresponding group in Heaven. This is meant… to emphasize that from the least to the greatest all in heaven are joyfully serving and esteeming the Bride that the Father elected for His Son's eternal inheritance."

I tend to feel that the most logical explanation of this verse is as Mike Bickle interprets it, a picture of the King's Court of queens, concubines and virgins symbolizing the heavenly court of angelic hosts - angels, archangels, seraphim, cherubim etc.

In this heavenly court Jesus is surrounded by a host of heavenly beings with different ranks and degrees of splendor, yet He says His Bride surpasses them all. It is suggested here that the heavenly beings that serve Jesus and the Bride are fully aware that this Bride has captured the heart of the King.

He said
I am surrounded by myriads of angels, all of different ranks and varying degrees of glory, but it is the church who has captured My heart. It is upon the church invisible and universal that I have bestowed My love. To human eyes it is a mystery that I am able to bind together in one body those who previously have been mortal enemies: Jews and Gentiles, bond and free, males and females. Once adversaries, they are presented to me as one Bride.[303]

In My love I gave Myself up for her in order to present her to Myself in glorious splendor, without spot or wrinkle, holy and faultless. I want you to know that I carefully nourish, protect and deeply cherish My church, My Bride.

Though I have many who serve Me faithfully, I seek for lovers above servants. Those who love Me truly, serve Me truly. Yet without that deep love relationship, service becomes tedious, absorbing all your faith and energies and leaving you empty and dry. Those who are *first lovers*

---

[302] Pastor Mike Bickle's study materials on the Song of Songs entitled "*The Ravished Heart of God*", Session 16

[303] Galatians 3:28/Colossians 3:11

and secondarily workers, find they are constantly nourished and rejuvenated by love. May this truth transform you into an intimate lover.

Verse 9A

My dove, My undefiled is but one . . . .
But My dove, My undefiled and perfect one, stands alone [above them all]... (Amplified)

My prayer
O Lord, You see Your church throughout the world as one body with many members, one house with many rooms, one garden with many beds of spices, and one building with many stones. And although there are many believers, we are one Bride!

Your church is glorious, unrivalled in Your affection. There is no need to compete for we are Your love, Your one and only inheritance, the unrivalled object of Your love. For this reason we, Your church, are the focus of Your love and the fulfillment of Your heartbeat. She is the only one You died for, the only one You live for.

He said
I could talk to you today about My church and how wonderful it is, but I come to you this morning to speak of My esteem for you.

I see you through My eyes. Where you see imperfections and flaws, My grace covers your humanity; where you question some of the ways in which I have directed you, My heart responds to your steadfast determination to honor Me through the fire. You have gone through the testing and you stand spotless and glorious in My love.

You have been assaulted by the enemy yet you have overcome all the strategies and attacks he has thrust against you. I see you standing in My love, clothed in My glorious dress and shouting My praises.

When you feel broken and distraught by the enemy's attacks against you, you fall down before Me and kiss My feet with your tears and worship. Do you know how that makes Me feel, My dove?

I say to you what you would never say of yourself, and I say what causes you to cringe when others say it of you. You are perfectly mature according to My design and purpose, and you are undefiled. You stand unrivalled in My affections. You alone are the one I have chosen to love forever.

As I speak to you like this I know you understand this is how I view My church corporately, but I want you to know it is also how I view you individually. This is a mystery and a paradox – hard to comprehend - yet a concept I want to impart to your understanding. As you declare this truth today, live in My love, revel in it and rejoice in it.

My prayer
I declare today what You have spoken over me. I declare I am not forsaken or alone. I am loved, chosen, a member of the Bride of Jesus Christ, given to Him by the Father.

I am not a pauper. I am rich and abundantly provided for.
I am not barren. I am fruitful, a mother in Israel with many children.
I am alone in Your affections, unrivaled by another.
I am the apple of Your eye, the chief among ten thousand, the only one that has captured Your love and affection!
I am covered with Your love. I am clothed in Your beautiful garments of righteousness.
I am empowered by Your grace, Your strength, Your joy, Your acceptance and Your love.
I am equipped by Your Word, by Your power, and by the glory of Your presence upon me.

And I am energized by Your life within me and by Your love that has totally captured my heart.
I declare that I am Yours forever. Nothing can ever separate me from Your love.
And I declare that Your purposes, Your will, Your design for me *shall be* totally fulfilled in my lifetime - here and now - on this earth where I walk and in the sphere of influence where I live.

O thank You, Jesus! You are awesome, You are great, and You are greatly to be praised.

Verse 9B

...she is the only one of her mother, she is the choice one of her that bare her . . . .

My thoughts

The Bible speaks of the church universal as "my mother" - the agency God uses to birth people into the kingdom of God.[304] Throughout history the church has been the mother of the redeemed. The favorite work of the church is bringing people to Jesus so they can become a part of the Bride.

He said

My church is My Bride, My favored one, My only love. In a corporate sense, My church throughout all of history and My church presently throughout all the world is My favorite one that I will love for eternity. Yet, *you* are My Bride - the one I have chosen to love. I have singled you out above all others, and My love is for you alone. You said of Me that I was the chief among ten thousand. I now commend *you*, and I say I love you above all others. I am satisfied with you alone. And yet . . . . I feel this way about each of My chosen ones.

The fact that I love each one in this way does not lessen my love for any individual. If nothing else, it should tell you that you are not inferior to anyone else or lacking anything that would draw Me to you. I love you alone as though you were indeed the only one, yet I love each one of My children in that same way.

I enable you to comprehend this love and acceptance today. You are not inferior in beauty or in giftings. You are totally awesome in your beauty and your love totally overwhelms me and satisfies My heart. *You* satisfy Me. *You* cause My heart to sing.

My prayer

Lord, please help comprehend this affirmation of Your love. It's just so difficult for my mind to grasp.

He said

I am speaking to your heart, *NOT* your mind. I want your heart to know that I love you alone, above all others, for time and for eternity.

---

[304] Galatians 4:26

And you are *not* inferior in beauty or in giftings. You tend to look at others and see why I would love them more than you and use them more than you, because you have a view of yourself as inferior to others. I'm telling you this is *NOT* so, for I see in you exceptional gifts and qualities that have endeared you to My heart over many years. I want you to quit looking at others and comparing yourself to them. I want you to know and understand the deep value I have placed in you and the untold beauty I see in you.

There is no other human being in all the earth quite like you. As My chosen Bride, you are My spouse for all eternity. Please do not turn My love away and say it cannot be so; I would never lie to you. Ask My Spirit to open your eyes to see yourself as I see you. Please receive these commendations and affirmations to your heart. I don't want a Bride who is constantly looking at others, demeaning herself, while hiding herself because she feels she is ugly and not good enough!

It's time for you to lay down the insecurities that so easily beset you and embrace My thoughts of you. To Me you are stunningly beautiful, inferior to none. I would not choose to love a loser. You are gifted, beautiful and totally loved and accepted by Me. Once again I call you to believe My words and to walk in them.

My response
Lord, I am beginning to see. As I lay aside my old way of thinking about myself, forgive me for not hearing Your heart.

I accept Your Word that declares my beauty through You, acknowledge the love bestowed upon me and believe that in You I am beautiful. By Your grace I assert that I am NOT inferior but rather, I am fearfully and wonderfully made and gifted with every spiritual blessing in high places. By grace I have been endowed with wonderful spiritual gifts that You desire for me to open and use.

I declare I am the chief desire of Your heart, Your one and only lover and friend. I am seated with You in heavenly places, clothed in Your beauty and covered with Your love. Having declared those truths, my heart rejoices even as it declares: Jesus, I am in love with You!

Verse 9C

...The daughters saw her and blessed her, yea, the queens and the concubines, and they praised her.

My thoughts

In the middle of His commendations, the King brings in the daughters, the younger, more immature ones who are growing in their relationship with the Bridegroom, and the older, more mature ones, for their estimation of the Bride.

They both express their great esteem for the Bride and now they further bless her and are delighted to add their praises to the King's.

Whatever others may have thought of the Bride, whatever the Bride may have thought of herself - the reality is, she was lovely inside and out, and those close to her saw this beauty in her and blessed and praised her.

My prayer

Lord, I believe You take note of the thoughts and words of Your people. You know what others think of Your servants and You record those thoughts and words. Since You do this, then it behooves me to think and speak of them in a way that is kind, loving, encouraging and positive.

I have been blessed when others have praised me or expressed their esteem and appreciation. I think most people are like me. We see our own weaknesses and blemishes, and even though we may know how You feel about us, it lifts our hearts to hear words of commendation, especially from those we highly respect and esteem in the body of Christ.

Many, even of Your servants, struggle with low self-esteem and feelings of inferiority. It's not that we depend on others' commendations for our security in You, Lord, but at the same time there are occasions where it is right and proper to give honor where honor and esteem is due.[305] Indeed, we are commanded to do so.[306] Help me, Jesus, to look for ways

[305] Romans 12:10

[306] Romans 13:7

to honor and bless people, especially those in places of ministry. I want to be a blessing to Your people, and I choose today to think and speak good things over them.

He said
I am delighted when you join with Me in My purposes and plans. It is in My heart to bless My people, and I want to do it through you! Be *generous in your praise* and encouragement of those in ministry, and be *stingy in your criticism.*

So many of My people are just the opposite: stingy in praise and generous in criticism. And it hurts My heart deeply to see My servants beaten down, not by the enemy, but by the very people to whom they show love. It is never wrong or out of order to show appreciation and thankfulness and to express encouragement and praise. It is imperative that My people learn this.

My church is coming into a day and a season where I will no longer tolerate unjust criticism and bad mouthing and putting down of My servants. I call you, My church, to accountability. You are responsible to Me for what you think and speak regarding My servants. This includes your pastors, your elders, your teachers, your parents and others who are over you in the Lord. I will deal very strongly with those who choose to ignore or disobey this warning.[307]

People function best in an environment of positive reinforcement and encouragement. You see it in families where children thrive under well-ordered discipline and in a positive environment and outlook on life. Relationships are built on love and trust and grow where there is the right amount of positive affirmation, encouragement and feedback.

Dear one, you know all these things and are walking in them. Be encouraged to continue in the things you have seen in Me and learned from Me. Speak well of My servants, speak well of My Bride, the church. *Look for Me* in My Bride and you'll be overwhelmed with her beauty even as I am.

---

[307] 1 Timothy 5:17

The Bride Is Compared to Four Objects

Verse 10A

Who is this that looketh forth as the morning, fair as the moon, clear as the sun, and terrible as an army with banners?

Comments

The Bride is here compared to four objects in a manner similar to the way in which she was compared to earthly cities.[308] Here the Holy Spirit asks, "Who *IS* she?"

My thoughts and prayer

You see me as one who shines forth like the dawn of the morning which "gives way to morning splendor"[309] Like the unfolding of the day, so You see the small steps of obedience and growth in the process that leads to my maturity. The light is overcoming the darkness.

Your path before me is full of hope and expectation. You lead me from glory to glory, from light to more light, until the day I see You face to face. It is there I will see You in Your glory, in the fullness of Your splendor reigning in the brightness of Your Throne forever and ever. You see no darkness in me. You are light, and because I walk in Your light, I have unbroken fellowship with You. O Jesus, I love walking in light with You. I love living in the light of Your presence.

He said

It is I who dawn on you like the morning light when the sun rises on a cloudless morning. Because I dawn on you, you are the light of the world around you. Your light cannot be hid. Everyone who comes near you is illumined by your light. Yes, you shine out as a bright light that keeps "shining ever brighter till the full light of day."[310]

The darkness in you is being dispelled little by little. You are being changed from glory to glory until that day you see Me face to face and you are pure light even as the sun shines in the brightness of her

---

[308] Song of Solomon 6:4

[309] Proverbs 4:18 Living Bible

[310] Proverbs 4:18, NIV

noonday glory. The Spirit of God is at work within you even today, and little by little you are becoming more like Me - more light - more glory.[311]

Verse 10B

...fair as the moon...

He said
You are like the moon on a dark night. It is beautiful, inspiring, attractive and bright because it mirrors the sun. I made the moon to give light at night, a light in the darkened heavens. Sailors navigate by the light of the moon. You are in a fallen world darkened by sin. The light in you is not your own, it is what I have placed in you. "Christ in you the hope of glory." [312] The glorious One, the Light of the world is in you. Like Mary, you sit in My presence having chosen the good portion which shall not be taken away from you. [313]

My thoughts
Though a dim reflection of the sun, the moon reveals the glory of the sun as it mirrors its light.

My prayer
Lord, I'm not getting it this morning; the "dots" are not connecting. Please come to me and speak to my heart. I need You, Lord, as I sit at Your feet today, ready to absorb Your light.

He said
Dear one, you are fair as the moon. By simply reflecting the glory of the sun it fulfills its appointed task as the light in the night; it has no light of its own. It neither attempts to be the sun, nor to fulfill its task on its own. Your life is like that, dear one. My people are like the moon in need of spending much time with Me in order to reflect My beauty and glory in the earth. You cannot be the light I've called you to be without spending time with Me.

[311] 2 Samuel 23:4/Matthew 5:14/Philippians 2:15/2 Corinthians 3:18
[312] Colossians 1:27
[313] Luke 10:42, Amplified

There is nothing more important in your life than the time you spend in My presence. As you absorb My life and strength, joy and beauty, love and hope, people will know you have been with Me; as you go out into the darkened, fallen world shining with My light and glory upon you, those around you will be attracted to that beauty. You are fair. You are Lovely. You are a beautiful moon that says to all the world, "God is love, God is light, God is good". Shine today, My lovely one. Let your light shine so people will see your good deeds and glorify your Father who is in heaven. No darkness of the night can put out your light for the darker the night, the more clearly shines the light.[314]

Verse 10C

...terrible as an army with banners

My thoughts
The word "terrible" in the Hebrew is from a word meaning frightful or to frighten. It is used earlier to depict an army with banners, a victorious, conquering army, terrifying to its enemies.[315]

This is how the Holy Spirit sees the people of God and me in particular. I am *NOT* a defeated, depressed, helpless victim. God's Word says I am more than a conqueror, and I am victorious over ALL the work of the enemy. I am a *Victor* - not a *Victim*.

Furthermore, His Word says that no weapon formed against me will prosper. [316]

Whatever is born of God is victorious over the world, and it is our faith that conquers the world.[317]

"Christ leads us in triumph [as trophies of Christ's victory] and through us spreads and makes evident the fragrance of the knowledge of God everywhere." [318]

[314] Matthew 5:16
[315] Song of Solomon 6:4
[316] Isaiah 54:17 and 1 Corinthians 15:57
[317] 1 John 5:4
[318] 2 Corinthians 2:14 Amplified

He said
I lead you in triumph over every work of the enemy. When submitted to Me, My people are invincible. In fact, the demons in hell tremble when they hear the weakest of My saints speaking My Word and My name. I have said that the very gates of hell cannot overpower or hold out against My church because it is a glorious, victorious army that I am leading to victory from glory to glory.

You are a part of that victorious army. I see you as one who overcomes every obstacle, conquers every difficulty in your path, and takes authority over every enemy or force that would come against you.

Because of your union with Me, you are totally victorious. Because I live, you shall live and live as an overcomer. Go in My strength today because since I overcame the world, you too can overcome in every circumstance of life. I have deprived the world of its power to harm you. Because I live within you, you have already defeated every work of the enemy. I am the Greater One - the Victorious One - the Conquering One, and I lead you in triumph today and every day.[319]

This is how each member of My church needs to see itself - a conquering army that is growing daily in numbers and in strength. Not only does My army cover the whole earth, it marches in victory today. It may not look like an army to those who do not know Me, but it is a glorious, victorious, triumphant army following in My footsteps and conquering every foe.

[319] John 16:33/1 John 4:4/2 Corinthians 2:14

The Bride's Garden Becomes The King's Garden

Verse 11A

I went down into the garden….

My thoughts

In separate references the garden is called "her" garden [320] and "His" garden. [321] Here we see that her garden becomes His garden.

In one passage [322] the garden is described as having pleasant fruits; she invites her Beloved to come into His garden, to take possession of it and make it His own. In response we see that He actually comes into the garden for the first time and finds there myrrh, spices, honeycomb, wine (vineyards) and milk (animals). [323] Next she says that her Beloved has gone down to His garden and describes it as containing beds of spices and lilies.[324]

Following His visit [325] we see that she now enters the garden of nuts and finds that it contains budding vines and budding pomegranates. The Bride invites her Beloved to go with her and describes the garden as having blooming vineyards and pomegranates. [326] Finally, we see that the Bride is living and interceding in the gardens. [327]

My prayer

Lord Jesus, You have done so much for me, and now I see Your heart is in Your garden where Your loved ones grow. Some plants are new and just budding, other plants are mature and bearing much fruit. A few plants are in need of attention if they are to become more fruitful.[328]

---

[320] Song of Solomon 4:12,15,16
[321] Song of Solomon 4:16, 5:1, 6:2 and 11
[322] Song of Solomon 4:16
[323] Song of Solomon 5:1
[324] Song of Solomon 6:2
[325] Song of Solomon 6:11
[326] Song of Solomon 7:11,12
[327] Song of Solomon 8:1,2
[328] John 15:1-8

I, too, want to be where You are, to be involved in the work You are involved in and committed to You and Your work. It is that commitment that brings me to the garden where I can meet You there and to partner with You in what You are doing.

I used to think that ministry was doing what I saw needed to be done and asking You to help me. Now I see ministry is being where You are, going where You go, and partnering with You in what You are doing. It is to this that I commit myself.

He said
Come, My fair one, My love, My daughter, My friend! How I have longed for this day where you would join Me in My love for the gardens. Take My hand, come with Me, let Me show you what a beautiful garden is Mine, and let Me share with you what needs to be done here.

In the garden of My Love
    There is a place for me
He calls me to His side and says,
    Come - let Me help you see.
My garden needs a helping hand
    The vineyards budding here
Will bear much fruit if pruned aright
    And watered with your tears.
I'll show you what My garden needs
    And give a full supply
You only need to take and give
    And leave the rest to Me.

Poetry written by Florli Nemeth

Verse 11B

I went down into the garden of nuts to see the fruits of the valley, and to see whether the vine flourished, and the pomegranates budded.

My prayer
Lord, You take special note of the Church, Your garden, and of every individual believer. Like the plants growing there, some believers are flourishing and fruitful in their ministries and could easily intimidate me, but I long to visit them, learn from them and be influenced by them.

Other believers are young, immature plants in Your garden, some are even sickly. It can be depressing or discouraging for me to be around these, but never for You. You would water these plants with Your own hands and nurture them to life and health and strength and to maturity.

I see *You* doing this, and I long to be like You, to minister with the love and grace I see in you. O Jesus, I long to see Your church in other places, to be connected to Your whole church, not just my sphere of influence and ministry. Open my eyes to see what Your garden is producing all over the earth.

He said
My dear one, I have embraced and nurtured you from your earliest days. Now I will take you to other gardens that are not yours. And I will use you to embrace and nurture others. You will not despise the young and immature, but you will love and encourage them and nurture them to life. Nor will you be intimidated any longer by those who have gone beyond you and are strong and mature. But rather, you will glean from them and allow yourself to be encouraged by them, even those who may be younger than you.

I have given you eyes to see the maturity and strength that lies in some of My young ones; in seeing them you will be blessed by them.

My response
Lord, I commit myself to the care of Your garden - to work in Your vineyard - to do what I see You doing.

He said
I have called you, chosen you, equipped you and filled you with My Spirit. Go in My name. Visit any part of My garden as you wish. You have full permission. I have called you not only to intercede for My church where you live, but to go to My church in many parts of the world with your prayers and encouragements.

You are an encourager like Barnabas. You will comfort and encourage many people in your latter years. I have called many into a more visible ministry in their latter years. Corrie ten Boom was one who ministered to My church way up into her eighties until I called her home. I know it looks impossible to you because your heart is saying, "How can this be?"

I'm going to send you to My gardens, and you will go with a message of strength and encouragement. I will put My words in your mouth and you will speak what I give you.

How will this happen? Even as I have prepared you, I will open the doors for you and make a way. You need to prepare yourself by being much with Me in prayer and in the Word. When the time is right, I will thrust you forth, and all the finances you need will be available to you. It will be a sudden, dramatic and possibly traumatic thing in your life because I know if you were to plan it yourself, it would never happen.

So don't be surprised when I open the door and like a strong wind, disperse you to the nations of the earth. It *will* come, and suddenly, quickly, unexpectedly you'll find yourself catapulted into other gardens.

When that happens, I will remind you of this conversation, and your heart will so rejoice. I have so many beautiful gardens all over the earth, and they all need My tender loving care. In the meantime, take care of My garden here, My Bride, My partner in ministry. I love you so deeply!

The Bride's Call to Serve in the Garden

Verse 12

Or ever I was aware, my soul made me like the chariots of Ammi-nadib.

My understanding of this scripture -
Before she is even aware of what is happening, her heart is enlarged for other parts of the Body of Christ. Her heart is suddenly reaching out to believers of other places or cultures, believers who do things differently or who still are immature.

My prayer
God, I find myself all of a sudden being drawn to others' ministries. You have put within me and other of Your servants, a mother's or a father's heart. That kind of heart sees beyond the immaturities and disturbances that young ministers sometimes make.

You are calling me to open my heart to these ministries, not to judge, criticize or evaluate them, but to encourage, serve and embrace them. Lord Jesus, expand my heart further so that I may fulfill Your calling to serve Your people.

He said
Yes, My child, I have called you to care for others and to cultivate My garden. You are experiencing the love I have for My church, My garden. Your desire to serve others there is the fruit of My filling your heart with love for others who are included in My Bride. You are called to strengthen My church, to love it with the kind of mother's love that looks beyond imperfections and immaturities, and sees what no one else can see: potential, possibility, preciousness and perseverance.

Your heart is moving swiftly toward My people - *suddenly, swiftly, secretly* in love not only with Me, but with My church. I have made you an awesome mother and you and your ministry are so needed. There are so few mothers and fathers in the kingdom who truly care for the needs of others *selflessly and fearlessly and tenaciously*. The devil lies to you and tells you you're getting old, you're not needed, your ideas are old-fashioned. In My name, refute these lies.

There is ever the need for those who will encourage and bless younger ministries. You are not called to change them or their ideas but to support, to pray, to encourage, to see what I see in their lives and most of all, just to love.

Isn't that what wise parents do? They affirm, confirm and support their children. That's what I'm calling you to do within your sphere of influence in the Body. Because I am filling your heart with My love from now on you will see things differently. You'll see the heart of My young ministers and you will be drawn to them in a supernatural way.

Verse 13A

Return, return, O Shulamite: return, return, that we may look upon thee…

My prayer
O Lord, You have put Your name upon me, even as the Shulamite bore Solomon's name. You have inscribed Your name on my forehead! I bear Your name wherever I go.[329]

Sometimes we are reviled and spoken evil against because we bear Your name but those who truly love You will, like the daughters of Jerusalem, truly love the Bride who bears Your name and want to be reunited with them.

He said
My name is upon you because you are married to Me and as such you share in all the benefits of this marriage union. Wherever you go, you bear My name.

Some will hate you because of My name upon you, and they will ridicule and persecute you. But others will love you because of My name and they will call you to return again and again.

Do not be discouraged when you are slighted or overlooked or even openly persecuted because of My name. Nor must you become proud when those who love Me recognize the beauty I've put within you and call you to return to them. Keep your spirit humble and dependent upon Me.

---

[329] Revelation 3:12/Revelation 14:1/1 Peter 4:14

There is also a sense in which I am calling you to return to our secret place where I may look upon your face and hear your voice before I send you forth into the gardens to look after that which is dear to My heart, the garden I love.

Remember, though, the call is always for you to return to Me, to return to that secret, intimate place where under the apple tree I may refresh you with My love. You will never be sent out to labor in the garden even for short periods of time without hearing My voice calling you to return to that place of intimate waiting upon Me.

No matter how far you travel in ministry, the call is *always* to return to intimacy. No matter how much you have to give, you will always need to return to receive more for yourself and for others. Furthermore, unless you regularly return to receive for yourself, you will eventually have nothing to give others.

My prayer

> I will pay my vows day by day
> I will praise Your name day by day
> I will come into Your courts with praise
> I will celebrate Your love each day
> I will run into Your presence here
> I will run into Your arms of love.

You call me by Your name, and You have placed Your Spirit upon me. I am Yours, and Yours forever - Yours alone! There is no place I'd rather be than in Your presence, before Your Throne.

> I bow me down, I bathe my soul, I adore You, O my God.
> I bless the One who made me whole, I adore You, O my God.
> I shed my tears, I bare my soul, I adore You, O my God.
> I worship You, I bless Your name, I adore You, O my God!

In earlier days I called *You* to return to me, but now it is You calling *me* to return.[330]

[330] Song of Solomon 2:17

In returning there is rest and strength. In returning to Zion there is joy and gladness.[331]

In returning there is love, mercy, pity and pardon.[332]

In returning there is intimate relationship.[333]

In returning there is healing.[334]

In returning there is quiet and safety and anointing to minister.[335]

I could go on and on in pursuits of every kind, but the best choice is to return every morning to the Shepherd and Bishop of my soul, my heavenly Husband who longs to see my face and hear my voice. O, how I love You, Jesus!

Verse 13B

What will ye see in the Shulamite? As it were a company of two armies.

My thoughts
There is some difference of opinion here as to who is speaking and as to the interpretation of the same. Some commentaries skip over this part of the verse without so much as mentioning it. I want for this purpose and at this time to interpret the question as coming from the Bride - the Shulamite - and the response as coming from the daughters of Jerusalem.

My prayer
Lord, sometimes it is difficult to know how to interpret some things in this love song of Solomon and the Bride. This is one of the statements that has caused some difference of opinion. However, I do identify with the question spoken by the Shulamite, "What do You see in *me*?"

---

[331] Isaiah 30:15/Isaiah 35:10 and 51:11
[332] Isaiah 55:7
[333] Jeremiah 3:14,15
[334] Jeremiah 3:22
[335] Jeremiah 15:19 Amplified

I feel that way when others compliment me or affirm me in my ministry. I feel that way after You speak so lovingly to me with such wonderful affirmations. I see my own weaknesses and failings, my immaturities and inconsistencies, and I ask, "What do *You* see in *me*?"

And when others compliment me I often ask myself, "How can I possibly fit that description? If you knew me better, You might not say that about me."

Lord, You knew Jacob too, yet You came to him and changed his name from Jacob to Israel because he prevailed with man and with God. You saw something in Jacob that he did not see in himself.[336]

Lord, You see things in me I cannot see in myself. Thank You. You see me as blessed and You see me not just as one army, but as two.

He said
Your beauty is twice as great as what has already been spoken over you by Myself and by the daughters of Jerusalem. Your effectiveness and your impact on others is doubled because I've anointed you with a double portion of My Spirit. Jacob got the double portion blessing by his conniving, but I have *given* you My double portion blessing by grace alone.

You excel even the angels in your ability to take hold of My heart and because of that you are blessed with a double portion of My love.

[336] Genesis 32:24-28

Chapter 7

The Daughters of Jerusalem Affirm the Bride

Verse 1A

How beautiful are thy feet with shoes…

My thoughts

Again, I find a variance in opinions as to who is speaking here: is it the daughters, or the spouse? I think the daughters are expressing their affirmations. Earlier the Bride gave Jesus ten affirmations;[337] now God has raised up a people to give her (the Bride) ten affirmations of her own.

The daughters first see her feet, a symbol of her success in evangelism, borne of her fearlessness in going wherever God called her to go. Her ministry was bearing fruit in the lives of others because she did not shy away from going into difficult places and situations. Nor did she go unshod but rather her feet were protected within sandals or shoes –a picture of her preparation for ministry and of her sure-supply for every need. In every way she was well furnished unto every good work.

He said

This is what My church, My daughters see in you. They see that you have prepared yourself to minister to them and they are delighted to see you. They look at you and see My abundant provision in your life,

[337] Song of Solomon 5: 10-16

and they are blessed and challenged by that. They are encouraged to believe Me as you have.

It brings Me great joy, dear one, when others see My beauty in you. Be encouraged to go wherever I call you, because I will give you every place on which the sole of your foot treads.[338] This was the promise I gave Joshua, and it's the promise I give you today. I will lead you to the "daughters" that need your ministry. You can trust Me to direct you and to prepare you for the people to whom I bring you. I make no mistakes.

I, too, think your feet are beautiful, My chosen one. Why? Because you have chosen to walk in My ways and to do My will. Because you are obedient and ready to go wherever I call you, I will bless you. Because you are willing to minister in places that are not familiar, I will minister to you with My own encouragement, provision and anointing.

Verse 1B

. . . O prince's daughter . . .
. . . O queenly Maiden . . . (Amplified)

My thoughts
The daughters see my kingly lineage and speak of my royalty. They say I am a daughter of royalty. They say my character within is beautiful.

He says
Daughter, you are beautiful within because I have bestowed My character upon you. You are beautiful both within and without because of what I have put upon you. I have clothed you with My beauty, My love and with My righteousness. As My own purchased possession I have called you out of darkness into light. In Me you are holy and pure.[339]

When I became your Father I gave you a new bloodline, a royal bloodline. That's why you can share with My sons and daughters their freedom. I have set them free from the bondage of sin. They are no longer slaves to their addictions; they are the sons and daughters of the

[338] Joshua 1:3
[339] Psalm 45:13/Revelation 19:7 & 8/Isaiah 61:10/1 Peter 2:9

King. In Me they are rich, lovely, and clothed in the choicest garments of salvation and the robe of righteousness.

Dear one, I am your inheritance and by that I have become everything you need and everything you have ever wanted. Don't look at your mistakes or your failures, they will always be present in your earthly life and they will always be there to discourage you. It is not My will that your eyes should be filled with tears of regret because there is no place for regrets in your life. I covered your sins under My blood and they are totally gone and forgotten. Not only that but I have overruled and turned around for good the mistakes that you have made.

You are where I've always wanted you - *at My feet in worship.* Nothing else really matters. I did not have an iron-clad plan for your life that if you missed, you would miss My will totally. That is rigid, unrealistic and totally legalistic thinking. I'm not a God in heaven dictating what you must do as if you were a robot of some kind. I allow My children the freedom to choose where you will live, whom you will marry, and how you will serve in My kingdom. You serve Me out of love, not out of the need to fulfill a set of rigid requirements in your life.

It is the joy and love in your life that brings Me joy and fulfillment. Don't let regret or feelings of sadness or depression fill your heart. My daughters will attest to your beauty.

You are in the center of My perfect will for your life, and you will always be My first love.

> Daughter, you are My first love, A daughter in My kingdom
> Clothed in garments pure and white, Most lovely without and within.
>
> There is no spot in you, You're perfect in My love
> O Child - I am amazed at you, Your beauty dazzles Me!
>
> My heart is love - your truest home, Your place of rest and peace
> My arms forever opened wide for you to come and hide.
>
> I hold you close, I whisper words of affirmation, love and peace
> I'll hold you close, forever held in arms of sweet release.

There's nothing that you face in life that you will face alone
For I am with you to the death, I am your Rock - your Stone!

So dear one, once again come close and lay your head right here
I shelter and protect and shield the ones I love so dear.

You're covered with My feathers, You're clothed in righteousness
You stand before My Throne in love, My bride in glorious dress.

My heart, it leaps, it dances too when you come near to Me
I sing this song of love to you, Your love is all I see!
Poetry written by Florli Nemeth

Verse 1C

...the joints of thy thighs are like jewels, the work of the hands of a cunning workman.
...the work of a master hand. (Amplified)

My thoughts
The daughters are commenting on her walk. They see her as strong and beautiful in her walk with the Lord. They see that it is God Himself who has strengthened and beautified her life. As Paul said in Ephesians 2:10, *"we are God's own handiwork (His workmanship) recreated in Christ Jesus [born anew] that we may do those good works which God predestined (planned beforehand) for us [taking paths which He prepared ahead of time] that we should walk in them."* (*Amplified*)

My prayer
Lord Jesus, You are a very skilled workman, a "master hand" and Master Designer of my life. Anything that others see in my life is there because You have placed it there, and You have made me beautiful. I am Your design and Your creation and Your workmanship

I didn't just "happen" to be who I am - You designed my life and prepared paths for me to walk in. I relate to another of Your servants, Bill Gothard, when He said, "Please be patient with me because God is not finished with me yet." Thank You, Lord and help me remember that I am Your creation, a work in progress; crafted according to Your design.

He said

Yes, dear one, you are the result of My workmanship, one among many of My own. Each one of My sons and daughters is a unique work of My hands and what I have formed is marked with strength and beauty. Sadly, though, there are times when My creations are marred or spoiled because of pride or rebellion or resistance to the hand of the Master Potter.[340] There was a time in your life when you, too, were in that state. During those times I wept for the loss to Myself and for the pain and loss you were to experience.

I never give up on the clay in My hands, though, and in My grace I made you another vessel, reworking the clay of your life *with My very own hands.* It is My intervention that brought you to the place where you are beautifully adorned, beautifully strong, beautifully designed to My perfection. Nothing but My beauty in you has made you thus.

"But this precious treasure - this light and power that now shine within us - is held in a perishable container, that is, in our weak bodies. Everyone can see that the glorious power within must be from God and is not our own."[341]

Because you are the work of My hand and I do not abandon My work, you will always be in My hand. I delight in you and take good care of you; you in turn, bring Me delight. I am pleased with what I have made of you – a perfectly designed and fitted vessel for My service.

My response

Others may see me and comment on my strength and beauty, but You and I both know that I am merely clay in Your hand. I am frail and weak, easily marred or broken but I rest in the knowledge that I am *in Your hands.* I am secure in the place of safety and design, for You are not yet finished with me.

Your hands are not only a place of security, though, for I have found that blessed place of yieldedness to Your will and to Your design; there is no other place that I would rather be. Continue Your work in me, my Father, as I yield myself totally to You and to Your purposeful design.

---

340 Isaiah 29:16 and 64:8/Jeremiah 18:1-6

341 2 Corinthians 4:7, Living Bible

Make me a blessing to Your church. I live only for You and for Your purposes in me.

Verse 2A

Your body is like a round goblet in which no mixed wine is wanting. (Amplified)
Your navel is lovely as a goblet filled with wine. (Living Bible)

Fear the Lord and depart from evil. It shall be health to thy navel and marrow to thy bones.[342]

When you were born, no one cared for you. When I first saw you your umbilical cord (navel) was uncut, and you had been neither washed nor rubbed with salt nor clothed. No one had the slightest interest in you. No one pitied you or cared for you.
On that day when you were born, you were dumped out into a field and left to die, unwanted [343].

My thoughts
The daughters are saying here that in contrast to a mother who abandons her own child and refuses even to cut the cord that made them one, this maiden's inner life is healthy and strong. Because she cares deeply for the ones she has brought to birth, she nurtures her inner life so that it is healthy. Her relationship with God is deep. She is balanced and well-nourished, making her well able to nourish others in their formative years – just as she is nourished by God.

He said
The early stages of one's life are so important both in the physical and in the spiritual. A well-balanced woman would never discard her own flesh and blood but rather care for her child, nourish and nurture it, providing a source of love and protection for her child. The daughters see you as such and they respond to your ministry because you love them.

In your calling as a mother in Israel you will need to love and nurture those who are yet unwashed and unclothed because they have been abandoned by the enemy. Their sin has left them distraught, deprived, depressed, delinquent and alone. Some of them have been thrown out

---

[342] Proverbs 3:7 & 8
[343] Ezekiel 16:4 & 5 Living Bible

on the dump heap of life with not a hope in their world. But every one of these left to die is deeply loved by Me, and in Me, each has a hope and a future.

This is the ministry to which I am calling My body – both reaching out to care for the abandoned, the hopeless, the dying and providing love and nurture and nourishment for these dear ones. I'm calling you to carry these on your heart and to love them to life. The enemy comes to kill, steal and destroy; I come to give life and hope and a future.

Will you partner with Me? You have so much to give because you are spiritually healthy and strong and well nourished by Me. Be on guard that you do not yield to the lies of the enemy who would say you have nothing to give. It is true you have not experienced the abandonment these have, but you have experienced My love and My provision, and that is what they need you to share.

My response
I'm Yours, Lord, be it unto me as You have spoken. Let me be a source of love and encouragement to others. Empower me to be the "mother" you have called me to be in Your house. Help me to remember that what I eat is important because it will affect those I nourish. What I do has implications that are far reaching.

Lord Jesus, I just want to be a passionate lover of God with an insatiable hunger for Your life-giving Word. I want to have a healthy inner life so I can minister health and life to others. Thank You for Your love over me. I yield myself to You.

Verse 2B

...thy belly is like a heap of wheat set about with lilies.
...your waist is a heap of wheat set about with lilies. (Living Bible)

My thoughts
The word for "belly" in the Hebrew is "womb". The daughters see the bride pregnant with a harvest - a *huge* harvest. She is on the brink of delivering this harvest, and it promises to be a good harvest, set about with lilies - surrounded with many truly transformed lives.

He is saying to His Bride corporately -

I see My church this way: My Bride is My church universal, the Church worldwide and she is about to give birth to the greatest harvest this world has ever seen. It will be a harvest of wheat, not weeds or tares. Many transformed lives will be as pure lilies in My kingdom. Contrary to what many pessimistic, antagonistic, and sarcastic people may be saying about the church being lethargic and full of division and problems, it is bursting at the seams, gloriously pregnant with the harvest I have long promised and foretold.

My church WILL fulfill its destiny in this world; it will conquer, will overcome, will be a light on a hill, and will prevail against the very gates of hell. My church will cover the whole earth, and My church will be ONE, even as I have prayed it would be. My church is facing its finest day in history. My church has a glorious future. My church is the only pure and beautiful thing to be found in this world.

He is saying to His Bride individually -
You, too, are pregnant with the dreams and visions I have placed in your heart, about to give birth to a harvest of good things in your life. These things will bless My church and hasten the harvest. You will continue to carry these dreams and visions until the time is right.

Do not be overly concerned with the timing. I am the One who brings to birth, and since I am the One who planted these dreams in you, I will bring them to birth for you. Your work is to continue to nurture and protect the visions I have conceived within you. The timing of their birth will be perfect - totally in line and in step with My will and purpose for your life.

Verse 3

Thy two breasts are like two young roes that are twins.

My thoughts
Not only did her Lover compliment her,[344] now the daughters are also commending her for not only is the maiden a beautiful bride, she is also a fruitful mother who nourishes and nurtures her children. Not only is she able to birth a harvest as we just saw but she is prepared to nurture

[344] Song of Solomon 4:5

the harvest. The "twins" speaks of her double-portion anointing and ability to nurture.

He said
The daughters see this in you. Not only have they been built up and edified by your life and ministry, your faithfulness has not gone unnoticed by Me. You have taken what I gave you and doubled it by using your gifts to bless others. Therefore, I will give you even more.

As long as you join with Me in ministering to the daughters and to the harvest, I will anoint you and strengthen you and fill you to overflowing. You will find that to nurture and build up others is easy when it is done out of the overflow of the way I love and care for and nurture you.

My promise is that My people would bear fruit even to their old age. So even in this stage of your life I will use your life to nurture others and to feed many.

My Word says you will flourish like a palm tree because you are planted in the house of the Lord. This majestic tree is not only a source of shade and protection from the sun; it is a source of food as well as a source of livelihood. My Word says you will still bear fruit in old age, and even in your aging, you will be full of sap - spiritual vitality and vigor.[345]

This is how the daughters see you and it is how I see you. I commend you for your commitment to Me and to My Word. According to My Word, this next phase or stage of your life will produce *double* fruit and blessing and glory.

My response
I give myself to You, dear Lord
A planted tree I'll stand
Within Your house, within Your courts
To flourish in Your hand.

[345] Psalm 92:12-14

For I am under Your own care
Your goodness is well known
For you are faithful to Your Word
And faithful to Your own.

So let me live and find in You
The Source of all I need
So let me share what you have given
To nurture, love and feed.

Poetry written by Florli Nemeth

Verse 4A

Thy neck is as a tower of ivory…

My thoughts
Earlier we heard the King say that her neck was like the tower of David. These words indicated her faith and obedience and compliance to the will of God, and they stated that every act of faith and obedience is as a shield of defensive protection and as a shield displayed in God's armory.[346]

Now listen as the daughters compare her neck to a tower of ivory.[347] They see that her dedication and obedience is a beautifully rare and costly commodity. Faith and obedience constitute a precious and a sure defence.

It is when we walk in wilfulness and disobedience that we have no defence against the enemy but when our will is submitted to Christ, the neck (the Bride) is moving at the will of the Head (Christ), *He* becomes our "*ivory tower*" and thus *we* become an extension of who He is – the "*ivory tower*", a place of safety and protection for others.

His thoughts
Faith and obedience, though costly and rare, becomes a beautiful tower of protection and safety both for you and for others.

---

[346] Song of Solomon 4:4
[347] Song of Solomon 7:4

Never underestimate the far reaching effects of obedience.

Remember that sin came into the world through one man's disobedience and as a result, sin and death spread to *all* men! No one earthly sacrifice could stop the power of sin and disobedience.

But you also know that now *many* reign as kings in life, delivered from the law of sin and death through one man's obedience - through one man's act of righteousness.

Through My Son, Jesus Christ, life has come to you, forgiveness, justification, and the gift of righteousness. All has come through one man's obedience.[348]

Your faith and obedience will inevitably affect many. That is why the daughters commend you. Like a tower of refuge, your faith has become a defense of love and protection for many. I see your faith and obedience, and it pleases Me greatly.

Just as I saw My Son's obedience and was pleased and delighted with Him, so I am pleased and delighted with you. He was My chosen One, sent to reveal justice and truth to the nations of the world. You too are My chosen one, commissioned to show forth My praises. I called you out of darkness into the light; once again I call you to be a shining tower of ivory in a world of darkness and despair.[349]

Verse 4B

...thine eyes like the fish pools in Heshbon, by the gate of Bath-rabbim:...

My thoughts
Her eyes were affirmed by the King in the following passages of Solomon's rhapsody.

Thou hast dove's eyes (1:15)
Thou hast dove's eyes...thou hast ravished My heart with one of thine eyes (4:1,9)
Turn away thine eyes from Me for they have overcome Me (6:5)

---

[348] Romans 5:12-21
[349] Isaiah 42:1

Now the daughters see that she has clear vision of God's purposes as well as of who she is in Christ and her purpose in life. She discerns spiritual things clearly, and she sees herself clearly.

The city of Heshbon was an Amorite city over which King Sihon ruled.[350] When Israel approached him, asking for permission to travel through his land, King Sihon of Heshbon refused, mobilized his army and attacked Israel in the wilderness. Through God's intervention Israel captured all the cities of the Amorites, including Heshbon.

A resort city, Beth-rabbin, boasted clear fish pools, filled with fish and clean, clear water like a mirror.

In another portion of Scripture Solomon declares: "*The wisdom of the prudent is to understand his way*" or "*The wise man looks ahead.*"[351]

Similarly the Apostle Paul exhorts believers: "*I pray that your hearts will be flooded with light so you can see something of the future He has called you to share.*"[352] He preceded that prayer by praying that God would give the Ephesian believers wisdom to see clearly who Christ is and that they would be granted insight into who He is.

He said
The daughters rightly commend you, My dear one. Your vision is not muddied by the world's belief system for you have come to know My Word and you see Me clearly. Because your vision is clear, your heart is flooded with light. You do not walk in darkness but in the light that comes with seeing Me clearly and seeing and understanding yourself clearly.

You know who you are and why you are here. I commend you, My dear one, for when your eyes see clearly, so does your heart.

Pray to be sharp in discernment, to see Me clearly and to see yourself and others clearly. As you behold Me in My Word, you will come to know Me more intimately and you will become more and more like

---

[350] Numbers 21:25,26
[351] Proverbs 14:8 KJV and Living Bible
[352] Ephesians 1:18 Living Bible

Me. You are constantly being transfigured into My image - My very own image! I will have sons and daughters who look like Me.[353]

You must understand, however, that your view of Me in My Word and your view of yourself is only a dim or blurred reflection of reality - the reality you will one day share with Me in My presence when you see Me face to face. Then you will understand Me fully and clearly, and you will also see and understand yourself as I see and understand you.[354]

In the meantime, be one who comes to Me daily to be anointed with eye salve so you can see. You purchase, as it were, vision from Me for I am the One who gives sight to the blind. Many of My children walk in a twilight zone because they do not walk in My Word. If you will walk in My light, which is My Word, you will experience fellowship with My people as well as beautiful, intimate, unbroken communion with Me. My promise to you is that My blood will cleanse you and keep you clean from ALL sin.[355]

This is My passion for you, dear one, that you would come to see Me more clearly and love Me more dearly, the deep, everlasting love for you encompasses eternity. My plan for your life doesn't stop at the end of your earthly life. At the end of your life you will realize you've only *begun* to know and understand My purposes for you - for time and throughout eternity.

As you live connected to Me and to My Word I will increase your ability to see and I will enlarge your vision of Me, of My church, and of your own purpose and life here on earth and in eternity.

My response

> O Lord, my God, open my eyes that I may see
> Glimpses of Your eternity
> Give me to understand and know
> All that You have for me to show.
> I just want to know You; I just want to see You
> I just want to be with You, My Lord.

---

[353] 2 Corinthians 3:18

[354] 1 Corinthians 13:12

[355] Revelation 3:18 and 1 John 1:7

I just want to follow, I just want to trust You
I just want to be like You, My Lord.
I just want to love You, I just want to cherish
I just want to be embraced by You.
I just want to serve You, I just want to seek You
I just want to walk in all Your ways.
I just will obey You, I just will believe You
I just will commit my life to You.
I just want to sit here, I just want to stand here
I just want to bask in Your delight.
I just want to bow down, I just want to worship
I just want to sit here at Your feet forever -
And until that day when You open heaven's doors for me
And I see You face to face
Let me look at Your dim reflection and be changed by Your love!

Poetry written by Florli Nemeth

Verse 4C

...thy nose is as the tower of Lebanon which looketh toward Damascus.

Things about Lebanon and Damascus

1. Defensive weapons were stored in Solomon's house at *Lebanon.* [356]
2. *Damascus* was the head of Syria, and the Syrians were some of David's fiercest enemies.[357]
3. *Rezin* was an enemy of Judah, and he reigned in Damascus.[358]
4. Solomon must have built a tower at his place in Lebanon, although there is no other mention of it in Scripture. The tower was built to watch over his chief enemy in Syria and to protect his people from harm.

My thoughts
The daughters saw the bride as having discernment and a keen sense of the enemy's activities. They saw her as a tower in Lebanon built to watch out for their fiercest enemies and to offer protection for them.

---

[356] 2 Chronicles 9:15 & 16
[357] 2 Samuel 8:5
[358] Isaiah 7:1-8

He said
My bride will always have enemies, and some more fierce than others. You must always be on your watch, for *you are not contending with physical opponents, but with despots and powers and spirits who are the world rulers of this present darkness.*[359]

I am your high tower; when you run into Me, you are safe. Yet, although My Word is your shield against every attack of the enemy, you have need to be on guard at all times. In your prayer life you stand as a tower of protection for those you pray over.

Verse 5A

Thine head upon thee is like Mt. Carmel . . . .

He said
The daughters see your wisdom and your hope. You know Me, You know My ways, My reputation, My love for you, and you are not easily led away or disturbed by theories or reasonings that are contrary to your knowledge of Me. Your mind is clear concerning truth because you have seen Me, the Light, and you are no longer blind. You have put on the helmet of salvation which is called the hope of salvation.[360] Your mind is filled with hope and wisdom and purity. Your thoughts are in line with My Word because My Word is your meat and drink.

You need to know that Satan's first attack is always on your mind because it is the control center of your heart. If he can distort your thoughts about Me, or about yourself or another, he has you in a very vulnerable position.

He tried to do this with Job by enticing Job to accuse Me. His wiles failed simply because Job had seen Me clearly and he refused to let go of his hope. Speaking to his supposed comforters, he declared: *But He knows the way that I take [He has concern for it, appreciates and pays attention to it]. When He has tried me, I shall come forth as refined gold [pure and luminous].*[361]

---

[359] Ephesians 6:12, Amplified
[360] 2 Corinthians 10:5/Ephesians 6:17/1 Thessalonians 5:8
[361] Job 23:10, Amplified

Job knew he was in My hands, and he clung to the hope of one day seeing his God, his Redeemer, he knew that he would behold Him not as a stranger, but as a friend.[362]

It is your understanding of My person, character and unchanging love for you that will sustain you in the deepest, darkest, most despairing trials of your life. It is your knowledge of Me that will keep your mind clear of the confusing, accusing and condemning thoughts of the enemy. And it is your understanding of My Word and your appropriation of it that will keep your mind (your control center) in perfect peace.

As you meditate on My Word, My Spirit will produce a beauty comparable to Mt. Carmel.

Mountains can be seen from a distance and their beauty admired from miles away. It is in their grandeur that streams are born; it is their towering strength that surrounds the valleys below and thwarts the power of the winds and storms. Not only do the mountains affect weather patterns and provide a hiding place and a living space for wild animals, they are unchanging in their beauty and stability.

Your hope in Me is like the beautiful, unchanging mountains. Your thoughts are stable and fixed on Me - the changeless One, the ageless One, the living One, the loving One. I commend you even as the daughters do, for they, too, see your stability and beauty. You are awesome in your love for Me, and I love you!

My prayer
Father, You are the One who is awesome. How can I ever love You enough? I don't always feel like "Mt. Carmel"; in fact, I sometimes feel quite devastated by the enemy. Yesterday it took only a few words to upset my entire equilibrium but as I began to worship You and pour out my pain and grief before You, I was lifted up and strengthened and encouraged and enabled once again to see You.

I see clearly that Satan's strategy is to attack the control center, the thoughts of our mind. If he gains control there, he is enabled to distort

[362] Job 19:25-27

every sense, rendering us unable to see or to hear and it is then that he has gained the advantage over us.

Where is my refuge? Where is my place of security and help? It is in You and in Your Word. Satan cannot stand Your presence or Your Word. Your Word in my mouth is like a two-edged sword in my hand. It is of interest to see that the helmet and the sword are linked together in Paul's letter to the Ephesians.[363]

Here we see hope and the Word of God intertwined. Note also, that as the agent of this verbal action against the enemy, it is the Sword that the *Spirit* wields. When I speak Your Word, Lord, the Holy Spirit goes to work against the enemy.[364]

I believe that when I speak Your Word, You stand in the midst of the lamp stands and from *Your* mouth there comes a sharp two-edged sword. This certainly falls in line with other scriptures that say *You* fight my battles, and *You* tell me to stand still and see the salvation of God.[365]

Yes, Lord, You are the Lifter of my head. You are my mighty *Warrior-King*. You call me to stand beside You as Your *Warrior-Bride*, invite me to partner with You. Thank You Lord.

You are an awesome Warrior-King. I am honored to stand beside You and be seen as Your Warrior-Bride.

Verse 5B

...and the hair of thy head like purple

My thoughts

The daughters saw the bride's resolute dedication to the King as something only God could work in her life. The word for "hair" in this verse differs in the Hebrew from other mentions of the word "hair" in this book. Here the word "hair" reflects the meaning of smallness or

[363] Ephesians 6:17

[364] Psalm 149:6/Hebrews 4:12/Revelation 1:16/Ephesians 6:17

[365] Revelation 1:13-16/Exodus 14:13

tenderness or it signifies a small hair decoration, and it is said to be like purple - precious, lovely, something only God can work in one.

In other words, the daughters are saying there is not the slightest thing in her that is out of order. Her whole life is adorned with grace. Her walk, even in the little things, is exceedingly lovely.

My prayer
Lord, the grace I have received is not without purpose. Given to me freely, it is the exertion of Your holy influence on my heart that draws me close to You and daily keeps and strengthens me. I have neither disregarded nor received it in vain.[366]

Lord Jesus, any beauty You see in me, any beauty others see in me, is the result of Your grace at work within me. My heart is so overwhelmed this day as I think of how Your grace has gently wooed and drawn me close to Your heart.

Jesus, You became poor - You who were rich - that by Your poverty I might be enriched and made beautiful. Your grace is enough for me: Your enablement, Your strength, Your power have become the substance of *all* I need. [367]

He said
Yes, My lovely one, I see My grace over you and I am not disappointed. As a pitched tent it dwells upon you and I know that My sacrifice for you has not been in vain. Even those who look on your life see the beauty of My grace over you, and they yearn to be like you. They see your dedication and the favor and mercy I have placed upon you, and they yearn to partake of My fullness even as they pray for you.

I hear the prayers of the little sisters, the daughters who are yet themselves immature and struggling and I promise you I will put My grace upon them as I have put it upon you. They too shall stand in My presence perfect, complete, mature, gracious and beautiful in their dedication to Me.[368]

---

[366] 2 Corinthians 6:1

[367] 2 Corinthians 8:9/9:14/12:9

[368] 2 Corinthians 9:14

Verse 5C

...the king is held in the galleries
...the king is held captive by its tresses. (Amplified)

My thoughts
This is the third time we see the King overcome with emotion over His bride. First, He said His heart was ravished with one look, with one act of obedience from her. He even asked His bride to turn away her flashing eyes because her gaze had overcome Him.[369] Here He is so overcome with emotion that even the daughters standing by can see it.

He said
I enjoy your presence so much that I am totally overwhelmed and held captive by your love. When you come into My presence and linger long, you think that the blessing is only for you. You will never know, though, the joy it brings when you come simply to be with Me. My heart is held captive by you and I am overcome with love and joy. I long for the day when we will be together forever!

[369] Song of Solomon 6:5

The King Affirms the Bride

Verse 6

How fair and how pleasant art thou, O love, for delights.
Oh, how delightful you are, how pleasant, O Love, for utter delight! (Living Bible)
[The King came forward, saying] How fair and how pleasant you are, with your delights! (Amplified)

My thoughts
Though it was His fruit that first was sweet to her taste,[370] now *her* fruit is sweet to Him. Here we see the King commending the external beauty and attractiveness (*how fair*) and also the sweetness and beauty of her inward person (*how pleasant*). Furthermore, He exclaims, *How fair* . . . .

In other words, with this exclamation He is showing how incomparable and inexpressible the bride's beauty is to Him. He cannot tell how fair and how pleasant. The bride's loveliness and the enjoyment of His presence go together. As we are complete in Him, so He is so completely satisfied with her,

He said
You have focused your worship on Me, lavishing Me with your praises and your love. Now see in your abandonment to Me, how beautiful you have become. My grace and love over you have covered you, creating in you an indescribable exquisiteness.

You have sat under the apple tree and enjoyed the fruit of My presence but I want you to know how much I value and enjoy the fruit of *your* company. You could be doing any number of things, but you have chosen to sit at My feet, morning by morning, receiving My grace and love and giving Me your love and adoration. No one is ever so beautiful as when their face is turned toward Me in worship.

You are lovely whether worshipping Me through your tears or in your joy. Your worship brings such joy to My heart because I know the sacrifice that attends it. Sometimes you have fallen on your face as Job in times of great pain and loss.

---

[370] Song of Solomon 2:3

Oft times you have wept in anguish before Me as David did repeatedly. You have stood before Me as Daniel did in intercession for the nation and you have wrestled with Me as Jacob, refusing to let go of Me in prayer until you saw the breakthrough. You've persevered in prayer in those desert times like Moses did when it seemed he had missed his destiny.

Child of My heart, Love of My life, I am delighted with you. I could sing of *your* love forever - and to be sure, I will do so. As do you, I look forward to that day when I will show you off to all of heaven and I will present you to My Father, pure and spotless. Stay with Me a while longer; let Me bask in *your* presence!

Verse 7A

This thy stature is like to a palm tree . . . .

My thoughts
Stature is made up of many parts in the body and all those parts in right proportion, fulfilling their rightful place.

"*He is altogether lovely*", or as the Amplified puts it, "*The whole of Him delights and is precious.*"[371]

Now He says of her that her stature is like a palm tree -

1. Upright - straight, not crooked
2. Fruitful, beautiful, flourishing and refreshing [372]
3. Long-living [373]

The branches of palm trees were used in joyful feasts or celebrations.

- The Israelites made booths with palm branches in order to celebrate the feast of tabernacles.[374]
- The people in Jerusalem took palm branches and went out to meet Jesus[375]

---

[371] Song of Solomon 5:16
[372] Number 33:9 & Deuteronomy 34:3
[373] Psalm 92:12,14
[374] Leviticus 23:40
[375] John 12:13

- Palm branches are in the hands of worshippers standing in front of the throne before the Lamb - a multitude of people of all nations, kindreds, people and tongues.[376]

A mature palm tree is able to stand and persevere under great pressure because its roots go deep. Its ability to endure drought and famine without itself suffering drought results from its ability to find sources of underground water.

He said
It is My desire that My church come to full stature, full growth and complete maturity. When this happens, every part of the body will function proportionately, accurately, flawlessly in perfection and unity.

Moreover, it is then that every part of My body functions in its God-given ability and task, endowed with godly maturity and completeness found only in Me.[377]

I see you, dear one, as a tall, beautiful and fruitful palm tree. Your roots are deep into My Word, you have weathered many storms and your fruitfulness stands as a source of refreshment to many.

Others find shade and protection under your branches, but not only that, their presence speaks words of significance. Even when winds of the enemy blow upon you, sent to bring destruction and annihilation upon you, your branches bend with the wind and keep declaring, "*Jesus is Lord - Jesus is King of kings - Jesus is victorious - Jesus is the sovereign Lord of lords - Jesus Christ is the conquering Lamb of God who is seated on the Throne and who has all power and might, wisdom and strength forever and ever!*"

The more the enemy tries to destroy My church, the louder the cry of victory and praise that ascends to the very Throne of God!

I have many such palm trees in My kingdom, therefore be encouraged for you are not alone. Do not forget that you are part of a *city of palm trees.* My church was formed to be a place of refuge and refreshment; I am faithful in raising it up for that purpose.

---

[376] Revelation 7:9

[377] Ephesians 4:13

My Church is a city on a hill - a city of palm trees - strong, mature, fully equipped unto every good work and growing in the knowledge of God. Lift your branches and give praise to the King this day.

Verse 7B

...and thy breasts to clusters of grapes.

My thoughts
The Bride has already rejoiced in that: *He shall lie all night between my breasts.*[378] Solomon said to young men regarding their wives, *Let her breasts satisfy thee at all times, and be thou always ravished with her love.*[379]

Her breasts were to satisfy her lover *first and foremost*, and only then were they to nurture others. A wife's love is to be first for her husband and then for her children. In the natural human relationships, it is so easy to become distracted from our first love and to focus on our children. Our babies and little ones need us, but *not* to the exclusion of our husband. Always he is to be our first love.

In this picture we see the spiritual truth: we can be so committed to the needs of those we nurture and nourish, and so committed to our ministry that we neglect our times with the Lord, our first love. He wants His Bride to know how refreshing our love is to Him.

He said
Dear one, your love for Me is so lovely. There is nothing that refreshes Me as much as your love. I am ravished with your love and satisfied as I gaze upon you. You bring Me such joy because you love Me so freely.

My prayer
The verse of an old, old hymn is My prayer -

> "And O that He, fulfilled may see
> The travail of His soul in me
> And with His work contented be
> As I with my dear Saviour."[380]

---

[378] Song of Solomon 1:13
[379] Proverbs 5:19
[380] Words by Dorothy Greenwell, Music by William J. Kirkpatrick in Songs of Joy & Gladness, 1885

Be fulfilled and contented with my love, my Lord. The love I have to give You is only what You have given me; my love for You the return of Your love to me.

He said
Your love is better than wine, nourishing My heart and strengthening others. You have learned well the lesson that in giving to Me, you bless others. The wife who honors and loves her husband is a crown of joy to her husband. Her children rise up and call her blessed because love brings security, joy and blessing into a relationship and into a home.

How a wife treats her husband deeply affects not only her marriage, but her children. So My dear one, because you love Me and spend time with Me, you are blessed, your spiritual children are blessed, and I am blessed. You are My beautiful bride, the one that I love, and you are so precious to Me.

Verse 8A

I said, I will go up to the palm tree, I will take hold of the boughs thereof…
I will climb up into the palm tree and take hold of its branches. (Living Bible)
I resolve that I will climb the palm tree; I will grasp its branches. (Amplified)

My prayer
O Jesus, You are determined and resolute in Your decision to reveal Your love to Your palm trees, Your people. You treasure Your people, Your church, above all others and in You delight in them. You want above all else to be close to them. It is refreshing and invigorating for You to be near the ones You love.

Your desire to reveal Yourself to us is not a passing thought or flippant desire. Your heart language of love for Your people is determined and deliberate. "I *will* go…I *will* take hold, or climb…". You have chosen to love Your people above all people of the earth. Your Bride is Your choice! You long to be near Your loved ones.

You chose us before You laid the foundation of the world. You picked us out for Yourself as Your very own. You spoke this truth through Your servant, Peter when You pronounced that we *were chosen and foreknown by God the Father and consecrated, made holy by the Spirit to be obedient to Jesus Christ and to be sprinkled with His blood.*[381]

Peter also said that we are a *chosen race, a royal priesthood, a dedicated nation, God's own purchased, special people* - ***God's*** people.[382]

You have good plans for Your people; Your thoughts toward us are good. In that love You are always planning for our welfare and for our best interests. Since You are in love with Your people, You long to reveal Yourself and manifest Your presence to them. We never have to beg You to come because You delight in us and *want* to be with us.

He said
You understand My heart. As the end of the age draws to a close, I am the more resolved to go to My palm tree and climb My beautiful tree. I want to be close to My Church, My Bride, and *you*, one of My palm trees.

You have won and captured My heart. I delight in You and embrace you today, cherishing you and loving you dearly. I love each one of My palm trees as if each was the only one in the world. None other will ever love you as I love you and in My love I come to reveal Myself to you.

You have said in your heart, *I will not let You go except You bless me*, yet in return, dear one, remember that I will never let you go. I am determined to reveal My manifest presence and glory to you. Though now through a glass dimly, You will see Me in all My glory and your heart will be satisfied. You will be refreshed and overjoyed at the strength and power and glory of My love for you. Bask in My presence. Bask in My love. I am here for you, My child.

Verse 8B

. . . .I will take hold of the boughs thereof . . . .
. . . .I will grasp its branches. . . (Amplified)

---

[381] Ephesians 1:4/1 Peter 1:2 Amplified
[382] 1 Peter 2:9, 10 Amplified

My thoughts

Enfolded in His arms
Where would I go from here?
Embraced in love secure,
What could I ever fear?
Empowered by His love
How could I be more beautiful?
Engraved upon His hands
His love so great, so bountiful!
Energized by strength so strong
The Lord my King, the Lord my Song!
Poetry written by Florli Nemeth

My prayer
Lord, I am *enfolded* in Your arms, and where would I ever want to go from here? Your love all around me, drawing me near, wiping my tears, removing all fear! You are awesome!

I am *embraced* in a love that will never let me go. You promised never to leave me nor forsake me. You said You would be with me night and day, wherever I go.[383]

I am held in Your hands - my name *engraved* - indelibly imprinted on the palm of each of Your hands. You have tattooed a picture of me on Your hands! Not merely my name, it's my picture You see on Your hands. There I find a place of rest as I place my total trust in Your hands for they bear the imprint of the nails that held You to the cross. It was the image of me that held You there for not even the nails could have held You there – it was that You saw me imprinted on Your palms, and for love You suffered the pain and endured the cross that I might be free[384].

I am *empowered* by Your love, clothed in garments of praise, salvation and righteousness, filled with the Holy Spirit, and adorned with Your gifts and graces. You have clothed me. You have covered me. You have adorned me.[385]

---

[383] Hebrews 13:5/Joshua 1:9
[384] Deuteronomy 33:3/Psalm 18:35/Isaiah 49:16
[385] Isaiah 61:3, 10

I am *energized* by Your strong arm as I live in Your embrace. It is Your arm that brings me into possession of Your promises; it is Your arm that pushes down my enemies.[386]

Your arm is mighty and strong, the strength and defense of Your servants.[387]

Yes, Your arm has been revealed to me. As the power of Your arm is unveiled I am strengthened, energized and overjoyed to live and walk in Your strength.[388]

He said

I'm here for you, My Child
    My love will never let you go
Thus held in love's embrace
    My deepest love to know.

My arms are opened wide
    For all to come and see
The love I have for you
    The Love that sets you free.

So come and live and stay with Me
    I'll do you only good
Be strengthened and empowered thus
    To love Me as you should.

Poetry written by Florli Nemeth

[386] Acts 13:17 and Psalm 44:3,5
[387] Psalm 89:13/Isaiah 33:2
[388] Isaiah 53:1 with John 12:38

The Bride Enters Into Mature Partnership

Verse 8C and 9A

...now also thy breasts shall be as clusters of the vine, and the smell of thy nose like apples.
And the roof of thy mouth like the best wine for my beloved...

He said
My dear friend, I bless you today with My presence. Because you have called out to Me in your desire to spend time with Me, I have taken hold of your branches, and I have come near to you. Your beauty is the result of the power of My presence that is changing you.

My presence will do three things in your life -

1. It will produce fruit in your life that will nurture and refresh others. The wine of the Holy Spirit in you will minister life to others.
2. It will purify your inner life so that your very breath is sweet and refreshing. Others will want to be with you because the words that come out of your mouth are sweet, healing words that refresh and encourage My people. I want you to know that your breath is also sweet to Me. Your words of love and adoration, worship and praise are delightful, bringing Me such joy.
3. It will bring you into a place of intimacy reserved only for My bride. I long for this intimacy with you. Don't neglect the time that you spend in My presence. For nothing else in life compares to this. I long to pour My love over you; I long to see your face and hear your voice. Your garden is enclosed for Me alone, and nearness to you brings Me such joy.

My prayer
Jesus, I want Your presence and I want the *best* of Your wine to flow freely through me and out to others. I want to breathe in Your breath that refreshes mine. I want my inner life to be pure and holy and undefiled. Breathe on me, breath of God. May my love bring You joy, may my love satisfy Your heart. I long for sweet intimacy with You, My God and my King.

Verse 9B

...causing the lips of those that are asleep to speak.

My thoughts
The bride interrupts the Bridegroom in the middle of His affirmations to speak of the wine and of how deeply committed she is to what comes from Him. This very special wine of intimacy, the best wine, is reserved only for Him.

My prayer
Lord, You have done so much for Your church, Your bride. Not only have You given her Your *best* wine, You are overcome when at last Your bride begins to drink the draft and then shares that wine with You. What consolation, what joy when one sinner repents and comes to you. But what pleasure it must bring to you when Your loved ones receive Your love and then give it back to You, responding in total surrender and devotion.

You have enraptured and captivated my heart yet I am equally amazed that in my response of love and reaching out to You, I have captivated *Your* heart! O what love! O what joy! To be totally Yours and Yours alone is my passion and desire. To know Your presence in an intimate way is my deepest longing and desire. Nothing less can satisfy.

He said
Daughter, you must come with Me to the height of ecstasy.

My response
Father, I feel overwhelmed at the depth of Your desire for me. Am I swimming in water over my head? Am I out of my realm? Do I need to step back from these writings or plough ahead to the end?

He said
Deep calls unto deep, My Child, and I am calling you deeper, not back to the shore. I'll give you understanding as you allow Me to reveal to you the depths of My love. The shoreline is well known to you but I want to continue to illuminate your heart to new truths and new experiences of My love. Take it one stroke at a time as you swim out into the ocean of My love.

This ocean has nothing to fear because there are no storms, no waves or billows, no tide that ebbs and flows, no frightening mammals or fish, no undercurrents. My love is just a beautiful ocean of pure water that will bear you up and take you to places you have never been and you will discover many things you have never seen before.

There is nothing to fear in My love nor do you have comprehend it all before you give yourself to the water and yield to its buoyancy. In fact, it is an uncharted way, unique to each of My children but I make a way in the sea, and most importantly, you are safe with Me.

Verse 9C

[Then the Shulamite interrupted] that goes down smoothly and sweetly for my beloved Shepherd, kisses gliding over his lips while he sleeps. (Amplified)

My thoughts
The bride interrupts and is speaking here. She speaks of four aspects of the bridal relationship in this section.[389] Here she sees her relationship with the King as a bridal relationship expressed in instant and complete obedience.

My prayer
Lord Jesus, Your wine goes down smoothly and I am able to receive Your Word, Your commands, without resistance. There is a growing "yes" in my spirit that yields to Your Word and to Your will without hesitation or questioning, doubt or disobedience. Your will is my command.

Jesus, You drank the cup of wine which involved the cross. You did not hesitate because You knew Your Father's love and You saw Your Father's heart of love for me and for all humanity. You never shrank from obedience; help me respond in the same way to Your will, to Your way, to Your cup of wine for me. I will obey You, Jesus, because of my love for You. I never want to grieve You in even the slightest way. Help me, Lord, to respond to You at all times with total obedience out of love, no matter how difficult that way may be.

---

[389] Song of Solomon 7:9 & 8:4

My heart cries, Not my will, but Yours, dear Lord. Help me to live and walk in perfect obedience and abandonment to Your will and purpose.

He said
My cup of wine may not always be easy to drink, but a yielded heart will make it go down smoothly, bringing much joy to you and to those who are blessed by your ministry. Many want only My power, but not My love. Your heart desires both, and both you shall see. My dearest Bride. I pour out on you today the wine of My Spirit.

Overview of Verses 8 & 9 -
This morning the last verse of an old hymn filled My thoughts. Searching through my entire Keswick Hymnal and then into the Alliance "Hymns of the Christian Faith" I found the entire work:-

"O Thou, in whose presence my soul takes delight
On Whom in affliction I call
My comfort by day and my song in the night
My hope, my salvation, my all.

"Where dost Thou, dear Shepherd, resort with Thy sheep
To feed them in pastures of love
Say, why in the valley of death should I weep
Or alone in this wilderness rove.

"Oh, why should I wander, an alien from Thee
Or cry in the desert for bread?
Thy foes will rejoice when my sorrows they see
And smile at the tears I have shed.

"Ye daughters of Zion, declare, have you seen
The Star that on Israel shone?
Say, if in your tents my Beloved has been,
And where with His flocks He has gone.

"He looks, and ten thousand of angels rejoice
And myriads wait for His Word
He speaks, and eternity filled with His voice
Re-echoes the praise of the Lord."

"Dear Shepherd! I hear, and will follow Thy call
I know the sweet sound of Thy voice
Restore and defend me, for Thou art my all
And in Thee I will ever rejoice."

Written by Freeman Lewis

Obviously, the person who wrote this hymn knew the Song of Solomon and had a deep understanding of the love relationship the Shepherd has for His little Shulamite maiden.

My prayer
Lord, Your church is that maiden - and I am one little maiden You love! Your voice restores my soul and defends me; one word from you and all heaven is moved to action. Your words of love and affirmation have so touched and strengthened and encouraged my heart, like wine, they go down smoothly, bringing joy and rejoicing to my heart.

Your promise to grasp my branches - to hold me - to come close to me - is infinitely precious. I hold You to me today for in my weakness, You are strong. In my grief and disappointments, You are near to comfort and to guide. In my joys, You rejoice with me and all heaven joins in the song. In my loneliness and in my sorrows You are with me, never to leave me nor forsake me. In those times when I am disappointed with myself You bring Your affirmations and declarations that I can do all things because You strengthen me.

You give me eyes to see the needs of others and a heart to love and to give. You give me life and health and strength of will to conquer and to live.

You, my God and King
My loving Shepherd dear
Your kisses like the best of wine
Your fragrance hovers near.

You hold me in Your arms of love
While all the world goes by
Forever let me rest secure
And in Your bosom lie.

My life, my strength, my joy, my all
        My Shepherd and my Friend
Your love, the dearest wine on earth,
        The joy that knows no end.

Forever I will sing Your praise
        Your worth in joyous swell
Forever I will love the One
        Who knows and loves me well!

So take my hand, and help me stand
        Beloved of my soul
Your love, my strength, Your joy, my pride
        Your pleasure, my sweet goal.

I live to love, I live to praise
        I live for You alone
I give my life, my love, my all
        My heart Your chosen home.

And one day when I stand before
        My God and Christ my King
My joy to fall before Your Throne
        My love and praise to bring.

Then for a million years I'll spend
        My life in love with Thee
My joy to be with Him I love
        For all eternity!

Poetry Written by Florli Nemeth

Jesus, my heart is blessed and strengthened and uplifted to be with You, my dear Shepherd. I felt so heavy before, but now I am full of Your love and joy. Thank You for coming to me in my weakness. I love you.

Verse 10A

I am my beloved's…

My thoughts
She comforts herself in her union with her bridegroom. She spoke this earlier.[390]

[390] Song of Solomon 2:16 and 6:3

It is good to speak of our love and of His love for us in those moments where we sense the manifestations of His presence and His intense love toward us. Then when clouds come and threaten the feelings of this love and tempt us to believe His love was just a delusion, we can rightly fix our confidence in His love, and our faith and trust will not be shaken or moved.

She sees herself as a lover of God. The affirmations of the previous verses led her to this great confession - *I am my beloved's.* She sees this as a definition of who she is.

My prayer
Lord Jesus, I am Yours and Yours alone. You do not define my life as others do. Others see me for what I *DO* in life. They see me as a teacher, or a musician, a mother or a grandmother. Some might see me as a failure or a misfit, a "has-been" or an "old foggy"! But *You see me as a lover, a friend, a confidant, a worshipper.*

I am *Yours* - first and foremost. I belong to You, and You are proud to associate Yourself with me, to walk arm-in-arm with me. I no longer harbour fleshly fear of You, and I am no longer anxious about how you view me. Nor do I any longer view myself as apart from You because *I am Yours, and Yours alone.* There are no other loves in my life for I am totally committed to You, to Your love and to Your desires for me.

Your thoughts and plans for me are for my welfare and my good. Since You are in complete control of my life, nothing happens to me by accident. I belong to You, therefore I have a stake in Your interests and in Your love.[391]

To the voices that whisper condemnation, I rebuke them by declaring: I am not a failure or a misfit; I am an extravagant lover of God. I am not a hypocritical saint but a passionate lover of God. I am a lover of God trying to overcome sin, not a sinner trying to love God. Your love empowers me to become who You say I am - a garden, a lily, a rose, a beautiful tree.

---

[391] Jeremiah 29: 10 & 11

Your love holds me fast in those days where clouds and storms would sweep my sky to obscure Your face. On those days I remind myself of Your desire to feed among the lilies and of Your declarations that Your heart is ravished with my love and held captive by my adoration of You. You have called me Your dove, Your undefiled one, Your perfect one, Your love. You have repeatedly expressed Your desire over me. You are my extravagant lover, and I belong to You forever!

I am Yours, whatever life may bring
I am my Beloved's
I am Yours, my heart will choose to sing
I am my Beloved's.

Clouds may come and clouds may go
Storms may sweep my sky
I will lift my voice to You, shout
Praise to God on high!

I am Yours, and You are mine
I am Your beloved
My heart is with Yours entwined
You are my Beloved!

Poetry written by Florli Nemeth

He said
My heart rejoices over you with joy as I sing songs of love over you. I will *never* accuse you, because I deeply love you. I rejoice over you with singing and at times just rest in silence as I gaze in love toward you.[392]

Because I do not remember past sins and failures; you will never be reminded of them, either. I see only the future I have prepared for you. It is true you will praise and worship Me forever, but it is also true that I will compose songs to sing over you for all of eternity. There is nothing I love more than a love song, and that is what I sing over you today!

You are My beloved
You, My dearest friend
You are Mine forever
Love that will not end.

---

[392] Zephaniah 3:17 Living Bible and Amplified

You are My sweet lover
Yours the song I sing
Satisfied and filled with joy
For the love you bring.

You are Mine - My chosen one
Called by My own name
Gathered to My heart of love
Given grace and fame.

You are Mine forever
Love that will not end
Fragrance poured out freely
Not too much to spend.

Passionate, extravagant
Confident and true
Is the love you have for Me
And My love for you!

Poetry written by Florli Nemeth

Verse 10B

...and His desire is toward me. and I am the one He desires. (Living Bible)

My thoughts

He wants to please me. His desire toward me is compared to a woman's fervent desire toward her husband.[393] He wants to make me happy, to satisfy my heart. He *enjoys* me!

My prayer

Lord, Your enjoyment of me empowers me to become the person You have called me to become. You believe in me. You shape my life and my circumstances to conform, or align themselves with Your will and purpose for me. I no longer live by what I think or by what others think of me. Others may dislike or even reject me, but You love me! You desire me! How can I ever fail with You beside me? You have promised

[393] Genesis 3:16

that everything would work together for good in my life; so I can trust You. I trust You because I know You are good. [394]

Lord, You enjoy me! You said You love me even as the Father loves You. My life is about Your love, Your enjoyment of me, and Your desire toward me. You don't just tolerate my friendship - You actually love me with a deep, deep love as a husband loves his wife, and as the Father loves You![395]

No wonder Paul prayed that our roots would grow down deeply into the soil of Your love. Will I ever understand how long, how wide, how deep, how high Your love really is? Paul prayed we would understand *and experience* Your love! And He said it was so great we would never see the end of it or fully know or understand it. Fill me up today with Your love, Jesus![396]

He said
My love for you will dispel every accusation of the enemy, every slander, every criticism, every persecution, every evil word he would ever throw against you. There is nothing in life that can stand against My love - no charge the enemy would lay against you, no trouble or calamity, no persecution, no peril or sword![397]

My love conquers all, and My love for you enables *you* to conquer all. Nothing can separate you from my love-

- Not death
- Not life
- Not angels
- Not the demons of hell
- Not your fears of present things today
- Not your worries of future things tomorrow
- Not success or achievements
- Not failures or discouragements

[394] Romans 8:28
[395] John 17:26
[396] Ephesians 3:17-19
[397] Romans 8:31-39

You are My bride, and I am committed to love you forever! There is never a moment where My thoughts are not toward you. You have totally captivated My heart! Yes, I have chosen to love you as a man loves his wife and tries to please her - not lording it over her, but seeking to know and fit in with her plans and desires just as she seeks to fit in with *his* plans and desires.

Husbands are to treat their wives with dignity and love, loving them as part of themselves and as loving their own body. In fact, Paul said a man does himself a favor when he loves his wife![398]

My dear child, this is how I love you and care for you! I tenderly hold your heart in My hand. You are a part of Me. I am a part of you. We are one! Forever!

My response

Lord, Your love **empowers** me
To be the best that I can be
Your love, it makes me strong.

Lord, Your love **releases** me
To live my life with dignity
To rise up with a song.

Lord, Your love **enables** me
To stand, to conquer, and be free
To do Your perfect will.

Lord, Your love **envelopes** me
Surrounds my life with destiny
And calms me to be still.

Lord, Your love **embraces** me
It holds me close to Thee
And will not let me go!

Lord, Your love **enfolds** me
Within Your arms so gently
Telling me what I need to know.

Poetry written by Florli Nemeth

[398] Ephesians 5:22, 28, 33

Verse 11A

Come my Beloved, let us go forth into the field, let us lodge in the villages.

My thoughts
The bride is speaking in the language of the bridegroom. The invitation she gives him is "Come, my Beloved". Earlier He had asked her to come away[399]. Now she expresses her desire for *Him* to be with her. In the closing book of Scripture the language of the Spirit and the bride is "Come".[400]

In her longing for Him, the bride is calling for her Lover to come. Now fully committed to His heart, she longs to be involved in ministry – in the things that touch His heart and in the things that He desires to do through her.

My prayer
Lord, my heart cries out for more of Your love and presence. Come to me, reveal Yourself to me. The more I experience Your presence, the more I long to be with You and to know the reality of Your promise to climb my palm tree and embrace it.

I call out to You today to do that very thing. Because I long for nearness to You, I am committed to seeking after Your presence, Your enabling, and Your heart for the nations. Your promise to me is that You would lay hold of me.[401] You called me to come away with You.[402]

Now I call out to You to fulfill Your Word by manifesting Your presence in my life. Empower me by Your Holy Spirit as You did on the day of Pentecost; send me to the nations of the world but come with me wherever I go today.

Come to me - come with me - come upon me - come for me!

[399] Song of Solomon 2:10
[400] Revelation 22:7
[401] Song of Solomon 7:8
[402] Song of Solomon 2:10

He said
I will come *to* you to reveal My love to you and to cover you with My presence just as I promised. I will come *with* you as you fulfill your daily tasks and as you reach out to touch the ones I love.

I will come *upon* you to empower you as I did the 120 on the day of Pentecost, and to enable you to fulfill your part of the Great Commission. As you step out to pray with people, to teach My Word, to share My love with others, I will empower and enable you to do the works I did here on earth, and even greater works.

And yes, dear one, I will come *for you personally*, and I will come *for My bride corporately.* As the darkness deepens and closes in on you, the cry of My bride for My return will become stronger and stronger until My Father hears that cry and gives the word. Then I will come with myriads of angels to gather and receive My own, My bride, into My presence forever and ever.[403]

I hear your cry and I come to you even now. What you feel is My love washing over you, cleansing and purifying your heart, and filling you with joy. I am with you today to bless you and to make you a blessing. I place My anointing upon you. I pour over you the oil of My Holy Spirit. Rejoice in My nearness and in My love for you.

Verse 11B

...let us go forth into the field...

My prayer
Lord, You have placed me where I am that I might gather a harvest with You. Each one of us who knows You is strategically placed in Your harvest field.

And Lord, I ask You to come with me. In answer to My prayer You have drawn and I have run with You, now come with me. Together we will reach out to minister to those You love. You love the sinners, the ones who do not yet know You, and I know Your heart is to touch them. I want to work in Your harvest, and I need You to be with me.

---

[403] Isaiah 27:13/2 Thessalonians 1:7/Matthew 25:31 and 24:30,31/Revelation 11:15

He said
Each one of My children has been given a field - a place where they will find a harvest if only they will seek it. You are not responsible for another person's field. It would not make sense for a farmer to go harvest someone else's field; his work lies within his own field.

That is also your job but you can never harvest it alone. I am the One who called you; I also will accompany you, strengthen and empower you to harvest your field. You do not labor alone. I am a partner with you. I am overjoyed to work with you, to go with you wherever you go, and just to be with you. You are never alone as you labor with Me.

Verse 11C

...let us lodge in the villages.

My thoughts
We hear the voice of the bride describing her desire to serve in small and out of the way places. She cares about the little isolated and unheard of places. It is in her heart to go where others are unwilling to go since she sees these places as important to God. She invites her Spouse to go with her, for she cannot live or minister without Him. She is constantly aware of His presence and of His working *in* her and *with* her. And yes, she wants to go out to the country villages so they too can feel the sweet and beneficial presence of Him whom she loves.

Previously God was working *in* her, but now He is working *with* her. She is totally united with Him to His will and purpose. No longer will He withdraw His presence from her, for He is united to her and they are one heart, one mind. His concerns are now hers, and she has embraced His concerns and longs to share His love with others.

My prayer
Lord Jesus, take me to the villages - to the out of the way places and out of the mainstream groups of people. Take me to those You love so we may pour Your love into them and impart a spiritual blessing.

And Jesus, I now see it's not about Your blessing *my* concerns - it's about my heart going out to those You love, and my asking You to come with me to minister through me. It's about expressing *Your* heart - *Your* desires - *Your* passion for people and then going to those places and to those people with You.

He said
You have put it correctly, My precious daughter, My lover, My friend. I will go with you wherever you go. My word to My church is to *go* and make disciples. My promise is to go with you on every occasion, every visit, every trip, and every phone call.[404]

You do the going and discipling, and I do the accompanying, the empowering, the strengthening and the anointing.

Yes, I gave specific instructions at various times to Paul and Barnabas and to Philip. But most of the time, in fact, the majority of the time, it's just in the *going* to the *villages* that I accompany you and minister through You. So do not be afraid to GO!

You are now at the place where you can take the initiative and invite Me to go with you. I've already given you permission to do that. So be blessed My dear, dear friend, My bride. As you go in prayer to the villages, you go in person and you take Me with you. I give power to you today to be a blessing to many.

Verse 11D

Come, my Beloved!

My prayer
Lord, You will always be my chief desire, the main focus in life. Fully committed to the priority of bridal love and bridal partnership, I want to live out the rest of my days in loving relationship with You and in a growing sense of partnership in our ministry.

It is not *my* work, *my* ministry, *my* mission. It is *Your* work, *Your* ministry, *Your* mission and yet You have chosen to invite and involve Your loved ones in Your mission. Realizing my frailties, I have no desire to be involved in Your work without a deep sense of Your presence, Your power and Your love over me. My time with You is vital; I must bask in Your love and open my heart to you. Our times together are

[404] Matthew 28:19,20

like fresh flowing streams of living water to my spirit and like sweet refreshing apples and raisins with wine.

You have said that You would come to me, would embrace me and nurture me with Your words. In Your coming I receive Your life and strength. You made known Your desire to be close to Your "palm tree" and to bring me to a place of intimacy reserved only for Your bride. And so Jesus, I call You my Beloved, and I whisper for You to come. Breathe Your life and breath into me, draw me near, hold me close. Whisper Your words of love and affirmation. You are my Beloved, my God and my King.

He said
You, too, are My beloved and I come to you today. You have thought these morning trysts were just for you, but they are for Me too. I am the One who planted My love in your heart, and today I am able to enjoy the fruit of My love. *You* are the gift the Father has given Me, and I treasure and value this gift so highly. *You* are My inheritance!

Yes, My bride corporately and each individual is the inheritance the Father gave Me. When My bride calls out to Me for more of My love, My heart is so overwhelmed I have to turn away My eyes. My heart is moved with your love and commitment to Me and with Your desire to serve in partnership with Me.

Do not get up and go away. Stay with Me awhile. Let Me hear your voice and let Me see your face, for your voice is so sweet and your countenance is lovely. As I reveal Myself to you here in this place, you will know My love anew. And when we go from here, we will go together to lodge in the villages - to touch those who as yet have not known My love.

We will go together - you and I
We will serve together - you and I
We are one forever - you and I
We will love forever - you and I
You will be forever, My pure Bride
I will stay forever, My dear Bride
You will live with Me forever, My chosen one, My Bride!
Poetry written by Florli Nemeth

Verse 12A

Let us get up early to the vineyards, let us see if the vine flourish, whether the tender grape appear, and the pomegranates bud forth...

My prayer
Let *us,* Lord, go out early to *Your* vineyards - *our* vineyards - to the vines You have entrusted to me. Lord, You have given each of Your mature believers a vineyard they alone are responsible to tend and nurture. You go with me to check on the vines to see if the vines are flourishing and to check on their spiritual progress. You sometimes call me to go to other's vineyards, and again, *we* go together to check on them. It isn't always convenient, Lord. Sometimes there is a sacrifice of time and energy and money, but You always go with me and we check things out together. It is not *my* ministry, but *our* ministry.

He said
I see your desire to be a blessing to other's vineyards as well as to your own and I also see the disappointment and discouragement you experience when the vines don't seem to be growing as they should or when there is a setback. But dear one, remember how I worked in your life when your vine was not flourishing? Do you recall how I drew you to Myself with tenderness and without condemnation?

Your remembrance of My love in bygone days will help you to keep going even when the vines are not flourishing or when the grapes have not yet appeared. A gardener always has an eye to the future and a sixth sense about what should be done when a plant or vine is languishing. I will show you what these vines need. Just ask.

My prayer
Show me, Jesus, the needs of plants in the vineyard across town. It's not my vineyard, but You and I have been visiting it. In my last visit I found a lot of immaturity and confusion about the truth of Your Word. There was uncertainty even about very basic, foundational truths. Lord, You see these budding vines. You were with me. Show me what I need to do for them.

He said
Water the vineyard and *all* the plants with your prayers. Go often to speak My Word over them.

It is said that plants grow faster if you talk to them. So speak My Word over and over and over again. It will settle on their hearts as the dew of the morning, and it will refresh and nourish them so they can grow.

The winds that blow on these vines and plants are sent by the enemy to dry them out and to bring drought and destruction, but My Word spoken over them, even in your prayers, will be as refreshing rain and dew of the morning to counteract the voice of the enemy and cause the plant to grow once again. We work together, My bride! It is as you labor that I receive your love.

Verse 12B

There I will give You my love.

My thoughts

Earlier the maiden desired to give Him her love only under the apple tree. She hesitated to follow Him to the mountains of ministry because she thought she might lose the intimacy she had experienced with Him. The fact of the matter is that God wants both intimacy *and* ministry. There is an established truth: ministry flows out of intimacy.

My prayer

God, You want to draw me into intimacy with Yourself so that I may run in ministry with You. You don't want a servant who works *for* You - You want a lover who rules and reigns *with* You. Your plan for me is that I become a working, loving bride at Your side -- a worshipping warrior, a lover-laborer.

Lord, I give myself to You to be an awesome lover of God *and* a bride committed to serving You no matter what the pressures or difficulties, hardships or persecutions. Lord God, I am committed to my being drawn by You into deeper love and intimacy in prayer and devotion *and* to our running together in ministry wherever that will take me.

I embrace both the first and second commandment - to love You with all my heart, soul and mind and to seek You for the needs of others - to love Your people and to embrace Your heart for the world.

He said
It is in knowing and experiencing My deep love that your heart will be expanded to love the people I love. You will always serve Me best from a position of love and intimacy in prayer. When you lose your love and your intimate times with Me, you will begin to burn out and dry up.

When you look to your ministry to define who you are, you will fall prey to discouragement and frustration.

When you begin to feel your work is more important than your inner love life with Me, you'll wear yourself out trying to be all things to all people.

When you labor out of fear or jealousy you will isolate yourself and fail to see that I have called other lovers of God to work alongside you.

The work will not fall apart without you. It is only a very narrow view of My kingdom that would cause you to feel you are the only one who can do a job the way it should be done. And isn't there also an element of pride that would provoke such an attitude?

My dear friend, do not be moved or distracted from the place of intimacy. There your heart is filled and watered and refreshed. There you are empowered and enabled to run with Me to the mountains, to the valleys, to the gardens, to the vineyards; it is there that you are made loving and endowed with a servant heart - serving and loving for all of your days. You are only effective in ministry when empowered by My love.

So do not allow anything or anyone to move you from this place of intimacy, for there I will give you My love.

My prayer response

> I will give You love no matter what the outcome
> I will stay with You and rest my soul awhile.
>
> I will sit beneath Your shade and bask in love divine
> I will spend my days with You, no thought of sense of time.

So draw me, Lord, into Your heart and let me feel Your love
Then run with You, my hand in Yours, to touch the ones *YOU* love!

So let me live my life in love, my heart entwined with Yours
So let me labor, Lord, with You, the work not mine, but *YOURS*!

Poetry written by Florli Nemeth

Verse 13

The mandrakes give a smell…and at our gates are all manner of pleasant fruits, new and old, which I have laid up for Thee, O my beloved.

My thoughts

The mandrakes speak of bridal love and intimacy. My love relationship with Jesus gives off a fragrance to others around me. The fruits speak of the results of the bride's ministry and also of the graces of God growing within her. The gates imply what is in her realm of authority and what is her own spiritual experience.[405]

My prayer

Lord, as Your graces grow within me, others are drawn to You. The fruit that is growing in my life is the work wrought by Your presence within me.[406].

Jesus, You are producing Your love, Your joy and peace, Your kindness, goodness and faithfulness, Your gentleness and Your self-control or continence in me. I can see that these things are growing within me, and I am encouraged. You don't ask that I be perfect in these graces, only that I am growing in them. These fruits need to be found within me, both new and mature. The joy I experienced yesterday is not enough for today; I need to build on the old, but continue to develop new fruit in my life.

---

[405] Genesis 30:14-16

[406] Galatians 5: 22 Amplified

Verse 13A

The mandrakes give a smell...

He said
Dear one, there is a deep fragrance emanating from your life, and it is the fragrance of My love. Our relationship touches every area of your life, coloring your choices and decisions and permeating everything you do. Your desire is to please Me and to serve others but do not forget that you serve others best by first serving Me with your love and affection. You have poured out your love over Me, and you continue to do so every morning.

Verse 13B

...and at our gates are all manner of pleasant fruits...

He said
The fruit, the revival, the move of My Holy Spirit is at your gates - at your door. The harvest is happening right in front of you! *You* will have a vital part to play in this harvest. You have been born into the kingdom for such a time as this. You – yes, even you - will experience deeper intimacy with Me than you have ever dreamed possible, and you will partner with Me to bring in the harvest. It is at your door, right before you.

Verse 13C

...pleasant fruits, new and old, which I have laid up for Thee, O my beloved.

He said
What I do is new in your life, but I do not discard the old. You have many hidden treasures in your heart as a seasoned warrior and these past experiences are vital for understanding what I would do today. Some want only to live in past experiences and fail to embrace the new things I give. Their arms are so full of the old, they cannot receive the new.

Others are so excited to embrace the new they throw away and completely disregard the former things, thereby losing the benefit and stability of a history in My presence. Your history is important. Your past experiences have made you what you are today. I do not change. I am the same, yesterday, today and forever. I build on the "yesterdays" of your life, and I do not disregard what you have experienced in prayer, in worship, or in the enjoyment of My presence.

But as you face the future, there is more. I long to load you down with new fruit, new wine, new revelations, new manifestations of My presence, new anointing, fresh fire. You need the "new fruits" to reach the "new harvest". You don't have to discount your old experiences - you just need to move on to the new things I have for you.

Chapter 8

The Bride Longs for the Church To Experience Bridal Intimacy

Verse 1

O that thou wert as my brother, that sucked the breasts of my mother! When I should find thee without, I would kiss thee; yea, I would not be despised.
Oh, if only you were my brother; then I could kiss you no matter who was watching, and no one would laugh at me. (Living Bible)

My thoughts
The bride is wishing she could be more intimate with Jesus in a public way. In Eastern countries expressions of love between brothers and sisters are displayed openly, but *not* between a wife and her husband, and certainly not with a fiancée. For example, in India women friends hold hands as they walk down the road, and men friends do the same but men and women do not do so. It is not proper for a man to hold hands even with his own wife in public. The bride here longs to express her love publicly, but she recognizes her need to restrain herself.

My prayer
Lord, I too long to publicly express my love for You but I recognize that I must hold back in places and situations where people may not understand these things. I want to be bold in my love for You, but find that in all practicality I must restrain my expressions of love when in the presence of others.

I believe You understand this. In like manner You would love to express Your love to me publicly and without restraint, but I know from experience that Your most beautiful expressions of love are given to me in the secret place where our hearts meet, face to face.

This is why it is so important that I develop an intimate prayer time with You for it is there that You reveal Yourself to me most deeply. It is in that solitary place of prayer that I hear You calling me to a higher level of adoration and intercession. It is to reveal Yourself to me more clearly, more dearly, and more deeply.

You call me to a higher level of worship, alone with You, I experience those things I can find no other place. O Jesus, You have my heart in this place of solitary prayer and worship for it is there that I can express my love to You as I so long to do.

The song Fanny J. Crosby wrote is in my heart today Jesus, and I sing it to You:

> "Here from the world we turn, Jesus to seek
> Here may His loving voice tenderly speak.
> Jesus, our dearest Friend
> While at Thy feet we bend
> Oh, let Thy smile descend,
> 'Tis Thee we seek.
> Come to our heart's delight
> Make every burden light
> Cheer Thou our waiting sight
> We long for Thee."[407]

These words truly express my heart, Lord Jesus. How I long for You to touch me. How I long to look deeply within Your eyes and say, "*I love You*".

He said

> In this holy, secret place
> Where you've come to meet with Me
> I will yet reveal Myself
> To your heart so sweet, so free.

---

[407] "Here From The World We Turn" No. 140 in Keswick Hymnal

You the one for whom I died
You the child for whom I live
You have chosen to be Mine
All your love to give.

I will yet reveal Myself
To your heart so very dear
In this holy, secret place
With My love, My presence near.

Come My dear and rest awhile
In this quiet, holy place
I am here to strengthen you
I am here to show My face.

Looking to Me here behold
Gaze of purest love divine
Held in arms of love secure
I am yours, and you are Mine!

One day I will come for you
You will live with Me
There forever in My arms
Experience My love eternally.

Poetry written by Florli Nemeth

I will always reveal My love to you in the quiet, secret place. There every need in your life will be met, every question answered, every heartache healed, every misunderstanding dissolved.

And you need not be restrained when in this place of prayer. You can pour out your heart to Me. Whatever is in your heart, you can share it with Me because I understand all, I know all, and I love you unconditionally. There is nothing in your life I do not know already, and as you love Me without restraint, I will pour out My love over you without holding back a thing.

Today the enemy has come against you with words in a vicious attack. Lay this at My feet, dear one, and let Me deal with it. Don't even let it possess a corner of your mind; cast it on Me. Did I not invite you to cast your cares and burdens on Me?[408] Give your burdens to Me. I can handle them and I will carry them - yes, I will carry you!

Verse 2

I would lead thee, and bring thee into my mother's house, who would instruct me; I would cause thee to drink of spiced wine of the juice of my pomegranate.

My thoughts
She wants to bring Jesus to the church. She has received a great revelation of passionate love and obedience and she longs to share it with those in her local expression of the body of Christ where she has had a long-term relationship. She has no desire to promote herself, she is just longing to promote Jesus. By honoring those who taught her in the ways of the Lord she blesses them and refuses to be critical of them. Her desire is to encourage and bless them.

My prayer
Lord Jesus, I long to see Your people come to experience Your bridal love and intimacy. It is my passion to bring the revelation of Your passionate love for Your people to the ones You so deeply love. I have tasted - only tasted - Your deep, deep love, and I long to go deeper. I want to spend the rest of my life experiencing deeper and deeper levels of Your bridal love and sharing this bridal love revelation with Your church.

It's not about *my* ministry - it's about bringing *You*, Jesus, and bringing Your presence and Your love to Your people. This is now my passionate desire.

And Jesus, I long to give my *best* to You. I want to give You the best and the highest, just as You have given me Your best. As You anoint me, I commit myself to minister to Your friends; in so doing, I cause *You* to drink. I would serve *You* by committing to the things that are on *Your* heart. Above all I commit myself to purity in my secret life, the life that is open only to You. I long that You would drink the juice of my pomegranate.

---

[408] Psalm 55:22. Here the word "cast" means to throw out, to hurl out, to throw down or cast off one's self

This inward purity is truly the foundation of any ministry or service. I understand that, and I commit to walk in purity before You.

He said
I receive your invitation. The desires you feel in your heart are the desires I've placed within you. I will enable and empower you to bring yourself to Me, and to bring the revelation of My bridal love to the ones I love and the ones you love. I receive the wine of your love. Not only that but I will keep your heart pure as you come before Me and allow Me to wash your feet on a daily basis. You are clean through the Word I have spoken to you. As you continue to walk in the light, you are kept clean by My Word and by My blood. I am that light, so as you walk with Me day by day, you are cleansed and kept pure within.[409]

Verse 3

His left hand should be under my head, and His right hand should embrace me.

My thoughts
She made this declaration in her earlier experience.[410].

My prayer
Lord Jesus, please support me; let Your left hand be under my head and please draw me to Your heart with the embrace of Your right hand. I feel frustrated and in a place of unrest. I need to pillow my head in Your arm and allow You to draw me close. I know it is only in nearness to You that my heart will find true peace.

How can I have come all this way and still feel the darkness of my own heart? The anxiousness of my own spirit? Lord Jesus, I just need Your touch, Your support, Your embrace in these days. I yield to Your love over me today.

He said
I will manifest My love and support today as you trust in Me and lean on Me. My left hand is holding you up, supporting and strengthening you, protecting and preserving you from the schemes and evil devices of the enemy. He is the one who brings unrest and uneasiness. But I say

---

[409] John 13:10/1 John 1:7
[410] Song of Solomon 2:6

to you today, lean your head on the pillow of My arm. Don't let your mind distract you or cause you to despair. Lean your head on Me.

I promise to draw you to My heart. On those days when you feel distraught - even when you rest your head on My arm - I am able to embrace and hold you close. That's My desire - to bring you close, to see you rest in My protection and love over you.

Don't fret, dear one. Your words of frustration bring a cloud of weariness over you but My words of love bring sunshine and clear, refreshing days to your life. Surrender to My embrace, to My love. Do not resist it. Do not push Me away. Come close.

Verse 4

I charge you, O daughter of Jerusalem, that ye stir not up, nor awake my love, until he please.

My thoughts
In her desire to avoid anything that would interrupt the presence of the Lord, she determines to watch over Him tenderly and carefully so that nothing would cause Him to withdraw. (There is again some difference of opinion as to who is speaking here. Some feel it is the King speaking to the daughters, asking them to avoid pressuring the bride with their religious agendas.)

Her mandate is to know and experience the deep love of her Lord and to minister out of that deep love relationship; His purpose for her is that she live her life out of this place of love. Hers is to be a ministry flowing out of love, a ministry perfectly blended together with love.

My prayer
Lord, could this not be interpreted both ways? When You reveal Yourself to us and we experience Your manifest presence, whether individually or corporately, it is no easy task to keep our hearts tender, pliable and totally submitted to the Spirit of God. You are easily grieved by our complacency or by our lack of immediate obedience. Lord, in those times of nearness to You I would hold You close and not let You go.

Further, Lord, I recognize You are speaking something very clearly here. You do not want me to be caught up in activities and even in ministry that does not flow out of love. You desire a lover, not a servant!

Remind me, though, my love for You is not to be at the exclusion of service. You are not saying You don't need me to work in Your harvest. You are just saying, "Don't disturb or distract her from these times of intimate communion and fellowship with Me."

He said
You are in a very strategic season in your life. You have yearned to know My deepest love, and I am now revealing My love to you. I speak to every distraction, every disturbance, every well-meaning disciple that would seek to lure you away from My presence and from the expressions of My intimate love.

My passion is for you to experience My love daily, to meet Me in the secret place daily, to enjoy and rest in My presence daily, and to know Me intimately. Then from that place I will send you out into My harvest field to glean, to reap, to work for Me.

Will a lover outwork everyone else? Oh, yes, of that there is no doubt. My desire over you is that the love we share will be the sacred impetus in your life and ministry.

When this is so, you will not burn out with overwork because you will have achieved the balance of loving relationship and dedicated servanthood. This balance between intimacy and ministry will largely affect the rest of your relationships as well. You will know their importance and their need to be guarded and nurtured. Your marriage will benefit and your family also will reap the benefits of a balanced walk with Me in intimacy and ministry.

You see, the question is *not* "*What do you do*?", but rather, "*How much do you love, and what ministry flows out of that love*?"

So, dear one, you need to say what I say to everything that would distract you from spending time with Me: - "*Do not stir nor awaken love*". It is not a matter of finding time in your busy schedule to spend with Me; it is a matter of organizing your schedule around your time with

Me. It must be a priority. It must take first place. It must be the one thing in your life that takes precedence over all other things.

Be assured that I am intentional in My emphasis on this issue. So many of My servants lose their first love and in the middle of their career they fall apart because their service did not continue to flow out of love. Do you know how that has grieved My heart? When the very ones I love, the very ones to whom I have committed My authority to serve in My kingdom lose their authority for lack of love, My heart is pained.

O My bride, My chosen servant, you are of great value to Me in My kingdom, but return to your first love. Put me before your ministry, before your schedule, before your commitments and speaking engagements. I long to pour into your heart as you wait on Me, and then you will go out to work, to live, to love, to speak with a new and fresh anointing upon you. **Make love your first aim. Make Me your first love!**

My response
Lord, I receive this admonition. I understand that You desire my love more than anything else I can give to You or do for You. My heart says "*Yes, do not awaken or stir up love until it please.*"

I want Your presence and Your love in my life more than fame, more than ministry, more than the applause of men. I want Your enjoyment, Your pleasure and delight, Your joy, Your love. I give myself to You. I commit myself to be first and foremost a lover of God. I want to be known not as a great pastor or missionary or worker in the kingdom - I want to be known only as a lover of God and a lover of the ones He loves! I give myself to You. I commit myself to be first and foremost a lover of God.

The Bridal Seal

Verse 5A

Who is this that cometh up from the wilderness, leaning upon her Beloved?

My thoughts
There are similar charges throughout this book as the previous verse and similar words to these: "Who is this that cometh out of the wilderness like pillars of smoke?" [411]

While once the question was asked of the King, here it is asked of the Bride as she leans upon the arm of her Beloved.

I love the old hymn -

"My faith has found a resting place
Not in device nor creed
I trust the Ever-living One
His wounds for me shall plead.
I have no other argument
I have no other plea
It is enough that Jesus died
And that He died for me."[412]

My prayer
Lord Jesus, You are preparing a loving and a leaning Bride, one who rises up out of this world victorious over the world, the flesh and the devil. You do not leave Your Bride in the wilderness of this fallen world. She arises to meet her Beloved, to walk with Him in white, to lean upon Him.

Lord Jesus, Your Bride walks with You thus here on earth, totally victorious over every obstacle the devil would put before her.

Jesus, I see my weaknesses, my inability to conquer in myself but You are the Lover of my soul. You are my joy, my peace, my Victor, my

---

411 Song of Solomon 3:6 and 8:5

412 My Faith Has Found A Resting Place by Eliza E. Hewitt (in "Songs of Joy and Gladness", No. 2, McDonald Gill & Co. 1891)

Conqueror, and I am one with You. Therefore I, too, am more than a conqueror. I, too have overcome the world, the flesh and the devil.

You are my strength, my wisdom, my hope, my life. All of my life is summed up in You and ends in You! You are the Source of my life, the Sustainer of my life, the Shining Star of my life!

The Holy Spirit has opened my eyes to see the weaknesses and inabilities and inadequacies of my own life. Even my heart that so loves you is capable of failing and denying the very One I love.

Through all this, Lord Jesus, I have come to a deeper understanding of who You are. Yes, I am dark. I saw that earlier in my life[413] and that was *all* I saw at that time. I could not see what You have always seen in me - in You I am lovely.

Now I see what *You* see, and as I lean on You, I see myself in proper balance. Yes, I once was a sinner, but YES - O glorious YES, You died for me on the cross. You took care of the sin question. Because You live in me, I can walk in forgiveness and wholeness, in victory and in complete protection and provision.

Jesus, You are a wonderful Saviour, a glorious King, and a marvelous Lover and Friend. I lean the weight of my life on You. I depend on You, not on my own understanding.[414]

Leaning on You I rise above the circumstances of my life! There is no place I'd rather be than right here beside You, leaning in total dependence upon You. Jesus, I love You.

He said
As a groom gives his bride his right arm, so I give you My right arm; as you take My arm, I put My hand over yours, holding you to Myself, never letting you go. There are many of My loved ones who truly love Me but have not yet learned to lean on Me.

---

[413] Song of Solomon 1:5
[414] Proverbs 3:5

I long for My bride to put her arm in Mine that we may rise together, conquering every foe, overcoming every attack of the enemy, and ascending to new heights of joy and peace in the experience of My love. This is My desire for My church, My bride. I know My bride loves Me but I long for her to look away from her own understanding and her own inadequacies and begin to lean on My understanding, My strength, My strategies to win the world and bring in the harvest.

When My bride begins to lean on Me, she will rise invincible in battle, a force this world has never seen. She will conquer every enemy, overcome every obstacle, and enjoy complete victory over even the gates of hell. I said in My Word that the gates of hell cannot prevail against the church, and you will see that kind of total victory when My bride takes her place of authority beside Me and rises up leaning upon Me.

You, too, My Child, will see this kind of victory and authority in your life when you rise up from the wilderness of your world and your circumstances and begin to lean upon Me, your Beloved. I see you as a leaning lover, one who is totally dependent upon Me.

Child of My heart, lean heavily upon Me allowing Me to support your weight. Draw your strength, your life from me. My heart is overcome with your leaning heart; I would do anything for you, My dearest love.

Verse 5B

...I raised thee up under the apple tree: there thy mother brought thee forth: there she brought thee forth that bare thee.

My prayer
Jesus, You are reminding me here of what You have done for me in the past. How well I remember the day You brought me forth into life. I can see the place where I knelt as a child and gave my heart to You. There were many who led me to You: my parents who taught me the Word of God and shared their walk with You; my church played a great part in bringing me to life and there were my pastors who impacted my life deeply and ministered Your love to me. I remember, too, an adopted aunt and uncle who prayed for me and impacted my life. There are

probably others who had a part in my coming to You that I will never know about.

It was Your church, Your people, who brought me forth to birth in Your family. Nor did the impact of their lives cease back then. From the days of my youth to where I stand today, I can proclaim that I have a *good* heritage and a wonderful spiritual root system.

I express my gratefulness to You for every person who is part of Your Body. Your church has touched my life making me who I am today because of those who poured into my life. I believe You are grieved when we despise our roots or are ashamed of our early beginnings.

Lord, I want always to appreciate the spiritual lineage You have given me. Forgive me for the times I neglected to do that.

He said
Yes, I know, dear one, how at various points in your life you have struggled with aspects of your spiritual heritage. But truth be known, you are what you are today as a result of what godly men and women poured into your life. They were not perfect but nor are *you*. As you recall how they held you to a standard, making you accountable and responsible, you have learned to value them highly now.

Remember that it was under the apple tree that I first spoke to your heart. The apple tree is a picture of My cross - the place where I died to show My love for you. And from that cross flows forgiveness and restoration, healing and wholeness, life and strength, refreshing and abundant life forever more!

When first you embraced the cross, your life was changed forever. The cross remains the place I have chosen to reveal Myself to you. It is no longer a place of death for Me but rather a place of life. As you come to My cross, My apple tree, I refresh you with My love. Did I not say, Look and live? In the Old Testament story of the plague in the wilderness where I commanded Moses to build a serpent on a pole, people had only to look, and they were healed.

Meet Me daily at My apple tree for there you will receive a revelation of My love and there I will pour out upon you *all* that you need. You are testimony to this truth for over the years you have come daily to sit under My apple tree. My people need to know how important this is for their growth in love and in maturity. There must be time in your day for love, a time for meeting me under the apple tree!

It is not a thing that will come easily because the enemy of your soul will fight this. He will try to keep you so busy you have no time to be with Me. And if he cannot keep you busy with life in general, he will distract you by allowing you to keep busy in serving Me. He doesn't mind if you work for Me as long as you don't sit under My apple tree. Why? Because he knows that you will eventually give up or wear out without the refreshing shade and fruit of My presence!

Be wise, My dear one, and remember where you found Me. Make it your chief aim in life to spend time with Me daily and often throughout the day. I wait there for you to come, and I long for your presence! I love our times together, and it is My joy to pour into your life again and again. So encourage My people to come to Me and to spend their love on Me.

The cross is a place of LIFE. It is death only to that which would destroy you. For the enemy, it is death; but for you, it is *LIFE.*

Verse 6A

Set me as a seal upon your heart, as a seal upon your arm . . . .

My prayer
Lord Jesus, my journey began with a desire for Your kisses and it ends here with a longing for the impartation of your love upon my heart. Seal my heart with Your royal seal of love.

Stamp my heart with your love! Then every time I look at my heart I will see Your seal that cannot be broken. That seal means everything to me: *Your promise* to love me and to protect me, *Your affirmation* of ownership and possession, and *Your Word* that is backed up by *Your authority.*

Stamp my arm with Your seal! Then all the world will know I belong to You, I am loved by You, I am protected by You, and I walk in Your authority here on earth.

He said
Dear one whom My heart adores, *the seal of My love on your heart is for you.* When you see My stamp upon your heart you will know I cannot break My promise to You. You are Mine, irrevocably Mine forever. Never will I cease to love those I purchased with Mine own blood.

Indeed, Mine is an everlasting love. It does not depend on what you do or don't do. I just love you because you belong to Me. I simply love you. [415]

My promise to you is that I will be with you to the end of the age and that I will keep you as the apple of My eye.[416]

I have promised

- To guard your feet.[417]
- To keep your city.[418]
- To keep your foot lest you stumble or fall.[419]
- To give My angels charge over you.[420]
- To keep you from all evil and to keep your life.[421]
- To guard you night and day and to water you every moment.[422]

These are just a few of My promises to you and remember, I do not change. [423] I will not love you today and cast you aside tomorrow. I cannot say this to you more clearly, My dearest love, My bride: I chose you, set my love upon you and all the world will see that you belong to Me.

The seal of love on your arm is for all who see you to know You are Mine.

---

[415] Deuteronomy 7:7 & 8/Jeremiah 31:3
[416] Matthew 28:20/Zechariah 2:8/Psalm 17:8
[417] 1 Samuel 2:9
[418] Psalm 127:1
[419] Proverbs 3:23
[420] Psalm 91:11,12
[421] Psalm 121:7
[422] Isaiah 27:3
[423] Malachi 3:6

There is another truth: Because the world hates Me, it will hate You, too, because You belong to Me. In their rage against Me, they will rage against you but I will open up to you a retreat in the wilderness where you will be safe. [424] Even there I will be your Refuge and your Strength because I am the eternal God. I am your Refuge and your dwelling place, and underneath you are My everlasting arms. I will drive out every enemy before you.[425]

In that day when you stand before Me, I will declare you are Mine before the angels and demons, before the beasts and elders, and before My Father. I have stamped My seal of love upon your heart and upon your arm and it is a seal that can never be broken. You are the bride I love, the bride I have chosen above all others. You are My joy and My crown.

And dearest one, I wear *your* stamp of love on My heart and on My arm. Every time I look at My arm I see you. Your love is always before Me and Your name is written on the palms of each of My hands. How could I ever forget you, My dearest love?

The things that hurt and wound you, hurt and wound Me. Even as the picture of Jerusalem's walls in ruin were before Me and I promised to rebuild them, so the things that have come against you to destroy you are before Me, and My promise to you is to rebuild those walls and chase away those who would destroy you.

Your enemies shall become your slaves and you will clothe yourself with them as a bride displays her jewels. These are My promises to you today. Let them enable you to lift up your voice and sing because your redemption is very near.[426]

He sang to me

> Your heart made tender - made tender with My love
> Like wax - like wax warmed by the flame
> My seal imprinted - imprinted on it thus
> My ownership, My very name.

---

[424] Revelation 12:6

[425] Psalm 46:1/Deuteronomy 33:27

[426] Isaiah 49:16 - 18

Your heart protected - protected by this love
And loved - yes, loved by Me alone
Your heart impacted - impacted by My touch
My dwelling place, My home.

I sang to Him
My heart transformed by love divine
His image pressed on me
I now live only for my God
His will alone I see.

My arm surrendered to His will
And yielded to His ways
My destiny to work with Him
Fulfill His plan each day.

Poetry Written by Florli Nemeth

Verse 6B

...for love is strong as death...

He said
My love fears nothing, overcoming all obstacles that would impede our union. My love for you is strong as death nor could you ever escape My love, for it will surely follow you wherever you go. My love will conquer every evil thing that would seek to attach itself to you.

There is no demon in hell that can stand before this love. There is no sin or bondage that can remain when you are sealed with My love. Through my love you will conquer, overcoming every demonic thing, every sinful thing, every inborn weakness and tendency to sin, every stronghold of the enemy in your family ancestral line that has come down to you and every strategy of the enemy to destroy you.

Ask yourself: how strong **is** death? Can you do anything to escape your appointment with death? Can anything in My creation escape it?

You know the answer ...and that is how comprehensively and completely My love works in your life.

My love will hold you fast and never let you go. It will conquer every enemy and defeat every foe. I proved My love for you at the cross where I conquered death and hell. I delivered you from the power of darkness and translated you into My kingdom through the blood I shed for you on the cross.[427]

I made peace through the blood of My cross and reconciled all things to Myself. I cleared the way for everyone to come to Me.[428]

Because I experienced death for you, I now can bring you into My very presence - into the presence of God.[429]

You stand before Me, justified, with nothing against you because your account has been paid for in full. Through My death, I have conquered all: all sin, all pain and sickness, all strategies of the enemy to keep you in bondage and to alienate you from Me. Even more, I promise you that one day even the sting of sin that causes death will be gone. As the Apostle Paul wrote, "death will be swallowed up in victory." [430]

Because I live in love, you too shall live in love forever and ever. You may die physically, but your spirit man, the real you, will be forever with Me in My home.

Yes, My love for you is strong as death - even stronger than death, for one day even death itself will be conquered by My love and life will reign forever. *You* will live forever with Me because the seal of My love is stamped on you.

Verse 6C

...jealousy is cruel as the grave: the coals thereof are coals of fire, which hath a most vehement flame.

My thoughts
Jealousy in a good sense is love at its highest peak. *Love demands everything or nothing at all!*

---

[427] Colossians 1:13
[428] Colossians 1:20
[429] Colossians 1:22
[430] 1 Corinthians 15:54 &55

God's love claims everything in my life. Like the grave that claims everything, so is God's jealous love – there are no exceptions to its demands. "*Nothing can escape the grasp of the grave, and likewise nothing escapes the holy power of this love. God will release a love upon us that is as comprehensive as death and the grave.*"[431]

God's love, like a fire out of control, cannot be quenched. The intensity of His fire burns away all that would prevent us from experiencing His love.

My prayer
O God, release over me this love divine, all other loves excelling! Charles Wesley knew this kind of love and wrote his beautiful hymn, "Love Divine" -

"Love divine, all loves excelling
  Joy of heaven, to earth come down
Fix in us Thy humble dwelling
  All Thy faithful mercies crown . . . .

Finish then Thy new creation
  Pure and spotless may we be......

Changed from glory into glory
  Till in heaven we take our place
Till we cast our crowns before Thee
  Lost in wonder, love and praise."

My prayer
Jesus, if Your love demands everything, it shall have everything: my body, my spirit, my soul, my home, my possessions, my goals, my family, my children, my friends, my earthly beginnings, my ends, *my heart, my love, my all.*

Let the fire of Your love consume all that is not of You in my life. May Your all-consuming love change my life from glory to glory, conforming me to Your image.

---

[431] Quote from Pastor Mike Bickle, "The Ravished Heart of God", Session 19 on Chapter 8, verse 6

I surrender to Your love
A love that will not let me go
I surrender to this fiery love
That now consumes my soul.
I surrender to Your claims
Demanding all I am
I surrender to this fiery love
And lay my life down for the Lamb.
I surrender to Your fire
A jealous flame of love divine
I surrender to consuming love
Refining till I brightly shine
- with Your glory, with Your beauty
- with Your love divine
- with Your presence, with Your holiness
Till all I am, is Thine!

Poetry written by Florli Nemeth

He said
I am committed to do this very thing. I am committed to our fiery love forever. One day in My presence you will shine but until that day, I desire to shine through you here on earth so that all may see My love - My glorious love in you.

My love in you is a consuming fire that burns like a raging forest fire out of control. Everyone that touches your life and everyone you touch will be set aflame with My glorious love. So spread My fiery love wherever you go.

Touch other people so they too will burn with My all consuming love. This is your calling, your destiny - to burn with fiery love for Me, and for My presence, even as My heart burns for you.

Verse 7A

Many waters cannot quench love [neither can the floods drown it]...

My thoughts
The love that God imparts to us cannot be quenched. Generally water extinguishes fire, but the love of God that rages within us cannot be quenched.

He said
My love is stronger than any sinful flame in your life. No matter what the sin or bondage, My love will loose it from you and extinguish its fire within you yet without quenching My fiery love within you. My love is stronger than the waters of affliction, trial or persecution.[432] Indeed, *nothing* can separate you from My love.[433]

Trouble or calamity does not come because I have ceased to love you nor do hunger or persecution beset you because I have deserted you. I will never cease to love you, and I will never leave you nor forsake you.[434]

Nothing can ever separate you from My love - not your fears or your worries, not where you find yourself emotionally, not the death of your loved one, not angels or the powers of hell. *nothing* can keep My love from reaching you, and *nothing* can take My love away from you.

In fact, My love will conquer every one of those things the enemy would throw at you to steal My love from your heart. These waters cannot extinguish My love in your heart.

My love is stronger than the raging waters of temptation.

The devil will use the desires of your heart that are right in themselves, but he will tempt you to satisfy those desires outside the boundaries of My will for you. The waters of immorality may come against you but I have promised to make a way of escape for you. My love is stronger than any temptation the enemy would bring against you and My love will overcome every power of the enemy in your life.[435]

My love is stronger than the waters of prosperity and riches.

The enemy attempts to use prosperity and wealth to draw your heart away from Me yet My fiery love in you cannot be quenched, not even by the pleasures of life that could distract you.

---

[432] Isaiah 43:1,2; Psalm 42:7 & 8
[433] Romans 8:35-39
[434] Hebrews 13:5
[435] 1 Corinthians 10:13

Your heart will *not* be distracted or deceived, discouraged or depressed or defeated, nor will My love in your heart be demolished or quenched or extinguished. My love for you will conquer; this is My commitment to you. I have promised that what I began in you, I will complete. The raging fire of My love within you will truly do the work I have called it to do.

I love you with an everlasting love. You may fail, and your heart may fail but My love cannot, it will prevail. Even you cannot stop this love I have for you! So rest in My love, yield to it for My unfailing, conquering love endures forever.

I responded
I will remember Your love more than wine! (Song of Solomon 1:4)

I will look to You, Lord when the trials come
I'll depend on Your love to overcome.
I will look to the Word when the storm waters rage
I'll remember Your love enduring age after age.
I will cry to my God when the enemy taunts
I'll escape to Your presence from temptation's pull and haunts.
I'll surrender to the love that will forever more endure
To the love that conquers all, to the love steadfast and sure.
I will conquer with Your love - the flames of love within
Will complete all You've begun till my heart is freed from sin.
Then I'll stand before Your Throne, The one You love, Your chosen bride
My heart still burning with the flame of love I cannot hide!
So keep me safe, my Lord, my God, impart this love to me
And let it burn within my heart for all eternity.

Poetry written by Florli Nemeth

Verse 7B

...neither can the floods drown it...

My thoughts
The word "flood" can mean something very destructive like a deluge or a torrent of water, or it can speak of a gentle drip or trickling of water.[436] Here, however, "floods" is from the Hebrew word "nahar"

---

[436] Isaiah 44:3

meaning to sparkle as the sheen of a running stream, Figuratively the word speaks of prosperity.

I believe He is saying here that not only are many waters of affliction incapable of quenching your love for Me, nor will prosperity, blessing, riches or fame drown it.

He said
Yes, My heart knows My end-time church will not be distracted or removed from their first love as was the church in Ephesus. My church will be faithful unto death in the midst of severe persecution.

I see in many parts of the world a rising rage of the enemy against My people who love Me but I also see that they are faithful, without wavering, and many of them thrown into prison and facing death. Even through all that they do not fear the things they are suffering, but have embraced their trials and even death.[437]

I know the things that are happening in various parts of the world.

I see the destructive floods of persecution engulfing My people. I see, too, My people prospering in other places, yet loving Me first, cherishing Me in their hearts, and using their prosperity to finance My kingdom work.

They have not held onto their prosperity for themselves; their love has not grown cold, and they are dreaming of, planning and strategizing ways to build My kingdom in the earth.

I know My people who have not left their first love; I know those who are pursuing Me with all their hearts. I know those who are not moved from their love for Me either by floods of persecution or by waters of prosperity!

The one who is persecuted is not better or more spiritual than the one who uses his or her prosperity to further My program. Both will receive their reward. The key is to be faithful, to remain steadfastly in

[437] Revelation 2:4, 9 & 10

love no matter what flood may come your way for love is the greatest of all things.

My church will overcome in these last days. My church will eat from the tree of life in paradise. My church will remain faithful even when facing death and will receive the crown of life. My church will be nourished by that hidden manna and will receive a stone engraved with a new name.

My overcoming church will be given power over the nations, My people clothed in white raiment. I will confess their name before My Father and the angels. My people will become pillars in My house, and I will write My name on them. My people will sit with Me on My Throne - My conquering church will sit beside Me even as I conquered and overcame and sat down with My Father on His Throne.

This is the glorious church, My beautiful bride without spot or wrinkle - My bride whose love cannot be quenched by waters of persecutions or floods of blessing and prosperity. This is My end time church - the church I died for, the church I love.[438]

And this is how I see you, My beautiful bride. O, how My heart longs for our wedding day when I may present you to My Father. I am so proud and protective of you. You are the joy and the rejoicing of My heart.

I want you to know that I sit upon the flood, no matter in what form it may come against you, I am in control and I am with you to the end of the age. You will never be left alone to face the flood. Lift up your voice and praise Me even as the mighty oceans thunder My praise. Clap your hands and dance before Me even as the waves clap their hands in glee.[439]

Praise Me in prosperity
When days are bright and you are strong;
Praise Me in perplexity
When storm clouds come and nights are long.

---

[438] Revelation 2:7, 10, 17, 26/Revelation 3:5, 12, 21
[439] Psalm 29:10/Matthew 28:20/Psalm 93:3 and 98:8

Praise Me in severity
Of storms and floods, of grief and pain
Praise me in sincerity
That hopes when lost and dreams again
Praise Me in complexity
When all is dark and makes no sense;
Praise Me when complacency
Would blind your heart to consequence.
Praise Me in community
When come together with My bride
Praise when opportunity
Would give you cause to run and hide.
Praise Me, yes, excitedly
With body, mind and soul
Praise My name exclusively
Be made to shine, and be made whole.
Praise with importunity
When sun is bright, when clouds hang low
Praise for all eternity
The One you love, the One you know!
Poetry written by Florli Nemeth

Verse 7C

...if a man would give all the substance of his house for love, it would utterly be contemned.

My thoughts
He is saying that the reward of love is ***LOVE.***
This love the bride longed for in the beginning of her journey is now imparted to her, she has been given the gift of love. She has the power to love Jesus with all her heart, soul and mind. She has found the Pearl of greatest price, sold everything and purchased the land.[440]

The bride gave up things of value to pursue this love, counting those things as rubbish compared to the beauty of God's love and affirmation in her life. Now she finds that the sacrifice was nothing in comparison to what she has received from God.[441]

[440] Matthew 13:45, 46
[441] Philippians 3:7-10

She has learned the truth that none can out-give God. The little sacrifices made that seemed so important at the time, slip into insignificance when God begins to multiply His love and grace into our lives.

My prayer

> O God, the little I have given you, the smallest sacrifice
> You take and multiply to me Your greatest love and life.
> My heart committed to this love, My life empowered by Your love
> My heart desiring only love, Your love - the gift of love!
>
> *Poetry by Florli Nemeth*

Jesus, I wanted only to love You more deeply, and here I have found so much more than ever I gave to You. I join the hymn writer in "pouring contempt on all my pride".[442]

Where I gave You trinkets and toys, You gave me gold, silver and precious pearls. Above all You gave me Yourself, the Pearl of greatest price. I gave You nothing more than rubbish and trash, You gave me everything I ever wanted and *more.* You are all I want, all I need, all I will ever desire. Thank You for Your great love. I will spend the rest of my life - and all of eternity - exploring and enjoying this Pearl of great price, You and Your great love.

He said
Explore, My child, enjoy My love. It is My gift to you.

And when I give you a gift it is not only for you, but for others too. As I impart not only My love, but the power to share My love with others I commission you to this task. It will not be a burden for you but rather a delight. It will become to you the greatest joy of your life to share and impart My love to others. This ministry of love will flow from you effortlessly because of My impartation over you and My calling.

I commission you this day to spend the rest of your life imparting wholehearted love for Me to others. This will be the main thrust of your ministry. So continue to bask in My love and when the time is right, I will send you into the limelight as I send you to the nations. When

---

[442] Isaac Watts in "When I Survey the Wondrous Cross"

you finish with the study of this book, it will be but the beginning of your journey into love. In actual fact, you will never be finished with this Song of Songs, a song you will sing forever. Every other book in My Word will take on new meaning because of your submersion into this book.

Do not attempt to make a way for yourself, just be available to Me. Walk in wholehearted love and I will promote you when the time is right. You are in hiding in the wilderness at this present time but I hide My loved ones in the shelter of My presence, safe beneath My hand. I have hidden you in the shadow of My hand, and I have made you a polished arrow.[443]

Right now I am holding you close and hiding you in My quiver, but one day I will take you, My beautifully polished arrow, and shoot you to the nations where you will fulfill My purpose and My destiny for your life.

It is not what you will do to get there, but what I will do to get you there. So be content to be held close to Me in My quiver. You have been called from the womb, even as Isaiah was, and I have made your mouth like a sharp sword.

When you speak My Word in prayer the enemy will flee. People will receive the words you speak and be set free from bondages and sicknesses and diseases. Whenever you speak My Word, your words will be like a sharp sword because My Word is a sword that is full of power.[444]

---

[443] Psalm 31:20 and Isaiah 49:2

[444] Hebrews 4:12

The Bride's Final Intercession and Revelation

Verse 8

We have a little sister, and she hath no breasts. What shall we do for our sister in the day when she shall be spoken for?

My thoughts
The bride is here moving into intercession. There has been a harvest[445] and now there are many young ones (sisters) who know how to feed on the milk of the Word, but they are yet immature and unable to minister to others.[446]

My prayer
Lord, I come to you in intercession for our little sister - the young babes who have just received You into their lives and for the many young people who are just starting their journey with You. What can we do for them to connect them with their destiny as the bride of Christ? How can we minister to them so they will begin to hunger for Your Word and desire to run after You?

Lord, I also intercede for those in Your church who, as believers for many years, have never connected with Your destiny and purpose for them. What can we do to help them see and understand that they are Your bride and that You long for them to know and understand Your love? I pray, as did the apostle Paul, that Your people would grow and in their journey to maturity, become laborers with God. Your servant encouraged them to work out their salvation, a relationship built upon a foundation he had laid.[447]

Lord, there are many in Your church who are still immature and lacking in spiritual discernment. I am asking You, what can we do for them? How can we convey to them the need to awaken to their calling and their inheritance?

[445] Song of Solomon 7:2
[446] 1 Corinthians 3:2
[447] 1 Corinthians 3:1-15/1 Corinthians 15:58/Ephesians 4:12

Lord, I see in a whole new way that, as Your bride, I not only come under Your love and protection, I come into a new agreement of partnership. We are workers together. You don't send me out to labor alone in Your vineyard. You come with me - or rather, I go with You. I find out where You are moving and what You are doing, and I get in agreement with You and actually partner with You in ministry! This is an awesome revelation. It's not my going out to labor and asking You to bless me and go with me but rather, it's my finding out where You are going and what You are doing, and then joining with You in that place of ministry.

So I'm asking You again, dear Lord, what can *we* do for the "little sisters" here in our local body of believers? What can *we* do for the "little sisters" around the world? For those who don't yet know You? For those who know You, but have not yet matured? I want to be involved in Your kingdom purposes. I want to be a co-laborer together with You.

He said
What can you do? Pray and intercede as you are presently doing. Intercede for those I put on your heart because where human efforts fail, prayer moistens and softens the heart-soil. Intercession is so important because as your pray, I will give you insights, revelation and even instructions and directions. Then do what you see Me doing. I have called you to preach the Word, lay hands on the sick, and cast out devils.

I have called you to make disciples of all nations. That involves teaching and mentoring, living your life before My people in such a way that they see Me in your life. Now I do not call you to do all of the above things at the same time. There will be seasons where you will reach out to the unsaved and preach My Word and there will be seasons where I lead you to connect closely with My people, teaching and mentoring those who are young and immature. At other times I will send you to the nations to preach and teach. Many times I will take you only to one or two people at a time; other times I will take you to many.

The key is to watch and wait at My gates in prayer, available and willing to go with Me at a moment's notice. I do not want you to wear out in this ministry, so there will be seasons of rest and refreshing where you may just bask in My love and presence. These seasons are very important in your life because you need rest and renewal on a regular basis. In the physical you need rest daily or else your entire body will lose its balance. Rest is absolutely essential to your physical health and also to your spiritual health.

So this is what we will do: We will rest and then go out to labor. We will return to rest again before going to another place to labor. Above all, though, remember that I will do the work through you. You may speak the Word, but I am the One who takes it and plants it in a heart and I am the One who causes it to grow and bear fruit. You speak the Word, you touch the sick, the blind, the maimed, but I do the work.

Then He gave me more encouraging words . . . .
What would you do for your sisters? For the church? I have given gifts to My people - apostles, prophets, evangelists, pastors and teachers. My intention in giving these gifts was to perfect and fully equip My people to build up My body, the church.[448]

The sister is a part of My body, the church I love and the church for which I gave My life. Don't ever speak evil of your sister. My intent for your sister is that she continue to develop until she arrives at maturity, fully grown and filled up with My life. Then she will "*no longer will be like children, tossed like ships to and fro between chance gusts of teaching and wavering with every changing wind of doctrine, the prey of the cunning and cleverness of unscrupulous men…*". Your *little sister* will then "*lovingly express truth in all things*" and she will be "*enfolded in My love*" even as you are now enfolded in My love.[449]

You see, dear one, I greatly love and value your *little sister,* and I am pleased that you also love her and are concerned about her. Under My direction, the whole body would be fitted together perfectly, each part in its own way helping the other parts, so the whole body would grow in love and be healthy. "*Every joint supplieth*" - every person is "*closely knit and joined together by the joints and ligaments with which it is supplied…*".[450]

---

[448] Ephesians 4:11-13
[449] Ephesians 4:14 & 5
[450] Ephesians 4:16

What I am saying here, dear one, is that every joint has something to give the body and has a function that only it can perform. This should answer your questions, "What shall we do for our sister".

My heart breaks when I view the attitude of some toward your sister, the church. Instead of building it up and adding to it, they tear it down with their critical words and they disregard that for which I gave My life! I am serious when I say that I love My church!

My heart weeps when I hear what some say about the gifts I gave to equip and build up My church. I gave apostles and prophets, just as I gave evangelists, pastors and teachers yet My church has misunderstood these gifts, criticized them, disregarded them and shut the door to their ministry. This grieves Me, dear one, and I call you to intercede for My body - your sister.

My heart longs for My church to come into full maturity, for when it does, the whole world will know that You are My disciples! They will know this when they see your love for one another. *Love is the maturity of all things. When you come into love, you come into maturity!*

My prayer
Lord, I purpose to intercede for our sister, the church, that she would come into full maturity, *built up* by the gifts You have given to bless her, and *brought into* unity as she begins to move into love. May I live to see the day this happens!

I give myself to You, asking You to fulfill my place in the body so that I do what You have called me to do. No matter how small my part may be, it is important. Every part of the body is an important part of the whole. May this become revelation truth to Your church.

Lord, it is vital that I be properly connected to the body and personally related to the sister. I cannot help something of which I am not a part. It is Your purpose and design that every believer be properly connected and related to Your body, the church.

O God, open the eyes and the understanding of Your people to see the value You place on the church and to see the great value You place on the gifts You have given to Your body. You will one day hold us accountable for the way we treated those you gave to us. So Lord, I determine never to speak a negative word against the ministries You have placed in Your church. I choose to receive Your gifts, embrace them and allow them to impart into my life the things I need in order to be built up and brought to maturity.

Lord, I also recognize that where I have rejected Your gifts, it has affected others in Your body. My attitudes affect the little sisters around me. Forgive me where my wrong attitudes toward some apostles and prophets and evangelists have stunted not only my personal growth but the growth of others. I repent of critical attitudes and ask You to change my heart. *I want to receive all You desire to give me so that I can become all You desire me to become!*

Verse 9

If she is a wall, we will build upon her a palace of silver; and if she be a door, we will enclose her with boards of cedar.

My prayer
Lord, I continue to speak with You about the needs of the church. My commitment is to intercede for my *little sisters* until "*Christ be formed in them.*"

There are those in my sphere of influence who are walls, ministries given to protect Your body, Your people.

I see this potential in some of my *little sisters*. Show me how I can come alongside and equip them in their God-given giftings. This is a day when you are building Your church, and I align myself with the Holy Spirit to build, to encourage, and to promote the growth of unity and maturity in Your church.

There are others in Your church who are doors - places of entrance, doors of salvation, people who live and breathe evangelism.

Lord, I want to surround these with *boards of cedar*, speaking of the presence and fragrance of Christ. Cover my *sisters*, clothe them with

Your fragrance as they reach out to the lost and as they present an open door for the lost to enter into Your salvation.

Lord, You are raising up pastors and apostolic and prophetic ministries - **WALLS** - that build and protect the body of Christ. I pray Your blessing over these ministries. I choose to come alongside in prayer and encouragement to see these young ones rise up to their full potential.

You are also raising up evangelists and teachers - DOORS - people whose passion is to see the lost saved and believers taught in the ways of the Lord. We need these ministries, Lord, and we who are mature need to encourage them in our prayers.

Lord, I pray that You will raise up the five-fold ministries spoken of in Ephesians. And I give myself to You to intercede for the strengthening, encouraging and maturing of these ministries in the body of Christ. I ask You to raise up intercessors who understand the functions of the five-fold ministries and who will come alongside with a prayerful heart to support these in prayer.

Father, I believe it is Your purpose to join the hearts of intercessors to the hearts of apostles, prophets, evangelists, pastors and teachers. I pray You will break down every wall of division, and I commit myself to the work of building walls of protection and opening doors of entry.

Father, forgive us as intercessors where we have raised ourselves up in pride, where we have exposed the weaknesses of those in ministry rather than lifting them up in prayer, trusting You to build strong walls in their lives. Forgive us where we have run ahead and chosen to walk independently, causing many to be disillusioned because of divisions and factions.

O God! Help us as intercessors to grow up into You, to be faithful builders of walls and openers of doors, to join our hearts with the apostolic, prophetic, pastoral, evangelistic and teaching ministries of the church, and to do whatever we can to strengthen and enhance these ministries that You have ordained to build Your church. Give to us a greater revelation of Your will and purpose for our *little sisters*.

Appendix A

How to Pray-Read This Book

---

1. Read one verse at a time, or one portion of a verse, and compare the Scripture passages with other versions of the Bible you may have. You may also use Internet resources to find other translations or paraphrases not readily available to you
2. Open your heart to receive what God is saying to **YOU**
3. Turn the scripture into **personal** prayer
4. Or take what God is saying and put it into your own words
5. **Write your prayer in your journal**
6. **Record in your journal what He is saying to YOU**
7. Look up word definitions in a good concordance (i.e. Strong's or Cruden's Concordances)
8. Study the portion of scripture and compare with other scriptures
9. Be open to receive what God would impart to you
10. In this way you will be embarking on your own personal journey of prayer in the Song of Songs!

It may take you a year or longer to complete this study, verse by verse, but when you have finished you will have ***BEGUN*** your journey of love to the high places! Remember, our love relationship with God is a life-long journey, so do you don't have to feel rushed or frustrated.

You are loved by God, and you are a lover of God!

Appendix B

Bibliography

The "Song of Solomon" by James Durham, a great Puritan theologian whose work was first published in 1668 and reprinted in 1723 and 1840. He was one of Scotland's most highly esteemed ministers in the 17th century. It is chiefly for his writings on this book that he is remembered.

The "*Song of Songs*" by Father Juan G. Arintero, O.P., a priest who lived in Spain from 1860 to 1928. His teachings on the Song of Solomon unlocked for many the mysteries of growth in holiness and intimacy with our heavenly Bridegroom, the Lord Jesus Christ.

"*Thy Hidden Ones*" by Jessie Penn-Lewis published first in 1899 in Great Britain, and again in 1950 (Sixth Edition). It was written not as a commentary on the Song of Solomon, but rather as a book expounding on the believer's union with Christ as traced in the Song of Songs.

"*Song of Songs*" by Watchman Nee, translated into English and first published in 1965 while Mr. Nee was still in prison as a persecuted believer in China. It is a devotional exposition of the Song of Solomon, illustrating the mystical union of the individual believer and his Lord.

The "*Song of Songs I & II*" by Mike Bickle of the International House of Prayer (IHOP) in Kansas City. As the son of a boxer he felt the call of God to study the Song of Solomon, a story he shares in detail in his video/DVD courses on the Song of Songs. He has freely shared his materials with the body of Christ at large, and I personally am *greatly indebted* to him for his obedience in sharing the things God gave him in the secret place.

Appendix C

About the Author

Florli was born in Chicago, Illinois, the oldest of seven children, and received Jesus into her life as a little girl of five. Her family moved to Stillwater, Minnesota when she was eight, and they found their spiritual home in the First Baptist Church where her faith blossomed and grew.

At the age of 16 Florli left home to attend a Christian high school in Three Hills, Alberta, Canada. When her parents followed her a few years later to be part of the staff of Prairie Bible Institute, the course of her life was changed forever.

In her years as a Bible college student and later as a student piano teacher on the faculty, Florli's passion to serve God continued to grow, and eventually, as a young woman of 26, Florli left her adopted country and family behind to serve as a missionary in Malaysia to missionaries' kids.

In teaching piano and caring for young children, Florli was living the dream of her life. A serious issue with depression, however, curtailed her ministry, returning her to Canada and causing her to doubt her call to ministry. She found a place of ministry in her local church in Calgary, Alberta, and was loved by young and old alike, but deep within there was an unsettledness, an emptiness, and a longing after God that she could not explain.

Then at the age of 34 she met Jesus in a powerful, intimate way, and was confronted with the Person and the power of the Holy Spirit. This experience radically changed her heart, her life and her ministry. It was a defining moment in her life which started her on a personal journey of intimacy with God that she continues to enjoy today. When she met her husband in 1976, she found a kindred spirit, and together they served God as missionaries to India until his passing in 2008.

It was through the encouragement of her husband that Florli pursued her music and eventually obtained her degree as a piano teacher in 1984 with the Royal Conservatory of Music at the University of Toronto. Later in her life he encouraged her again to become ordained as a minister of the gospel, a dream that in her youth was never even on her radar screen!

Florli has served as a musician and worship leader all her life –a wealth of treasures to share which is evidenced in the courses she has taught on worship and the workshops she has developed for piano teachers and worship pianists and keyboardists.

Today as a widow, her life has changed, but she is still enjoying her piano students, teaching in her local church and ministering both here in Canada and overseas as opportunities arise within their churches in South India and in other places in the world.

If you were to sit down and enjoy a cup of coffee with Florli today, you would discover the secret to her contagious joy and love of life is found in her love for Jesus, her intimate walk with God and her passion to communicate and impart this message of God's love to others. She would like to be remembered only as a lover of God and as a lover of the ones He loves. That is her legacy to her family and to you, her spiritual sisters and brothers!

'SIA information can be obtained at www.ICGtesting.com
'ed in the USA
V120932240812
36LV00002B/10/P